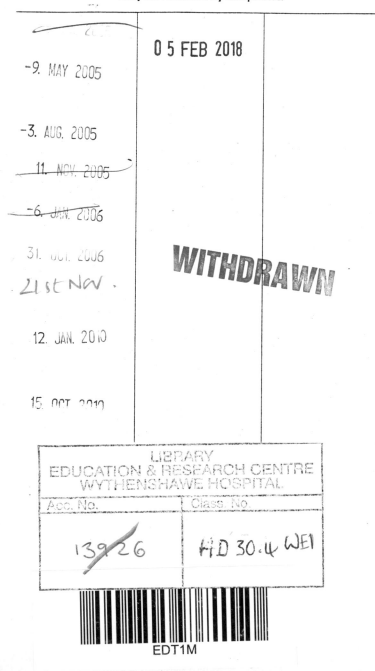

ACTION LEARNING

A Practical Guide
Second Edition

Krystyna Weinstein

© Krystyna Weinstein 1999

First edition published 1995 by HarperCollins Publishers

This edition published by
Gower Publishing Limited
Gower House
Croft Road
Aldershot
Hampshire GU11 3HR
England

Gower Publishing Company
Suite 420
101 Cherry Street
Burlington, VT 05401-4405
USA

Reprinted 2001, 2002, 2003

Krystyna Weinstein has asserted her right under the Copyright, Designs and Patents Act 1988 to be identified as the author of this work.

British Library Cataloguing in Publication Data
Weinstein, Krystyna
    Action learning: a practical guide. – 2nd ed.
    1. Active learning 2. Executives – Training of
    I. Title
    658.4'07'124

    ISBN 0 566 08097 4

Library of Congress Cataloging–in–Publication Data
Weinstein, Krystyna.
    Action learning: a practical guide/Krystyna Weinstein. — 2nd ed.
        p.   cm.
    Includes bibliographical references and index.
    ISBN 0-566-08097-4 (pbk.)
    1. Executives – Training of. 2. Active learning. I. Title.
HF5549.5.T7W387 1998   98–25001
658.4'071245–dc21   CIP

Typeset in 10pt Century Oldstyle by Saxon Graphics Ltd, Derby and printed in Great Britain by MPG Books Ltd, Bodmin, Cornwall.

Contents

List of figures

Preface

In the few years since the first edition of this book appeared, action learning has become almost mainstream in the field of development – both of people and organizations. And yet there are many who claim to be 'doing' action learning which bears only a passing resemblance to the real thing. Four elements in particular seem to be missing, and it is with these in mind that this second edition gives added emphasis to: the importance of working on, and implementing, real work-based projects over time (for it is sometimes forgotten that action learning is also a powerful way of resolving daily business quandaries); the role of the set adviser; the underlying values of action learning; and the emphasis on learning.

Some aspects of the book have been reorganized in an effort to improve clarity, but like the first edition, this edition emphasizes the six elements that constitute an action learning programme. However, Chapter 1, 'What is action learning?', now gives an expanded introduction to action learning, with more instances of the benefits that it brings, and a simple model of 'the four Ps of action learning'. Chapter 6, 'The set adviser', gives more thought to the role, tasks, and skills of the set adviser, and describes how this role is one that many participants subsequently use as a new model for managing. In addition, a number of brief case examples of how and when action learning has been used by a variety of organizations are included to give readers a flavour of action learning's wide applications, and a new Chapter 10, 'The future of action learning', includes insights on how action learning can be applied successfully in non-work environments.

Although there are now more books available on the subject of action learning than when the first edition appeared, this book still has the distinction of focusing on the voices of participants to describe the experience of action learning. In fact, the original idea for this book emerged from my frustration at never having anything easy and readable on action learning to give people when they asked me if I could recommend something 'basic' to read. They also wanted to know what people gained from such programmes.

For giving me access to participants on their action learning programmes, I would particularly like to thank W.H. Smith, TSB, Motorola, Lever Brothers, BUPA, Seagrams, Surrey and Hampshire County Councils, Nottingham Trent University, Brighton Borough Council and Sun Life. I would also like to thank IMC (International Management Centres), Manchester Metropolitan University and Brighton University, for giving me access to students from a variety of organizations on their post-graduate management-by-action learning programmes.

I would also like to thank all those in the following organizations – and others – who discussed their programmes with me, and enabled me to create some case examples of how action learning is being or has recently been applied: Woolworths, Zeneca, Hackney Borough Council, ICL, Thames Water, Price Waterhouse, the National Health Service, and the Corporation of London.

Thanks are also due to the many colleagues running mixed-company programmes, and all the participants on these programmes, who were willing to let me come and talk to them. They came from diverse organizations, including finance institutions (pensions, insurance and merchant banking), the civil service, small businesses (building, bakery and computer software).

I would also like to thank all those participants on varied in-company and mixed-company programmes with which I have worked during the past few years (for example, Nationwide-Anglia, Oxfam, Conoco, as well as HDL's distance learning programmes for developers, and Reading University's distance learning MBA), and whose thoughts and comments feature widely.

My thanks, too, to Bob Garratt and Julia Scott, who suggested several important amendments. And finally, I need to acknowledge the influence of Jean Lawrence, who first introduced me to action learning, and whose experience and knowledge I greatly value – some of which I hope is reflected in this book.

Krystyna Weinstein
London
January 1998

Introduction

This book is intended for managers, consultants, trainers, developers – anyone, in fact, who works with others in any capacity and is interested in improving the quality of their own and others' actions and behaviours, and in seeing tangible business, as well as personal, results. It is written primarily for those who know little or nothing about action learning, but I hope that those who know something of, or have already experienced action learning, will also gain insights and ideas.

The book explains the practical elements that make up a programme, and uses the words of participants to express what they experienced, achieved and learnt; it explains the theory, beliefs, and values that underpin action learning, and the steps involved in designing action learning programmes, with guidelines on how to ensure their success.

Action learning is not a course. It is a programme which combines action on real work-based issues with real learning. In addition, it has provided many participants with a new way of working, managing – and being. It is geared to people, no matter what their seniority or job, and the benefits spread beyond the immediate task or learning objective, for participants take from action learning a new set of behaviours and beliefs which can be applied no matter what task they are undertaking, or where they are working.

Action learning has become a key approach in enabling people engaged in all walks of working life to tackle the ever-increasing demands made of them. It does this by engaging their energy and commitment, because it focuses not on what they need to learn, but on how to resolve the daily questions, quandaries and confusions that beset us all at some point in our work: how to accomplish something, how to deal with difficult people, how to engage the energies of staff, how to be more creative in our work, and how to interact more productively with each other in teams or across networks, using all our talents and skills.

Action learning, as I hope this book will show, manages all of these, because those who participate in action learning programmes focus on what is troubling them as they tackle their working days; it also helps them – with the support and challenge of others – to find solutions, rather than simply listening to experts for solutions (although this may be useful at the right time!). They become engaged in finding their own solutions, and in the process become empowered, gain confidence, and gain a sense of achievement.

Action learning also has another major attraction, for its structures and processes bear an uncanny resemblance to a learning company in microcosm. Many questions are being asked about how we can make this seductive idea of a learning community come about. How can we make sure that all the learning, all the experience each of us gains, can be shared with others, to everyone's mutual benefit? How can we take learning out of the classroom and anchor it firmly in our everyday lives, at work, in leisure – anywhere? Here is one answer.

Some proof of the value of action learning is its spread, for it has found a foothold in the UK, the Netherlands, Sweden, Norway, Denmark, Germany, Austria, Belgium, the Czech Republic, Italy, the USA, Canada, Australia, New Zealand, India, Japan, Singapore, Hong Kong, South Africa, Kenya, Tanzania, Swaziland, Colombia and Argentina. In all these places, programmes are being run in many organizations, including major international corporations, in local government, health services and hospitals, small businesses, educational institutions, charities and community projects.

The idea for this book arose out of my experiences – as a set adviser, and as Secretary to IFAL (the International Foundation for Action Learning) – of people wanting to know more about action learning and its applications. The questions they asked related not so much to the theory, or how to be a practitioner, but what happened in such programmes: what did participants do, what did they gain – and learn – and how did they do this? In particular, how is it possible to learn without teachers and experts; what did a project consist of; why does it take so long (other courses are no longer than one week, normally)? And, of course, what prompted organizations to adopt action learning, who such programmes are for, and for what purposes are organizations using action learning?

Those I interviewed for the book came from functions and positions which covered the entire work spectrum: managing directors, chief executives, senior functional managers, engineers, IT specialists, marketing and sales personnel, retail and banking employees, surveyors and police administrators, lecturers and teachers, and those responsible for training and personnel.

On concluding my interviews, I was left with the following thoughts and insights. The majority felt that they had learnt a great deal more than either they or the organizers of the programmes had anticipated. This led me to divide the learning into two component parts:

- **anticipated learning** – what participants had planned or hoped to learn (because they had, in most but not all instances, relatively clear ideas of why they were on the programmes)

- **unanticipated learning** – what they gained as a result of this programme, and its elements (many of which were not what participants had been expecting).

In the course of tackling such issues as effective management of people, events and resources, participants gain new insights about themselves. The creation and putting into place of new strategies was obviously important to participants, but what they mostly talked of was the personal development they were experiencing as a result of learning to manage themselves.

Action learning legitimizes, and brings out the value of, giving people space and time to stand back, think, reflect and see things in perspective. It brings out the value of sharing doubts, successes, questions and mistakes with others. Two participants' insights are revealing here: 'I know I need to sit back and reflect, but unfortunately our time sheets don't allow allocate space for this' and 'Reflecting, stopping to think, has saved me from plunging in and making mistakes as I go along.'

The longer the programme, the more the participants felt they had benefited, for this allowed their development to take place, and their confidence to grow.

The depth and breadth of learning was greatest where: individuals worked on their own projects rather than on group projects; the participants were responsible for or participated to some degree in implementing what they had proposed; the set adviser was 'qualified'; there was some action learning-related taught input as part of the programme (in addition to a one-day introduction to action learning at the beginning of a programme), or where some other development programme had preceded it.

Most outstanding of all, everyone mentioned that their self-confidence had increased.

My last insight was that action learning, at its best, is capable of 'reaching those parts that other programmes do not reach'.

I was left with a very strong impression that for a successful action learning programme, all the six elements that constitute a programme must be present. It is with this in mind that I have structured the book to record in detail what these elements are; for if some are missing, the programmes are that much the poorer, and the participants and their organizations the losers.

This book is thus an *attempt* to describe the experience of action learning. It is an attempt, because even the participants in programmes, whose words and experiences form the main bulk of this book, found it difficult to sometimes express in words what it was they had gained and learnt – or even how it had come about. 'I know I've changed – that I'm not the person I was ... but I'm not really sure how it happened,' was how one participant put it. Others went into detail about a more effective way of communicating, working and generally relating to others, as well as a greater intellectual and emotional honesty.

These are not 'road to Damascus' revelations. It is just that words – although adequate to describe specific skills and achievements gained – often prove inadequate to chronicle how we feel changed, how we sense we are different. There is also a sense in which words cannot convey *experience* – they convey only information about it. In fact, it is probably a paradox to be even trying to write a book about action learning, which has experience or action as the starting point for learners.

HOW THIS BOOK IS STRUCTURED

This book aims to cater for people with different levels of knowledge of action learning, and hence different interests.

If you know very little about action learning and want to know more, but keep it brief and practical, you may find it best to begin with Chapter 1, 'What is action learning?', and then move on to Part 2, 'Action Learning in Practice'.

If you want to know about the theory of action learning and take time to reflect on the philosophy that underpins it, you may want to read Chapter 2, 'The theory and philosophy of action learning', first.

If, on the other hand, you know something about action learning already and have a number of questions about it, such as 'What happens on an action learning programme?' and 'What do people get from it?', and want to hear what participants have experienced, you may choose to go straight to Part 2 first.

Lastly, if after reading these chapters you want to plunge in and try running a programme, turn to Chapter 11, where you will find the basics of what you need to do to start up and run a successful programme.

A warning: A few of the programmes that the participants interviewed for this book were on did not fully meet what I would now define as the criteria for successful action learning. Nevertheless, it is only by uncovering the limitations of some programmes and analysing why they were less than successful (as described in participants' own words) that we will know what makes for programmes which will 'deliver the goodies', and which ones merely scratch the surface and never reveal the full depth, breadth and complexity that is the potential of a well-run programme.

Part I

Definitions and Theoretical Background

Part I of this book contains two chapters. The aim of Chapter I is to explain action learning to those readers who know little about it, and would like to know:

- What is action learning?
- What does an action learning programme consist of?
- What makes it different from other methods of learning?
- Why do organizations run such programmes, and why do individuals attend them?
- When are they helpful?
- What are the benefits, and what do people say they gain from them?
- Is it for everyone?
- What are the various types of programmes?

Chapter 2, by contrast, focuses on the theoretical and philosophical underpinnings of action learning.

1 What is action learning?

Action learning is a process underpinned by a belief in individual potential: a way of learning from our actions, and from what happens to us, and around us, by taking the time to question, understand and reflect, to gain insights, and consider how to act in future.

There are two other important elements to action learning: it involves a group of people who work together on their 'doing' and their 'learning'; and it requires regular and rigorous meetings of the group, to allow space and time for the questioning, understanding and reflecting.

So, when applied at work, action learning means working and learning simultaneously. Participants on an action learning programme will focus on work-based issues, problems and questions, which could be their own managerial and personal development, team-working or managing their staff, consulting, managing change, or indeed any other issue that is of concern to them. In other, non-work situations, the same applies: learning from what we do.

This sounds simple and obvious, and in a way it is. But there's a great deal more to it than that, otherwise there would be no scope for a book!

It is precisely because action learning involves a *group* of people that it is so effective for introducing change into organizations: changes in the way people work together, in the way they behave and think (culture change). Changes also occur because participants from a programme begin to influence others, which may in turn bring about changes in the structures, systems and processes within an organization:

> Lasting behavioural change is more likely to follow the reinterpretation of past experiences than the acquisition of fresh knowledge. (Reg Revans)

> Action learning encourages all those engaged in it to learn and change, and demands that they move forward; repetition, old answers to old questions, is not enough. (Jean Lawrence)

ENDLESS OPPORTUNITIES TO LEARN

The belief underlying action learning is that our daily activities provide us with endless opportunities to learn. Nowhere is this more true than at work – in the organizations where so many of us spend at least a third of our waking hours. The same is true of learning opportunities when we 'play'. Yet we persist in thinking that learning is something that takes place only in a lecture room or on a course.

In fact, we are learning all the time – be it at work or elsewhere. And we learn as much from our mistakes as from our successes. But we do not make it a conscious activity. Nor do we make it explicit. We rarely share our learning with others so that they can benefit. Neither do we question whether the conclusions we are individually drawing all the time, and subsequently acting on, are valid. We don't always check out our assumptions or prejudices. We tend to act on our own judgements only. Yet others' insights can prove very valuable – if we create the opportunity to work and share with them in a constructive manner.

Action learning creates an opportunity to become conscious of what we do, how we think, and what we believe. In so doing, it eventually encourages a climate of learning within an organization.

A QUESTIONING APPROACH

Action learning is a questioning approach. The questions that participants ask one another as they work in the set – always with a focus on the project or task they are working on – are an invitation to stop and consider, rather than to rush in with answers, solutions or justifications. So participants learn to ask helpful and thoughtful questions. They also learn to listen – not as easy as it sounds!

Reg Revans, the 'founding father' of action learning, describes learning (L) as consisting of two elements: programmed or taught learning (P), coupled with asking questions (Q). But it is the emphasis on the Q that is the more important. By asking ourselves and others questions, we challenge, and are challenged. For the purpose of questions posed in action learning is to prompt thought and reflection, from which will emerge effective actions.

WHAT CONSTITUTES AN ACTION LEARNING PROGRAMME?

In an action learning programme:

- Everyone works on a work-based project, or series of tasks.
- The group of people who join a programme learn to work in a constructive and effective way.

- The emphasis throughout the programme is as much on achieving visible results as on learning from everything that takes place, within and outside the set.

The six main elements of an action learning programme are:

1. **the set** – the small group of five or six people who meet regularly, ideally once a month for a day, to work together in a supportive yet challenging way
2. **the 'learning vehicle'** – the work-focused, real-time projects or tasks that each person (or the set as a whole) focuses on during the programme
3. **the processes the set adopts when working** – each person has their own 'airspace', in which to work on their project; the set meanwhile adopts a helpful questioning approach (no advice, and no general discussions)
4. **a set adviser** – who helps the group as it works and learns
5. **the duration of a programme** – normally three to six months
6. **the emphasis on learning** – which emerges both from working on the projects and from working in the set.

Each programme needs to have clear objectives; participants need to be chosen carefully (and given the choice of whether or not to take part in the programme), and the 'projects' or tasks (the quandaries, questions or issues) that they work on need to be of importance to the organization, and be ones that they will play a part in implementing, rather than simply involving research. The projects should also meet participants' individual development needs.

Once the programme has begun (Chapter 11 gives the details of how to put an effective programme into practice), the set meets regularly, usually with a set adviser (at least initially). The set adviser's role is to help the set with their processes, and to make them aware of their learning. And if at any point set members decide they would find it helpful to have a taught input, they themselves, or the set adviser, may arrange this.

Each of the six elements is discussed in greater detail in Part 2, and is illustrated by quotes from participants describing their experiences of each element.

TACKLING PROBLEMS, NOT PUZZLES

In action learning, the task or projects that participants work on should be what Revans calls *problems*. He makes a useful distinction between what he calls 'puzzles' and 'problems'. We are dealing with puzzles when there is a known 'answer' to our questioning and probing, only we don't yet know it. Probably another course or some more reading will give us the solution. By contrast, problems are those issues, challenges, opportunities where there is no one answer, no one way of doing things, no one solution. It's a question of juggling with insights, ideas, experience, and deciding what is the 'best' solution in these particular circumstances.

So someone who is learning to use a word-processor would gain little from attending an action learning programme. But someone given the task of determining whether staff in a given department would benefit by having individual word-processing facilities would find this a useful project to work on in an action learning programme.

The following distinctions are crucial:

- **Puzzle** – an embarrassment to which a solution already exists, where there is one right answer.
- **Problem** – an issue for which there is no existing solution; different people in different circumstances will suggest different courses of action.

If the word 'problem' sounds too negative (as many participants feel), there are a host of other words that maybe define more clearly the issues that action learning deals with best: quandaries and questions, dilemmas, uncertainties, irritations, challenges or opportunities, those occasions when there is no one solution but a range of possibilities, thereby opening the door to choice and decisions.

Increasingly, people in all walks of life, and in most organizations, are faced with new issues, and hence decisions that they have not had to take before. They are often unaware that anyone else may have faced a similar dilemma. It is in these circumstances – where something entirely new is being tackled, and where so-called expert knowledge can't help except maybe in pointing to some possible directions – that action learning is helpful.

So action learning is useful where there is no single way forward, or one answer; where the solution will depend on circumstances, people, history, on what is to be achieved – on a host of often unpredictable forces. Likewise, action learning is helpful where change of any sort is involved, for change brings in its wake uncertainties, doubts, fears and hence problems.

As one action learning veteran said: 'Action learning is explorative and inquisitive – it encourages that spirit in participants.' Another participant explained: 'Someone who isn't prepared to ask questions, to investigate and explore is probably part of the problem.'

IS ANYTHING TAUGHT ON AN ACTION LEARNING PROGRAMME?

On a classic action learning programme, there is no teaching. This is probably one of the most difficult aspects of action learning for new participants to understand. How can you learn without being taught?

It *is* possible, as participants come to realize. They each bring so much experience and knowledge, and as they share with one another, they gradually perceive that between them they often have insights and even answers, and do not need experts to come along and tell them.

This is not to dismiss experts or expert knowledge. But there is a time and place for them. Action learning programmes are often run after taught courses, to help consolidate the knowledge that participants have acquired, either through lectures, case studies or reading.

Some action learning programmes do in fact have minor taught inputs on subjects that are either of direct relevance to the projects or the learning that the programme is hoping to achieve.

WHAT'S SO SPECIAL ABOUT ACTION LEARNING?

The thinking behind action learning is that learning is not solely about acquiring knowledge of a skill by reading a book or listening to a lecture. Learning is about doing something differently; about applying and making use of a skill or of new knowledge; or about thinking differently, or having a new set of values and beliefs. Only when we can transfer our knowledge, skill, behaviour or beliefs and insights to something practical, thus providing evidence that we are able to apply it, can we claim that we have really learnt. In other words: *learning is about changing*.

The best way to learn to do something differently is to focus on that 'doing' – on something we have an interest in, an issue we need to tackle, an opportunity to grasp, or a problem we need to resolve – and learn from that experience, discovering as much from our successes as we do from our mistakes.

But simply doing something different is insufficient. We need to *learn* from what we do, to progress and develop, to avoid what doesn't work (understanding why it doesn't), and equally to learn from our successes (understanding how they came about). Stopping to carry out this reflection, to gain insights, and to do something different in the future (or repeating it if the previous action was successful) is the basis of learning.

AN EQUAL FOCUS ON ACTION AND LEARNING

Action learning stresses the simultaneous achievement of actions and learning.

Everything we do reflects our skills, qualities, beliefs, values and assumptions. By becoming aware of how these underpin our actions – and recognizing which are 'positive' and which may be 'negative' factors – we can begin to take stock of what we need to change, discard or rethink if we are to become more effective in our relationships with others.

Because of its emphasis on communication processes and learning, action learning provides an ideal mirror in which we can begin to see ourselves more clearly.

LEARNING WITH AND FROM ONE ANOTHER

One of the tenets of action learning is that we learn best and most effectively when we learn in the company of others who are also learning. None of us has a monopoly on knowledge or insights. We all have a host of questions, which we voice or keep silently to ourselves. By working and learning with others, we are able to share knowledge, insights and perceptions, as well as hear each others' doubts and questions, and realize our own potential:

> Managerial learning is a social exchange in which managers learn with and from each other during the diagnosis and treatment of real problems (and opportunities). (Reg Revans)

> Swop your difficulties, not your cleverness. (Reg Revans)

> A living community ... is a network of conversations with feedback loops. One of the best ways to nurture the community is to facilitate and sustain conversations. (Fritjof Capra)

Returning to work after a set meeting, tackling their project, and then coming back to the set and talking about what they've achieved – or failed to achieve – and doing this several times over a period of some months: for participants, this 'rhythm' is essential to anchoring the learning.

IT TAKES TIME

Action learning takes time. It takes time to learn – and unlearn. It takes time to build up trust among a group as they work and learn together; it takes time for members to feel free to discuss some issues that they may never have discussed with anyone before; it takes time to build up confidence to do things differently, and it takes time to practice and perfect what we are doing differently.

THE VALUES OF ACTION LEARNING

There is one other important aspect to action learning: the values and beliefs that underpin it. Revans is very clear about this. Honesty with one's self and with others, respect for others and their viewpoints, trying to understand, rather than judge them, and accepting responsibility for what one does: these are fundamental to successful action learning. Without them, there is little real achievement (although there may be results), and certainly no learning.

The emphasis in action learning is thus on taking responsibility for one's actions, on helpful questioning, thinking, avoiding the impulse to give advice, pass judgement on anyone, or find easy solutions to problems. The problems presented initially are often symptoms of other deeper-lying problems. It is those that action learning aims to get at. Figure 1.1 encapsulates all these elements of action learning. If one of them is missing, the full benefit of action learning will also be missing.

WHAT CREATES A GOOD PROGRAMME?

A good action learning programme will encourage participants not only to 'crack the shells of their ignorance', but also 'the shells of their understanding' – and discover something about themselves. The learning may be about:

- gaining new knowledge and information
- reasoning differently
- behaving differently
- becoming more aware
- gaining greater understanding of oneself and motives
- altering beliefs and values
- acknowledging feelings and their impact.

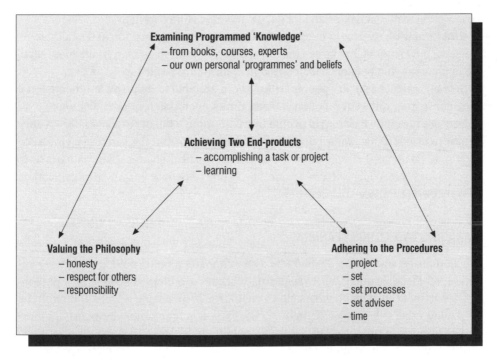

Figure 1.1   The four Ps of action learning

All of this is part of action learning. A good set adviser will encourage participants to become aware of these changes.

For those readers interested in reading more about the thinking that underpins action learning, Chapter 2 goes into greater depth.

WHO IS IT FOR?

Action learning is for *everyone*. The participants quoted in this book probably provide the best answers to this question. They included engineers, shop floor staff, sales and marketing personnel, trainers and developers, middle managers of a variety of hues and in different functions, clerical assistants, senior managers and managing directors, hospital administrators, para-medical staff, nurses, social workers, teachers and lecturers, shop retail staff, bankers, a baker, a builder, and several people in IT.

But the possibilities don't stop there: it is for secretaries and supervisors, social workers and managers, doctors and solicitors, accountants and farmers. Programmes have run in every conceivable type of organization – from local government, education and the health service to blue-chip finance, service and manufacturing companies, to small companies and partnerships – from building and farming to small companies and individual business entrepreneurs.

Programmes have run in every type of organization – education and health service, local government, banks and building societies, manufacturing companies, service companies, the police, charities, and in community projects.

Sets are selected so that people within them are able to help one another, even if they come from different functions – sometimes even different organizations.

Sets are normally made up of people from the same level of responsibility – a very senior manager and a junior person are unlikely to work in the same set. However, they may do so very successfully when such a 'vertical-slice' set has as its task to resolve an issue which affects a wide spectrum of people within an organization. (For more on this, see Chapter 3.)

MANAGING AND ACTION LEARNING

We all manage something. It might be a switchboard, a multi-million-pound organization, an IT department, an engineering workshop, a clerical section or a personnel department. It might be managing a customer or managing a project. It might be managing others, be they a team of six or sixty. It might simply be managing ourselves or our career.

Whatever it is we manage, we need to manage it effectively. No matter what it is, questions and queries, dilemmas and quandaries will arise. We will face minor hiccups or major problems. We will have challenges and opportunities – even if we don't always recognize them.

To manage better whatever it is we manage, we need to learn. And we learn by stopping and taking note of everything that impinges on our managing, reflecting on this, and gaining insights and clues about how to manage better next time. For no matter what we manage, we will have successes, and we'll make mistakes. And we can learn from both. We can also learn from other people, and their experiences, if we're willing to share. We then need the confidence to recognize all this, and maybe to take some personal, and even professional, risks. Above all, we need to learn to think and to ask questions.

Action learning helps participants tackle all this. In particular, working in the set offers participants insights into new ways of managing.

One action learning participant, as long ago as 1978, had the following comments to make:

- Lack of information and communication in organizations leads to problems and non-involvement.
- Hierarchy and structure impede the taking of responsibility.
- Management philosophy ossifies individuals' involvement, and devalues them.
- The *raison d'être* for organizations is not clear – people lose their way into other avenues.
- Change needs standard bearers.
- We may solve today's problems, but there are new ones lurking around the corner.

WHEN IS IT USEFUL?

An action learning approach can be applied to the following circumstances:

- when we are confronting a new situation we have never been in before
- when we are working with a new group of people we have never dealt with before
- when we want to test out new ways of working with people we already know in teams, or simply managing staff or relating to colleagues
- when our jobs or work roles change and we're not sure what our responsibilities are, or how to relate to other staff
- when the organization we work for is facing a major dilemma and needs to move forward
- when we feel there are untapped human resources around us that we are ignoring – when involving people in working on resolving issues that affect them in organizations

- when the organization we work for is faced with challenges in the future, and needs to establish strategies and plans
- when trying to deliver this elusive concept called 'empowerment'
- when we want to change the way things have been before
- when we want to change something in our own personal make-up – the way we do things, the way we react – and our personal development
- when, as part of an NVQ or MCI initiative, we need to attain competence in a given area.

Action learning is effective for organizational development, team development and personal development. In reality, the three intertwine, and it is often difficult to know where one ends and another begins: without individual development there is no team development; without the latter, there is little organizational development.

Through action learning:

- We learn to communicate openly and freely.
- We learn how to solve today's problems, and thereby gain insights on how to tackle tomorrow's.
- We learn to value and respect everyone.
- We learn to listen.

Action learning also has a powerful role to play in any training or development programme: as an integral part of 'development' programmes; as a follow-up to/or integrated into more traditional courses – to anchor and consolidate the learning; as an integral part of distance learning programmes, to offset the 'loneliness of the long-distance learner', and on practice-oriented professional programmes, to offer opportunities to share experiences.

Above all:

- It is an opportunity for networking across an organization, helping members to understand the different functions within that organization, and the issues and quandaries that colleagues deal with.
- It is a forum where people can share difficulties and problems, without fear.
- It provides a model of a new way of both communicating and managing.

The processes of action learning encourage particular ways of communicating which for many participants prove to be more helpful than standard, everyday discussions. For the emphasis is on 'dialogue' with others (see page 39 for a more detailed discussion of the distinction between dialogue and discussion). Participants learn to listen (not as easy as it sounds!), to ask helpful questions, to help others resolve their own queries and issues through encouraging them to think and reflect. In fact, several participants have likened being a member of the set to having a group of mentors.

WHY HAVE ORGANIZATIONS USED ACTION LEARNING?

The reasons given for running – or attending – action learning programmes are many and varied. Some companies had tried all the 'traditional' courses that were available, but found that little learning was being transferred back into work. Several felt that action learning was an important adjunct to taught two or three-day courses. Many were looking for developmental programmes, and felt that action learning, because of its practical work focus, would be most pragmatic. Many wanted to engage their staff in more hands-on projects. A number believed that this was the best way of creating working networks across their organizations. Many were attracted by action learning's emphasis on learning, rather than simply achieving 'bottom-line' results. The majority felt sure that the best results occur when participants are trying to resolve their own day-to-day problems.

Surrey County Council, which runs many action learning programmes for all its staff, listed the following reasons:

- It is a good support mechanism for managers.
- It provides very useful thinking time.
- It provides space for reflection.
- It counteracts stress – it slows down the pace of work.
- It highlights experiential learning.
- It is very empowering.
- It is good for self-development and manager development, working on real management issues.
- It is very powerful for individuals.
- It enables the development of counselling skills.
- It enables the development of consultancy skills, analytical questioning and problem-solving.
- It provides space for self-discovery.
- It produces ways forward on work issues.
- It unlocks and unfreezes.
- It helps with the management of change.
- It provides cross-departmental and external exchange opportunities.

A major retailer's reason for using action learning – in a programme that had encompassed staff in all parts of its multi-outlet business – was that it was simply the best form of developmental 'training' they knew of. And an institution of higher education, where departments were very separate entities, created a programme with the aim of 'engaging senior managers in real management problems, and changing the culture'.

Action learning is also being built into university-run management, and management-related courses and programmes, be they full-time, part-time or distance learning. It offers participants the opportunity to share with one another, to test out their learning and how they are applying the new knowledge they have acquired, and to gain feedback, as well as new ideas and insights from fellow 'students'.

WHY DO INDIVIDUALS ATTEND PROGRAMMES?

When asked why they had participated in an action learning programme, participants had different reasons. Some individuals in mixed-company sets were simply curious to find out what it was about, and whether it was appropriate and of interest for their organization or department.

One senior manager in a small firm had come on a mixed-company programme because he had found no other programme that catered for his needs or questions. He came, however, in trepidation: 'I'd had no formal education and thought I'd be out of my depth. I soon found I wasn't, and it was one of the most interesting and rewarding experiences of my life.'

In that same set was an IT manager from a large insurance company. He had some doubts about a mixed-function, mixed-company set. 'I came to investigate whether it was a programme that we could usefully use. I think we – my staff – would gain more by working together in an in-company set, and resolving our own specific issues.'

Participants on another mixed-company set came because they had all taken part in a week-long management development programme, and the issues raised by it were of such impact that they wanted to continue 'to consolidate our learning', as some of them put it. In fact, several of them stated that they personally could not imagine joining an action learning programme without such a previous course.

Few organizations use action learning in this way, however – although it is ideal for such consolidation, and for testing and experimenting with the new knowledge and ideas gained on courses.

WHAT ARE THE BENEFITS FROM AN ACTION LEARNING PROGRAMME?

Practitioners and participants have highlighted the following benefits of action learning:

- **It resolves real business problems** – 'It's a bridge between analysis and implementation. Its rigour comes from benchmarking and improvement. It's not a fad; it has a long scientific pedigree ... It focuses on improving actual performance, not analysis.'
- **It improves social processes** – 'Action learning is itself a social process and organizations are realizing that social processes underpin their success.'

- **It empowers people** – 'Content is a false trail. Experts don't provide the answers. Someone will always know more! We need to encourage people to say, "Let's try it," and have confidence in their abilities and insights.'
- **It improves leadership qualities** – 'Being authentic is the only way to be a true leader ... Learning to manage yourself has to come before managing and leading others. Action learning makes people examine themselves and their actions and motivations.'
- **It improves coping with change** – 'More traditional programmes don't deliver the change and differences looked for back at work ... It's the only programme I know where you can actually see people change.'

At the outset of any programme, the outcomes it hopes to achieve are stated. During the course of the programme, these are addressed through the projects that participants work on. Thus, one of the benefits is that these highlighted issues or 'problems' are resolved, and action is taken in areas that the organization feel are important. These might include setting up a new sales deal, hammering out and implementing a new strategy, reorganizing and improving the efficiency of a department, successfully setting up and running a new training scheme, and so on.

DISCOVERY AND DEVELOPMENT

In addition to the projects completed, most participants also mentioned their own personal development that had occurred – often unanticipated, and much of it stemming from the way the set worked. Participants' discoveries included:

- The way you 'instinctively' wanted to manage, but in which you had been thwarted, is possible, even acceptable.
- You have the ability to redesign a workplace even if you are only the workshop staff.
- If you're a manager, you have the ability, by using your own behaviour as an example, to give your department a 'facelift'.
- You don't have to become a different person to 'sell'.
- Others are a helpful resource, a network to be used and developed.
- By behaving less competitively and working 'constructively' with others, you can achieve more.
- You can contribute directly to strategic decisions even if you have little responsibility.
- You're not alone with your quandaries and dilemmas, or even your doubts and fears.
- The commonest problem that everyone faces is their relationships with others.
- Communicating is more than talking and arguing.
- Managing means managing yourself as well as others.
- You can achieve more and be more effective by being 'yourself'.

Participants also discovered that all they hoped for was not always achievable instantly; that some organizations – and people – may not be able or willing to accommodate their 'new' way of thinking, working and being.

When it came to their own development, individual participants felt it was taking the form of:

- learning to work in a more disciplined way
- beginning to achieve what you want
- realizing that you have choices
- gaining the confidence to accomplish what you want
- taking initiative and responsibility and asking 'What can I do about X?', rather than waiting to be told or asked
- helping others to develop, and developing mentoring skills
- giving your staff (if you are a manager) the space, time, opportunity and support to develop and grow
- acquiring skills that permit real communication to take place between you and those you work with
- learning to network productively
- beginning to know and understand yourself – and others
- knowing that your own integrity, and being honest with oneself, is crucial
- realizing that being open and honest is less stressful than playing games or covering up.

Thus an action learning programme – if effectively managed – produces people who are able to think clearly, who challenge, who have gained self-confidence, who question, seek responsibility and a sense of achievement, who listen to and value different perspectives, and who know the benefits of collaboration rather than confrontation. It results in a questioning, democratic, networking form of organization:

> It produces a radical change in how you operate. You are personally challenged. The onus is on you as a person, and not simply on you as a role-player in some larger organizational theatre. It makes you confront who you are, how you want to be – what's stopping you, what you're doing to yourself and to others.

For those who want to take more control of, and responsibility for, their lives and their work, it is an ideal opportunity to learn how to do so more effectively, with more personal power, and with greater confidence: 'It releases you, it creates a sense of freedom.'

More pragmatically, others commented: 'It's about problem-solving – a firm structure to help you tackle projects, problems, any issue you face at work, where you have to take decisions, find solutions, evaluate them. It encompasses all of these.'

One engineer expressed amazement that 'The common issue we all had, regardless of how our projects were defined, was dealing with people – staff, colleagues or bosses.' Which in turn gave 'comfort that I'm not alone with this problem. Others experience it as well. And having a common issue means everyone's insights are likely to be helpful and provide good ideas.'

To many, it was 'a programme which forces you to face up to and tackle the real problems – and not the symptoms'.

Many participants also commented that they transferred the working processes they had learnt to use in the set back into their working environments, with benefits for their staff and the way they work as a team: 'If only people at work would behave more like set members! Instead of being supportive and asking questions, [at work] you're given information and advice. Neither is very helpful.'

For a manager in a local authority, it was: 'the challenge and exploring that I found most useful. It was unlike the confrontations and the sense of being exposed that you get at work when you're questioned. It's really helpful to forage around as you can do in the set.'

> The action learning discipline has given me a template of how people can work effectively together. You sense the atmosphere when a group is working well – and I don't mean agreeing with each other. They're listening to each other, and you know because you see how what they say relates to what the previous person said, and builds on it, rather than destroying it. And disagreements are approached constructively, by trying to work out where they spring from. Silences are OK, too, and body language tells you a lot.

BECOMING EMPOWERED

Definitions of empowering – or rather, becoming empowered – refer to individuals gaining in confidence, feeling they have something to offer, knowing how to put across ideas, how to ask questions, how to take responsibility, as well as being given – or taking – the opportunity to become more active and involved.

For managers, empowering may mean removing the blocks that prevent their staff from carrying out their jobs effectively. But empowerment cannot be bestowed by one human being on another. The simple act of bestowing perpetuates dependence – and power. Nor can anyone, in the end, empower someone who does not wish to become empowered. It has to come from within the individual. Others can merely create an environment in which becoming empowered is made possible.

> We are enslaved by despots – institutions or beliefs or neuroses – which can be removed only by being analysed and understood. We are imprisoned by evil spirits which we have ourselves – albeit not consciously – created, and can exorcise them only by becoming conscious and acting appropriately.[1]

Action learning provides some useful models which – if followed – are the stepping stones to both being empowered, and to empowering – and hence managing – others.

NOT ALL ORGANIZATIONS ARE READY FOR ACTION LEARNING

Action learning may not be suitable for all organizations at a given point in their life, however. They may simply not be ready for it, may not have the culture to contain people who feel empowered and confident, and who think and question – or indeed, may not *want* to create such a culture.

It might be apt to use a homeopathic image, and say that drops of what may appear poison to a particular organization will ultimately cure it. So, because of its investigative, questioning approach, action learning can be dangerous for some organizations. As one participant put it: 'It's not only radical ... it's the most dangerous course I've been on. Dangerous because it makes you question everything.'

For some organizations, action learning can be said to be subversive because:

- It values everyone.
- It's democratic.
- It stresses questioning.
- It stresses listening.
- It insists on actions.
- It gives courage.
- It encourages responsibility.
- It examines everything.

For action learning to work – to take hold – the culture of the company is important. If it is authoritarian, fragmented and structured, with egoistic managers, where someone is always blamed, and where mistakes are pushed under the carpet, then the programme is likely to ruffle feathers, and expose people who prefer to hide:

> The culture of many organizations is the antithesis of action learning beliefs and principles – they're competitive, individualistic.

> It's too revolutionary for many companies: it teaches you to ask questions.

> Action learning threatens some people. If they are a little insecure, they don't like to lose control. If they give people power, they feel it reduces their authority. Some managers feel they need total control.

However, another view might be that action learning could be used to kick-start some radical changes in an organization, provided the idea is bought into by the most senior managers, and they themselves endorse and support such programmes.

Action learning cannot be viewed simply as just another form of workshop – a bolt-on. For, as participants' comments highlight, action learning changes the way people work, think and view each other. It is based on a profoundly democratic philosophy, and gives participants confidence in themselves and their abilities. As such, it may be deeply disturbing for those who fear any change in existing structures, status and beliefs.

ORGANIZATIONAL READINESS FOR ACTION LEARNING

The following questionnaire, reproduced with kind permission from *Action Learning for Managers* (Pedler 1996), has been devised to help organizations assess the chance of action learning working in their organizations.

For each statement, score the company from 1 (not much like us) to 5 (very like us).

In this organization:

People are rewarded for asking good questions.	1	2	3	4	5
People often come up with new ideas.	1	2	3	4	5
There is a fairly free flow of communication.	1	2	3	4	5
Conflict is surfaced and dealt with, rather than suppressed.	1	2	3	4	5
We are encouraged to learn new skills.	1	2	3	4	5
We take time out to reflect on experiences.	1	2	3	4	5
There are plenty of books, films, packages and other resources for learning.	1	2	3	4	5
People help, encourage and constructively criticize each other.	1	2	3	4	5
We are flexible in our working patterns, and used to working on several jobs at once.	1	2	3	4	5
Senior people never pull rank, and always encourage others to speak their minds.	1	2	3	4	5

Now total up your score. If you scored:

10–20 – Action learning probably won't work in your organization until things open up a bit more.
21–40 – Yes, action learning should work well to help you achieve your purposes.
Over 40 – You don't need action learning – but maybe action learning would help you develop your critical faculties?

Interestingly, three programmes investigated for this book were in companies which by and large did not espouse the values and processes of action learning. The problem this posed was that after attending the programme, the participants became dissatisfied with their employers, and many admitted that they were looking for an opportunity to leave:

It changes you, the participant, but if the company you work for doesn't really want to change, you end up feeling frustrated.

This is what happened to a group of clerical staff in a civil service department after a powerful experience on an action learning programme. The participants were given a responsible project to work on, came up with interesting ideas and solutions, gained in self-confidence, and realized their own potential – only to then be returned to their old desk-bound, structurally limited jobs.

As several participants said: 'Organizations need to be aware that they will not get back the same people they sent on the programme.' Those responsible for introducing action learning need to make this clear to those who back the programme. It changes people, and they may become disillusioned and unhappy if their organization fails to realize this.

In fact, many participants from action learning programmes make career changes and other work-related moves very soon after such programmes. This is partly because they have developed, have gained visibility through being on the programme, and have made new contacts while working on their projects (just one of the unanticipated gains!).

Although if it is taken to its logical conclusions action learning can prove to be too revolutionary for many organizations, taken slowly, it begins to change the culture of an organization and to build a very different, more committed and more fulfilled workforce.

Inevitably, though, some participants were sceptical of action learning, and their comments are discussed on pages 193–194, and Chapter 9.

ACTION LEARNING AND THE LEARNING ORGANIZATION

A great deal is currently being written about the value of a learning organization: one where learning is a way of life. Yesterday's answers are not necessarily those for tomorrow, and the challenge is to enable the entire organization – the individuals who constitute it – to share their learning, their knowledge, experiences and insights, with others.

As Bob Garratt, author of the book *The Learning Organisation*, has put it: 'Action learning is a process for the reform of organizations and the liberation of human vision within organizations' (Garratt 1994).

The authors of the book *The Learning Company* say: 'Action in the learning company always has two purposes: to resolve the immediate problem, and to learn from that process' (Pedler, Burgoyne and Boydell 1991). This sounds suspiciously like action learning in action! And the action learning set begins to resemble a learning company/organization in microcosm:

> You can't create a learning organisation, but you can enhance people's capacities to learn and align their activities in creative ways. (Gareth Morgan)

The challenge, then, is: how to create an action learning ethos throughout an organization?

A recent study on how learning takes place in organizations, carried out by the Institute for Research on Learning in Palo Alto, California, came up with the following conclusion:

> The most powerful organizational learning and collective knowledge-sharing grows through informal relationships and personal networks – via working conversations in communities of practice.

Peter Honey, in an article entitled 'Establishing a learning regime' (Honey 1994) postulates ten learning behaviours, which – as those readers who read the rest of this book will discover – are remarkably similar to the learning that participants claim to gain on action learning programmes (see Chapter 8).

But this alone is not sufficient to create a learning organization. It merely creates the behaviours that 'oil its wheels'. A learning organization also needs:

- the will to become one
- the 'structures' that enable it to function as a learning company (see Morgan 1993)
- opportunities to work on a daily basis as one.

Action learning provides a programme for developing the behaviours and skills. It also provides some insights into the other three elements. By demonstrating the benefits of such working, it can provide the impetus or 'will' to become such an organization. It also provides one model of structures that enable working and learning to occur simultaneously, and a matrix for a networking form of organization, rather than a hierarchical one. Furthermore, it provides an insight into how to create opportunities that enable learning to be 'extracted' from the work process.

It also creates a forum in which knowledge is shared. And knowledge, as most organizations are now recognizing, is one of their most important assets. Yet most are confronted not only with the question of how to enable knowledge to be passed around, but how to create a climate in which knowledge is willingly shared, rather than equated with power, and kept under lock and key.

One could, in a sense, claim that the basis of a learning company is a network of like-minded people, who enjoy the challenge of working in an action learning way. They form a powerful network which will share and exchange insights and information, provide help and support for each other in their work and personal 'experiments', will ask questions and challenge supportively, and give feedback. In other words, they will learn with and from one another, and in the process 'transform' themselves and the organization they work for.

WHAT TYPES OF PROGRAMMES CAN BE RUN?

Programmes may be run 'in-company' (where only people from one organization attend, though they may be spread geographically across the country), or may be 'mixed-company' (where participants are from different companies and organizations).

Within these programmes there are four types of projects:

1. in-company programmes where everyone works on projects within their own department or section – a setting they are familiar with
2. in-company programmes where they work on projects in unfamiliar departments or sections
3. mixed-company programmes where they work on a project based in their own work area, but in another organization
4. mixed-company programmes where the project is not only in a different company, but also in an unfamiliar department or section.

The most common are the first two. The third and fourth are normally for more senior, rather than junior people.

An example of the fourth are programmes run in multinationals or organizations containing many separately managed companies. An instance of such a programme took place in a ferry company, with operations in many European countries. The participants came from each of these countries, and represented many functions; each set then focused on an issue to be resolved in one particular field of activity – such as finance and freight.

Another possibility is a mixed-company set with participants drawn from separately managed companies within a vast conglomerate (indeed, one of the sets interviewed for this book was made up of employees from separate businesses which came under one large umbrella organization).

To be successful, action learning programmes need to be designed carefully. Here are some of the elements that need particular attention:

- Be clear about the objectives of the programme, and communicate them to all who are concerned and actively involved.
- Be clear and explicit about the nature of action learning, and how it changes people.
- Engage the support of senior managers and participants' managers.
- Clarify the design of the programme – will it be part of a 'taught' programme, will it be a free-standing programme, and will participants be given access to resources during the programme, such as taught inputs, books, videos or visits, or simply given access to money which participants themselves decide how to spend?
- Determine what will be evaluated – the action implemented, the participants' development and its effects?

- Determine how the programme will be evaluated – by written reports, by some 'bottom-line' measurement?
- Determine by whom it will be evaluated – participants themselves, their managers, clients, or even their staff?
- Select carefully who will participate – who will benefit from the design, coupled with the programme's objectives and hoped-for outcomes.
- Allow those selected to *choose* whether to participate.

Once an organization has become familiar with action learning, however, it may well experiment with variations on this theme.

IN-COMPANY PROGRAMMES

An in-company action learning programme tends to be championed, and hence introduced, by either the management development or training manager, a line manager or a senior manager. In-company programmes are run for people at all levels of responsibility, with the possible exception of the most senior managers and chief executives. But this may depend on the purpose of the programme (for example, a culture change programme would have to involve everyone, including all senior managers).

Precisely who will participate will depend very much on the aims of the programme. If it is a company-wide initiative – such as culture change or Total Quality Management (TQM) – then a wide cross-section of staff is likely to be involved. In this instance, the sets might be 'horizontal', with all set members from the same 'level' within the organization, or 'vertical', where people from different levels work in the same set. If it is for more loosely defined management development, such as a graduate development programme, then participants may be more specifically selected. And if it is to address some other issue, such as creating a new staff appraisal system, then participants could be selected according to their interest and perhaps knowledge (as was the case in one programme mentioned in this book).

One sales manager pointed out that company-wide programmes: 'begin to remove tribalism from a company. You build teams into bigger teams, and create huge networks, whether you're in a big company or a small one. In a small one it's easier because you already know people better. But you still need to identify a common issue, such as TQM, for instance.'

'If you want to introduce a culture change into a company, you've got to have a company-wide programme, with everyone involved – and probably it needs to begin by involving senior managers first, and then cascading down,' was the observation of an IT manager from a major insurance company.

Thus programmes, and hence sets, can be made up of people from any function. They may then either work in mixed-function sets or single-function sets.

Participants on one of the largest in-company programmes in the UK, run some ten years ago in the Prudential Assurance Company listed, among a host of other insights, the following (from Lewis 1994):

> I realized that I did not have to toe the party line. I was my own person and could make things happen.

> Old-style status takes a long time to change. Action learning helped to build the foundation from which we could make this change.

> It gave me a lot of self-confidence, realizing that I could demand things of the organizations if well argued, rather than just accepting demands of the organization.

> It stretched our thinking and made us go well outside our normal parameters.

> I know of no other form of management training activity which transformed line managers into zealots – missionaries wanting to get their staff involved.

MIXED-COMPANY PROGRAMMES

In mixed-company programmes, as the name implies, participants will come from different organizations: public and private, large and small. But programmes run for separate businesses which nevertheless belong to the same parent company are also, in a sense, mixed-company programmes.

As with in-company sets, participants may again be from different functions or all from the same one.

Mixed-company programmes are often attended primarily by more senior managers, because very senior people have no obvious peers within their own organization. Experience has shown that the issues they are working on and tackling daily are best worked on with other managing directors and chief executives, and in an environment where they feel free to express their doubts and queries. (For more on programmes run specifically for senior managers, see pages 194–196. For more on the advantages and disadvantages of mixed-company versus in-company programmes, see pages 66–67.)

The majority of the many university-based management MSc and MBA programmes run along action learning lines also form students into mixed-company sets; although sometimes personnel from any one organization may all attend the same management programme and hence choose to work in the same set (as is the case, for instance, with action learning-based programmes being run for National Health Service personnel).[2]

HOW DO PARTICIPANTS REACT TO ACTION LEARNING?

Although participants had problems defining what action learning was, they were quite clear about what the experience had meant for them:

The questioning goes to the heart of everything, to fundamentals. It's given me a set of 'tools' to work with the unknown.

Others commented on the value of sharing:

I've realized that if you rely exclusively on your own thoughts and presuppositions you come a cropper. I've so often failed to see others' points of view. Action learning stops that.

Another participant put it slightly differently:

Others see things you don't ... but it's the way you learn this that is the hallmark of action learning. You see this through listening and observing and hearing them talk and being non-judgemental, just taking things in.

Many participants talked of the action learning 'spirit':

What distinguishes the action learning spirit is that it's not about answers to questions or decision-oriented, but about questions and space to talk and think. Nor is it about getting advice or information.

This was an observation that came up time again: the time and space to think and reflect. The programme legitimizes taking up others' time and gaining their insights, 'without feeling you're poaching, prying or encroaching on their territory'.

A nurse-manager was:

... excited by its common sense. It takes away the feel of ignorance – which becomes instead a strength, because you've identified what you don't know and that's a first step to begin to learn, ask questions, and apply in the everyday situations you operate in ...

The action learning discipline has given me a template of how people can work effectively. You sense the atmosphere when a group is working well – and I don't mean agreeing with each other. They're listening to each other, and you know because you see how what they say relates to what the previous person said, and it builds on it, rather than destroying it. And disagreements are approached constructively, by trying to work out where they spring form. Silences are OK, too, and body language tells you a lot.

I'll be encouraging my senior women managers to go on such a programme – to help them gain more confidence. Men, on the other hand, gain in different ways – usually to be more open and less authoritarian.

For a manager with a local authority, it was:

the challenge and the exploring that I found most useful. It was unlike the confrontations and the sense of being exposed that you get at work when you're questioned. It's really helpful to 'forage' around as you can do in the set.

A young participant said:

It's about empowering people. It pushes responsibility and duties – even power – back to staff.

For another participant, it was:

> ... like putting together your own programme ... You find that in addition to your project, the ostensible learning vehicle, you're simultaneously working on time management, empowerment, presentation skills, assertiveness ...

And to a young manager in his first job, it was:

> ... magic ... in that it draws on everything you know, and uses it.

More dramatically, one participant said:

> It's the most dangerous course I've been on. Dangerous because it makes you question everything.

Another young participant, in a rather similar vein, said:

> This may sound melodramatic, but I entered the programme as a boy, and left as a more mature adult.

NOTES

[1] Isaiah Berlin, (1969) *Four Essays on Liberty*, Oxford: Oxford University Press.

[2] In 1998, the following UK universities were running action learning-based management and management-related programmes: Brighton University, Nottingham Trent University, Manchester Metropolitan University, Salford University, Wolverhampton University, Huddersfield University, Lancaster University, Middlesex University, Surrey University, SouthBank University, Guildhall University. The International Management Centres (based in the UK, but with locations around the world) run all their programmes along action learning lines. Action learning was also being used on several non-management programmes.

2

The theory and philosophy of action learning

Any attempt to give definitions of action learning highlights how elusive a concept it can be. As Reg Revans said himself: 'Action learning takes so long to describe because it is so simple.'

Maybe this is because, as some participants said, action learning provides 'a philosophy for life', and opens doors of perception for them. In the words of one academic, action learning is 'rather like a Möbius strip, where the surfaces join up in one continuous strip imperceptibly – rather as action and learning are linked imperceptibly, and both are part of the same "surface" '.

SOME DEFINITIONS OF ACTION LEARNING

Revans defines managerial learning as: 'a social exchange in which managers learn with and from one another during the diagnosis and treatment of real problems'. Although Revans's original definitions talk about 'managers' learning, this approach is clearly applicable and available to everyone and anyone. Various other action learners have tried to define action learning, and perhaps those quoted here will begin to give an insight into what action learning is:

> It is learning by doing ... We learn by doing from the cradle on. In action learning we go further by making arrangements – often very simple arrangements – to enhance the opportunities to learn from our experiences, and to speed up the process. (Lawrence 1986)

> Action learning is an approach to the development of people in organisations which takes the task as the vehicle for learning. It is based on the premise that there is no learning without action and no sober and deliberate action without learning. On the whole our education system has not been based upon this principle. The method has been pioneered in work organisations and has three main components: people who accept responsibility for taking action on a particular issue; problems, or the task that people set themselves; and a set of six or so colleagues who support and challenge each other to make progress on problems. Action learning implies both self-development and organisation development. (Pedler 1997)

A manager's tools are knowledge, skills and an accumulation of years of thinking, acting and discovery. Together these make up 'experience', with which he or she faces the problems of management ... Every problem tackled adds to that experience and from it he/she acquires a new mix of experience to take forward into the future. By sharing problems with others ... every manager can use their experience and their perception to enlarge their own experience and enrich their learning. (David Sutton, unpublished paper)

Revans also writes: 'Action learning suggests that we may best master whatsoever unknown challenge appears, by working with others who seek to triumph in the same way', and goes on to say that this is the prime reason why 'programmes should be collectively designed and launched by those who hope to profit from them'. Furthermore:

The primary occupation of managers is to treat their problems (or to seize their opportunities) ... in other words, managers must make up their minds about what to do and settle for doing it. All secondary activity should be linked as closely as possible to this everyday task. For this simple reason, action learning is cradled in the very task itself ... (Reg Revans)[1]

When participants on action learning programmes were asked to define action learning, or explain what it meant to them, they also found it difficult to encapsulate this in one brief phrase or sentence: 'It's difficult to explain,' said one young scientific research officer. 'It seems very simple at the outset: a group of people who each has a real work project which they work on and learn from that, with the help and support of the other participants ... but then it begins to get more complex.'

'It's about doing something and learning from it,' was another participant's response, but she went to say: 'but that's too simple because it's how you approach that action, and how you learn that are important ... and that's when defining action learning begins to get complicated!'

'It's a process of looking at an issue in front of others – of trying things out and reporting back,' was another attempt at a definition.

A managing director who has been involved with action learning for the past ten years explained what it was for him: 'There are a great many things that I learnt as fact, but they only have curiosity value until I can find ways of applying them. Learning by doing takes care of that and the experience provides a much more indelible memory than a transient fact.'

THE FLAVOUR AND 'SPIRIT' OF ACTION LEARNING

The comments quoted above came from people who, in spite of their inability to put into precise words a definition of action learning, had spent several months on action learning programmes, gaining and learning. 'I wish I could bottle it: it's so difficult to describe' – one participant's cry – implies that maybe you can't fully understand what action learning is about until you've tried it, rather like a gourmet dish, sex, marriage or having a child. But in order to tempt people into tasting it, something of the 'flavour' of action learning needs to be captured in words first, despite their limitations.

The participants' accounts in this book will convey some of that 'flavour'. But the words and even deeds alone do not convey the 'spirit' of action learning. That spirit has more to do with the energy and confidence that such a programme can give participants. 'I always come away full of energy and revitalized,' is quite a common comment. Yet paradoxically, the spirit of action learning that provides this energy demands that we put a stop to the 'busyness' we are so embroiled in and recognize the value of 'space' – 'simply having the time to stand back and gain a perspective, to have time to think' – a sentiment echoed by almost everyone on an action learning programme.

Others will tell you that the spirit had something to do with being honest and open, valuing others, having courage, and developing self-confidence – particularly after working with people, being listened to, being valued, being supported and yet pushed intellectually and emotionally.

One of the problems with action learning is that it means different things to different people. Yet there is a great deal that is common to all participants, and the best way for me to convey this is by using their own words. But even these do not fully convey the experience. It's rather like driving past a beautiful landscape: from the car you can describe the hills, streams, trees, but until you stop the car, get out of it, walk, smell, feel and sense it, you don't really experience it.

So let me try some simple signposting – for becoming involved in action learning is like going on a journey. You begin with the clear signposts, and the route seems straightforward. But the further on the journey you go, the more the side routes and detours become significant. It is in this sense that action learning is a journey of discovery and development.

WHAT IS ACTION LEARNING ABOUT?

I hear and I forget ... I see and I remember ... I do and I understand. (Chinese proverb)

Action learning is a process that young children use continuously: they learn by doing something, by testing it out. They learn to walk by taking the risk of testing what it's like to stand hazardously on two legs, and not four! Later, they learn to ride a bicycle. But they only learn when they get on it and try out the balance, veer around crazily, probably fall off, and thus, through practice, they soon get to the stage of being so good at balancing that they can steer without even having their hands on the handlebars!

But as we get older, our learning by doing seems to get shelved, shunted to the sidelines. Instead, we read, we listen to others (for example, lecturers) talk about things. Gradually, we begin to believe that because we have taken information/ knowledge in cognitively, we have learned. And so we have, at one level. We now know *about*; but this doesn't mean we know *how*, and *when*, and *what if*.

Some of the participants I spoke to had taken this 'adult' approach to action learning. They had read about it – rather like the reader of this book! And their comments? As one said:

> I'd read quite a bit about action learning before coming on the programme, and it all seemed logical, pretty straightforward, almost common sense. But 'it' didn't happen as I'd anticipated. As an engineer I'd expected to solve my 'problems' in a 'straight-line' approach – here's the problem, here's a solution – but it's not like that. You begin to work on whether what you have identified as the problem really is the problem ... and that's when the real work of action learning begins.

Hands-on experience is in the end the only way to acquire the answers to these questions. Craftspeople take this approach when they learn a skill; training for certain professions (for example, doctors) contains elements of this approach to learning. But training for the rest of us has been slow in taking up this practical approach.

Instead, we go on one- and two-day courses or workshops which may even include some role-play to help consolidate and anchor our learning. But when we return to work, we are often still left with those nagging questions about how we can really apply what we've learnt, still feel there are questions we have which weren't covered, or parts of the course that we didn't write down sufficiently clearly in our notes.

We try out some of the new ideas we've memorized, and if we're lucky, we feel we've been successful. On the other hand, we may not achieve what we hoped to, but don't quite understand why. And at the back of our mind is a series of gnawing questions. But what can we do about them? Who can we ask?

Too often, the temptation is to put this newly acquired theoretical knowledge into a metaphorical drawer, file the beautiful binder we were given during the course on a bookshelf, and carry on as before:

> Cognitive learning no more makes a manager than a swimmer. The latter will drown the first time she jumps into the water if her coach never takes her out of the lecture hall, gets her wet, and gives her feedback on her performance. (H. Mintzberg)

> Anybody in management education can tell you that lectures and bookwork alone are not sufficient for developing people who have to take decisions in the real world. (Reg Revans)

Such was the experience of one manager on his return from a course on 'motivating your staff'. He didn't know how to begin to tackle his staff's lack of motivation. Should he talk to them each individually? Should they do something collectively?

Where to start? So he did nothing. And it wasn't until he joined an action learning programme to help put this acquired knowledge into action that he came to the realization that in fact the issue was not how to motivate his staff, but how to motivate *himself*!

THE OPPOSITE OF 'CHALK AND TALK'

'It's the opposite of chalk and talk,' is one way I often describe action learning. From chalk and talk, we gain knowledge. But we can't know whether we're able to transfer that knowledge into practice until we try.

That's where the action comes in – action on some work-focused issue that is close to the participant's heart. For it's through applying what we think we know, or behaving in ways that we think will be effective, by making mistakes and thus discovering what we don't know or understand, and by celebrating our successes and understanding how they came about – through recalling, reflecting on, asking questions about and analysing all of this – that we gain insights, and understanding, and learn. We gain insights into how to be, to behave, and what might be useful next time we find ourselves in similar situations. But only 'similar', for nothing is ever the same again!

It is this process that is at the heart of action learning:

> It's a process that encourages and allows managers to blossom. It shows them the power of discovery and gives them greater sophistication as managers.

As one participant put it: 'It's unlike traditional courses where you work on make-believe projects, and then come Friday you go back to reality and you're not sure what, if anything, you can take back, until you've tried it.'

As mentioned in the Introduction, there is something paradoxical in writing a book about action learning. You will learn about action learning by reading, and become aware of the steps and stages of an action learning programme, and what you might learn and gain by participating in a programme. But you won't really know the 'how' of it until you've tested it out, run a programme, been part of one yourself – experienced the 'how it works' in practice. It's the experience of living through it that consolidates book-based or course-based knowledge.

Action learning is about working on real issues, taking actions – not merely talking about them – and learning while doing so.

It was during lecture-based courses that Revans originally, and others subsequently, became aware that their student managers were relatively passive and lacking in energy in the classroom. They came to life, though, when they discussed their own 'back home' problems with one another – usually in the bar. The message came over loud and clear: managers are people of action, who learn from action (unlike lecturers and academics, whose action and learning is based around thoughts and ideas). The other message was that managers will help each other in the right environment, are prepared to share their experience and insights, and that they represent a great seam of untapped wealth. Any one room of, say, ten middle managers, or ten functionally experienced staff, has within it over a hundred years' experience – often untapped and unshared.

And this, in a sense, is where the essential message of action learning originates: that we learn best when we have a real issue to resolve. We are more involved in, and committed to the action – and the subsequent learning – if what we are trying to resolve, change or manage is something we are responsible for, something we have to tackle – maybe something we have never had to do before. So our problems or challenges could be around such issues as: how to get a team working well together, how to involve people in issues that affect their lives, how to introduce new working practices, how to tackle a new work role, how to increase sales, how to reduce costs, and so on.

That is why an action learning programme requires everyone to work on such a real project. In this sense, action learning is about working and learning simultaneously – work provides a valuable learning opportunity.

The essential idea in an action learning programme is that participants don't just come up with a possible, elegant solution on paper – as in a case study. As in any real actionable project, they have to work through various stages, such as investigating, talking with people, planning, designing, resourcing, evaluating as they go along, recommending and – ideally – implementing what they are recommending. In this way, participants take responsibility from start to finish. Only by testing their ideas in practice will they know whether or not they were effective, practical, what problems they caused, what issues they had not considered and how to tackle these in turn, what to do differently in the future, and so on.

We're all aware that the skills and knowledge we have aren't always sufficient to help us with the uncertainties and questions, the challenges and opportunities that we face. In so many instances, we find ourselves feeling unsure, puzzled, juggling with several options. An issue we are tackling suddenly appears less straightforward than it seemed at the outset, simple techniques don't work, our body of knowledge or skills seems unable or inadequate to provide easy solutions. The answers still elude us.

So, as we come face to face with some issue/challenge, we become aware of our own questions, uncertainties, even doubts: Revans's problems (as opposed to puzzles). That's the time when we are most likely to learn, because resolving those issues is central to our being effective and successful. In other words, we learn best when we have some concrete issue on which to 'hang' our learning, rather than trying to learn in abstract:

Activity is the only road to knowledge. (George Bernard Shaw)

The real voyage of discovery consists not in seeking new lands, but seeing with new eyes. (Marcel Proust)

A person does not gather learnings as possessions but rather becomes a new person. (Gib Atkin)

When you read, you gain knowledge; when you 'do', you gain experience; when you reflect, you gain an understanding of both. (Anon.)

LEARNING WITH OTHERS

'Learning with and from others similarly engaged' is one of the basic tenets of action learning. It is built into the nature of the programmes. 'Comrades in adversity' was Revans's way of describing action learners (others have since come up with more positive definitions, such as 'comrades in opportunity'). A group of people will resolve issues in a more effective and imaginative way – if they work together effectively – than one person.

None of us has a monopoly on good ideas, insights, or even information – there is now too much of it for any one person to grasp, maybe even to understand. Moreover, we always bring our own perspective to everything – inevitably! That perspective will colour what we see and do, and may not alter from year to year, so it may prevent us from growing and changing; it may also create a block for others who wish to develop and change.

But when we work with others who are also concerned with trying to understand what is really happening around us, we gain from the searching and questioning that each one of us goes through. Improbable as this may sound initially, it is something that participants refer to time and time again: how beneficial it is to work with others, even on others' issues.

Revans is fond of quoting Lord Rutherford of the Cavendish Laboratory in Cambridge in the late 1920s (where Revans then worked), who, after an afternoon's 'action learning' (the term was not yet coined) with a group of colleagues (their task was to find some means of financing their laboratory and its research, which were threatened with closure), exclaimed: 'Gentlemen, I have in the course of this afternoon become aware of the depth of my own ignorance. What does yours look like to you?'

The challenge of others revealing their doubts and their unknowns, and working with them to create more insight and clarity is as helpful to those examining their actions as it is to the rest of the 'comrades in adversity'.

I was asked, while preparing this book, whether it was possible to undertake action learning as a solo activity – on your own. Intellectually, it obviously is – though only up to a point. We are, after all, thinking beings. 'It's something that I need to learn to do without others – on my own,' was the comment of one young participant after her colleagues in adversity had quizzed her, pushed her, and made her think of issues that hadn't occurred to her. But doing so on our own is weaker, because we lose the benefit of others. How can we guarantee that on our own we won't merely pursue our own inclinations, that we will challenge ourselves as much as a group of others will force us to? Do we really have such faith in ourselves?[2]

LEARNING WITHOUT EXPERT INSTRUCTION

Action learning places a high value on each individual, coupled with a strong belief that we can learn without experts, lecturers, and specialists. This may seem like heresy to many – and such a bold statement does require some modifying.

In a 'classic' action learning programme, there is no taught element. The programme centres on the combined expertise of the set members. The thinking behind this is that all of us have a great deal of knowledge and experience which, when combined with others' knowledge, experiences and perspectives, is often as valuable as having an expert come in to teach:

> ... in true action learning it is not what a man already knows and tells that sharpens the countenance of his friend, but what he does not know and what his friend does not know either. It is recognised ignorance not programmed knowledge that is the key to action learning: men start to learn with and from each other only when they discover that no-one knows the answer but all are obliged to find it. (Reg Revans)

We have been brought up to believe that experts know best. We undervalue ourselves, are in turn undervalued, and lose confidence in our own insights and abilities. So we bring in experts, who often confirm what we have been thinking – which is in itself useful! There are, of course, areas of specific knowledge where an expert can add considerable value. But frequently, someone within a set has that expertise already. And when it comes to knowing our own situations and circumstances, each of us is the expert on that.

Action learning stresses the value of the so-called 'non-experts' – handing back to each of us our own 'power'. Revans is provocative when talking about experts, for they are mostly, as he puts it, experts of past knowledge. The past, however, is not necessarily a guide to what will be useful or relevant in the future. Moreover, experts are frequently pedlars of packages and solutions that fit all problems! More useful, according to Revans, is the ability to ask questions, and thus to see where past expertise may have some relevance, but also where it is of little use.

How often do we go on a course and hear ideas and suggestions that we have silently thought and felt would be effective or relevant, but subsequently fail to implement them for a number of complex reasons – there wasn't time, we didn't want to stick our necks out, it would be rejected anyway, we'd be told it had been tried before, no one ever listened, and so on? Alternatively, we go on a course, only to find that much of what we hear is only of marginal relevance to our own circumstances. Or we are told so much, we simply forget whole chunks of it – remembering only bits that are relevant today, and not knowing what may be relevant tomorrow, but by that time it's too late, for the lecture was today. Or, worse still, we don't fully follow or understand what we've been told, but there is no chance to stop, examine it, ask questions and try to understand. Anyway, maybe everyone else present fully understands, and it's only us who don't. So we remain silent – and confused.

What happens in an action learning programme is that our belief in ourselves is restored. We realize – through having to think and work through issues we face – that we often have the answers to our questions and problems. With the help and support of the group with whom we work, we test out our own ideas in practice, evaluate them, and learn from doing so: 'I kept asking questions and seeking others' answers, until I realized that the answers were in me.'

Action learning programmes create an environment where participants go through this process of recalling, analysing and thinking in the company of others who are similarly engaged. Such a group becomes supportive and challenging, ready to give participants feedback, to help, and to question. When this begins to happen, action learning becomes complex and very rich.

OUR OWN EXPERIENCE IS THE BEST TEACHER

Action learning is based on the premise that our own experience is one of the most useful teachers – if we know how, and are prepared, to make the most of it.

Over a lifetime, we gather a huge mass of data about our work, our relationships at work and elsewhere, and about our own and others' behaviours. This accumulation or experience forms the basis of our opinions, generalizations, convictions – our 'theories in use'. But, in the words of one participant: 'Experiences, like dreams, need interpreting.' Or, as T.S. Eliot said: 'We had the experience but missed the meaning.'

To realize the true value of our experience, we need to learn to reflect on it, to put our 'theories in use' to the test by sharing them with fellow set members who will respond with insights and questions of their own. Together, we can learn from our multiple experiences, both 'good' and 'bad', successful and less successful. This is a process that requires time, openness, and often courage.

L = P + Q

The stress on the learning means that sets usually need to work with a set adviser, at least in the initial stages of a programme. Without the set adviser pulling the set back from rushing into yet more actions, and asking them 'What have you learnt?', action learning becomes merely another action-focused programme, where the 'experience' and the action are not fully explored and reflected on. Yet without such 'feedback', we learn little.

$$L = P + Q$$

This is Revans's shorthand for: 'Learning consists of Programmed Knowledge plus Questioning.'

P – 'Programmed Knowledge' – is the expert knowledge, the knowledge in books, what we are told to do because that is how it has been done for decades. But it may not be the most useful knowledge for the present or the future.

Q – Questioning – is just that: questioning what aspect of this previous knowledge and experience is useful, relevant or helpful here and now, as we deal with our immediate issue. This questioning is also a way of admitting to our own ignorance, of saying, 'I don't know. ' And by questioning others, we increase the scope of our – and their – searching.

L – Learning – results from the combination of the other two: P (all the knowledge we accumulate through reading or going on courses and listening to lectures – the knowledge of the experts) and Q (asking questions about that programmed knowledge and about the circumstances you find yourself in).

But there is a further P which we each need to examine. Everyone has a mass of accumulated life encounters from which we create our own beliefs and theories, on which we then proceed to act. This forms our own personal 'Programmed Knowledge' which, like the knowledge in books, we need to question.

Revans has another interesting equation:

$$L > C$$

Learning has to be greater than Change. He means: to survive, to keep up with changes around us, our learning, and the speed at which we learn, has to be greater than change. This obviously has implications for the world as we enter the 21st century. We hear everywhere that change is accelerating, that nothing is static, everything is constantly changing. So, if we accept the equation $L > C$, it means we have to learn $(P + Q)$ at a fast rate. But the faster the change, the more rapidly P will become outdated. That leaves us with Q. The better our questioning, the greater the opportunity for accelerated learning.

Asking questions – examining, thinking – these are fundamental aspects of action learning.

Action learning is thus an excellent complement to standard teaching courses – you learn about X, Y and Z, but real life isn't as neat and tidy. When you're back at work, you begin to wonder how to use what you learnt, what would be useful. You find you forgot some parts of it, or don't seem to be applying others as effectively as you hoped – that's when action learning programmes come into their own: to help you apply your learning and consolidate the knowledge.

We know that we have learnt when we can do something differently. This may result from seeing things differently, gaining a different understanding of them, being able to think differently or ask different questions.

Put simply, learning – as we use the word in everyday language – is often applied to memorizing (as exhibited in some television quiz shows), or to simply understanding intellectually, after reading something or hearing a lecture, or applying some newly learnt skill – doing something differently, or developing and changing in some way, after an experience. So:

L = memorizing

L = understanding something intellectually

L = applying some newly learnt skill – taking action and doing something differently

L = experiencing – an inner development which touches on beliefs and attitudes, and which leads to development

One branch manager from a major building society said:

> I was sent on this programme because, although I'd attended every management course available in the company, I still wasn't performing or achieving. And that was because, although I knew a great deal 'about' various managerial topics, I was unsure of how to apply them, and what to do if I didn't get things quite right ... and then I'd lose confidence, or find it was easier to simply behave as I had before ... This programme has enabled me to use – to test out and apply – all that 'chalk and talk' that I'd absorbed and kept in my head, but not really applied in any coherent fashion.

We need to be able to examine and ask ourselves questions about these expert or theoretical solutions or ways of doing things. We need to apply our own critical assessments and insights, and either choose what we think will be helpful, or devise some other ways of resolving the issues we face.

Participants on action learning programmes are made to focus most of all on asking questions, and are discouraged from giving advice (a form of programmed knowledge).

Questioning oneself and others who are on the programme does not try to find answers, but rather to explore, uncover, unpeel (as the skins of an onion), to get at the core issue, and to get insights and begin to understand:

> Through being asked questions and having to give explanations or answers, you hear yourself talk, you hear your own inconsistencies or doubts, or you confirm what you think ... but doing it out loud is different from asking yourself 'in your head'. You hear things – in fact you say things – you don't necessarily think in the silence of your head.

> Questioning – more and more discriminating questioning – is at the heart of action learning ... The simple nudge of a question occurring as one responds to another can change the way we see ourselves and be a permanent unrepeatable eye-opener.

Questions always lead to more questions, and perhaps to more discriminating questions. It seems unlikely we will be able to make progress on the vast organisational problems in businesses, government and society without developing the skills of asking and responding to more and more discriminating questions. It is certain that we will not find in any book an answer to how to distribute food to the starving; how to enable computers to arrange to do heavy, dangerous and repetitive work without causing hardship to people; how to ensure that we give adequate health care to all new born babies; or how to house even our present population. (Lawrence 1986)

A REFLECTIVE ELEMENT

Built into the processes of action learning is a large reflective element. As we are asked – or ask ourselves – questions, we are pulled back or propelled forward in our thoughts. Participants on a programme are made to look back and reflect on what they did (the action) or did not do, and on what happened. But equally importantly, participants are also made to look back on what they said and felt, and on what others said, or did or did not do. By replaying events, conversations and feelings, we can begin to understand why we did or did not achieve something, or what was stopping us. We may also reflect on what else we could have done, or what we could have done differently, and what results that might have brought.

Reflecting – recalling, thinking about, pulling apart, making sense, trying to understand – is crucial to our learning. It makes us more aware of ourselves, of others, and of what is happening around us. The process of action learning gives us the time to do this. It also legitimizes reflection, points up the benefits. Reflection is a stage in the learning cycles which participants in action learning (and other learning programmes) are introduced to and encouraged to follow to a greater or lesser degree (see pages 40–43), and by reflecting on past actions, we can become aware of what to do – or not do – in the future.

We can thus begin to expand the basic action learning equation to look like this:

$$L = P + Q + A + R$$

Here, A represents the Action (or the conversation or thoughts and feelings), and R is the Reflection.

As one participant said:

> It gives you time and space to stand back and reflect, unfreeze your thoughts, rise above everyday problems, bring things into perspective, get others' perspectives – all in a non-judgemental, supportive yet challenging way ... and say: 'So what can I/you/do about it?' – take responsibility and ownership. It's very exciting, if at times daunting. But you get a great sense of achievement.

Others said:

It gives you the time and ability to move away from tasks and activities and see and understand and learn about – and learn from – what you're doing. At work, we're simply achievers of activity.

I've realized that the time out for thinking and reflecting is crucial. I now often go out for a quick walk and take my 'problem' with me for a walk!

DIALOGUE VERSUS DISCUSSION

By giving each person in the set the time to focus on themselves and their work, and by applying the questioning process, the set is engaging in a 'dialogue' with that person, rather than having a 'discussion'. David Bohm (1993) makes a useful distinction between dialogue and discussion.

The word 'dialogue' comes from the Greek *dia* ('through') and *logos* ('word'). A dialogue emphasizes the idea of a meaning that flows between people from which emerges a greater understanding – possibly even a shared meaning.

'Discussion' (from the same root as 'percussion' and 'concussion') emphasizes analysis, breaking up/down, and different viewpoints.

'A discussion,' says David Bohm, 'is like a ping-pong match, with people batting ideas around in order to win a game … in a dialogue there is no attempt to gain points … in a dialogue everyone wins'.

In a dialogue, there are two sorts of questions: those that are person- and project-focused, and those that, like pebbles, are thrown into a pool to create ripples.

LEARNING, DEVELOPING AND CHANGING

This constant emphasis on learning, and how it is achieved, is one of the distinguishing hallmarks of action learning – the asking of the question 'What did I learn from that?' which becomes second nature. (There are other learning and experiential programmes that bear some resemblance to action learning, but which differ in many fundamental ways: see below.)

The task or project (the action) part of a programme provides – at least initially – the main vehicle for learning. As time goes by, participants find more learning opportunities. In fact, the set and its process become major sources of learning (see below).

THE KOLB AND REVANS LEARNING CYCLES

Learning from our actions thus involves undertaking some action – a 'project' which consists of various tasks to be carried out, behaviours, conversations, and so on –

recalling them, being questioned about them, reflecting on them, trying to understand what was happening, coming to some conclusions or having some insights,
preparing to do something differently next time, and then beginning on some 'new'
actions (a continuation of a task or project). Such learning cycles are represented in
Figure 2.1.

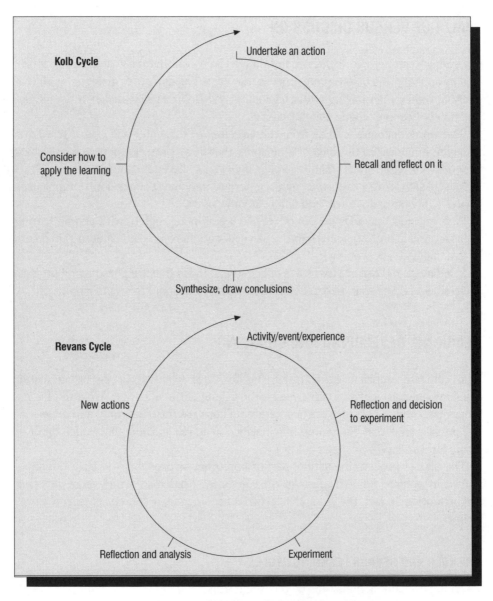

Figure 2.1　　The Kolb and Revans learning cycles

In a sense, though, they need to be depicted as learning *spirals* (as shown in Figure 2.1), for the intention is that we will not return to the same place from which we started. That would not be learning. We move to a different place. Hence the notion of something moving and changing – a spiral.

Moreover, placing 'reflection' at one location in such spirals is also misleading. The whole point is to develop an ability to reflect at *every* stage, all the time, whether we are undertaking an action, planning a new one, or even reflecting: we can be aware of what we are bringing into our reflection, and what we are choosing to leave out, and why (see Figure 2.2).

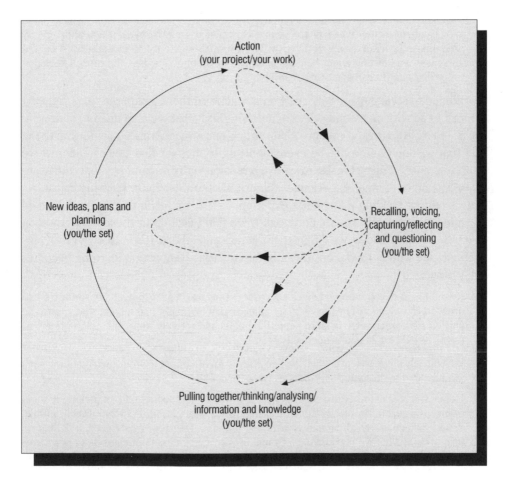

Figure 2.2   Reflections at each stage

AN INNER LEARNING CYCLE (OR SPIRAL)

In order to learn, more than action is required. We have seen that to learn, we also need to question, to understand and to reflect not simply on our actions, but on our thoughts and our feelings. These are equally important if learning is to take place. Changing actions – behaviours – without changing underlying beliefs and assumptions will be a short-term affair. To change, we need more fundamental shifts in beliefs and feelings.

A useful distinction between 'action' and 'experience' has been made by Logan and Stuart:

> A distinction can be drawn between an outer and inner world of human existence. Activity is focused upon and enacted in an outer world, whilst experience is located in an individual's inner world ... Juch comments that '... those who devote their major attention and efforts to the world outside them ... dealing with people and tasks and situations in the environment ... may become out of touch with their inner capacities or purpose in life ...'. That inner focus – which characterises experience – may be bypassed or short-cut by predominantly outer-oriented activity. The more that activity is characterised by the 'busyness' and flitting about behaviour typical of action managers, the more likely that this will occur. (Logan and Stuart 1987)

In addition to recalling and reflecting on our actions, there is an *inner* experiencing – more to do with our feelings and inner thoughts – that we also need to address if we are to really learn and change. 'Confronting our own ignorance', owning up to the fact that we don't know, maybe even admitting to the fear this causes and how we therefore cover it up by bluster or even aggression, or by remaining silent: these are some examples of inner experiences. Figure 2.3 shows an inner learning spiral.

It is only by tackling these inner experiences that we begin to gain the full value of action learning, and see its potential. If we don't face up to these very common and human experiences, we diminish ourselves and others. It's at this level – if participants are willing to explore these inner caverns – that action learning becomes truly powerful:

> It is not hard to stand behind one's successes. But to accept responsibility for one's failures, to accept them unreservedly as failures that are truly one's own, that cannot be shifted somewhere else or onto something else, and actively to accept ... the price that has to be paid for it: that is devilishly hard.[3]

> We will only begin to learn when we become aware of – admit to – our own ignorance and are prepared to do something about it. (Reg Revans)

> Denial is a way of life. More accurately, it is a way of diminishing life, of making it seem more manageable. Denial is the alternative to transformation. Personal denial, mutual denial, collective denial. Denial of facts and feelings. Denial of experience, a deliberate forgetting of what we see and hear. Denial of our capabilities. Politicians deny problems, parents deny their vulnerability, teachers deny their biases, children deny their intentions. Most of all we deny what we know in our bones.[4]

> We do not see things as they are, we see them as *we* are. (The Talmud)

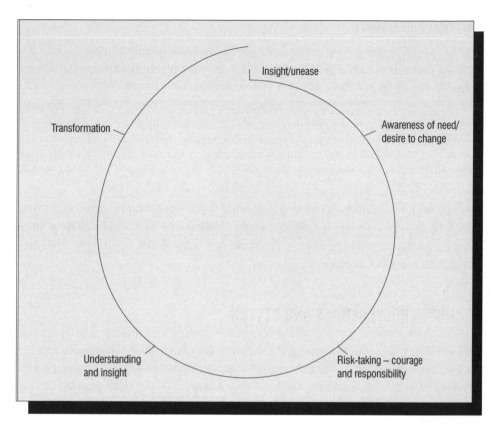

Figure 2.3   The inner learning spiral

THE VALUES UNDERPINNING ACTION LEARNING

The three fundamental values that underpin action learning are:

1. being honest with oneself and with others
2. respecting others and their viewpoint
3. taking responsibility for our own actions.

Honesty with oneself is essential if we are to develop, and change. We may be able to hide from other people, but hiding from ourselves is counter-productive. It's living a lie. In the end, either we are caught out or we become cynical, negative, and cease to grow.

Respecting others, listening to them, appreciating their viewpoint (maybe they really do have something to tell us?) regardless of who they are is increasingly important in working organizations. Those nearest the 'coal-face' have so much to offer.

FREEDOM AND LIBERTY

Taking responsibility for our actions and our behaviours is part of being honest. It's so easy these days to blame others for what goes wrong, or doesn't work, or isn't done. This may be justified, but often it's another smoke-screen:

> The answer to the question, 'who governs me?' is logically distinct from the question, 'How far does government interfere with me?' It is in this difference that the great contrast between the two concepts of negative and positive liberty, in the end, consists. For the 'positive' liberty comes to light if we try to answer the question, not 'What am I free to do or be?' but 'By whom am I ruled?' or 'Who is to say what I am, and what I am not, to be or do?'[5]

Dealing with our own dishonesty, and hearing – and admitting to – the 'sub-texts' which lie behind what we say and do, means dealing with our 'shadow'. How often do we really acknowledge openly, to ourselves even if not to others, what lies behind our words or actions?

LEARNING PREFERENCES AND STYLES

The challenge for action learning is to enable people to be more effective in the future, and not simply in the one project that set members work on during a programme. The power of action learning is that it gives us tools to help us face future problems and challenges more confidently and effectively.

Learning is concerned with acquiring new facts and figures or new skills and behaviours. It is also about gaining new understanding, and becoming more aware. It may lead to us changing our beliefs and attitudes. In this sense, learning carries with it the implication of doing things differently, of changing.

But, it seems, we also have preferences for how we learn. To paraphrase a whole volume of work (*The Manual of Learning Styles*, complete with questionnaire), Honey and Mumford (1986) have divided learners into four categories (which are not exclusive, but indicate preference):

1. **Activists** prefer immediate action, and maybe stop and consider later.
2. **Reflectors** prefer to stop and think, and tend to be cautious.
3. **Theoretists** integrate what they have seen or done into sound, rational schemes.
4. **Pragmatists** are keen on trying out ideas, theories and techniques.

These four styles of learning coincide with the stages of the learning cycles/spirals:

1. doing something – what they call 'experiencing'
2. thinking about what happened – reviewing
3. drawing some conclusions – concluding
4. deciding what to do in a similar situation – planning.

According to Honey and Mumford, if you are 'an all-round learner, you are likely to manage each stage of this process consciously and well. Your activist tendencies will ensure you have plenty of experiences. Your reflector and theoretist tendencies will ensure that afterwards you review and reach conclusions. Your pragmatist tendencies will ensure that you plan future implementation' (Honey and Mumford 1986).

Thus we each choose activities that are most congruent with our style of working/learning – which we need to be aware of. But, as Honey and Mumford point out: 'if you want to be fully equipped to learn from experience, you will need to develop styles which at present you do not use' (Honey and Mumford 1986).

One way of doing this is by working in a set, seeing how others work, and benefiting from their 'approach' – which will be clear from the way they tackle their learning, the way they behave in the set, and the language and concepts they use. Thus set members can not only learn from colleagues with differing styles, but also begin to appreciate the value of such differences. Activists, for example, by being asked questions and almost being forced to reflect before piling into the next activity, will start to use another style, and may begin to see the benefits. Set members with other styles will similarly learn from their colleagues with differing styles.

In order to gain the most from others, we need to acquire learning skills: those behaviours that help us learn. Mumford (1993) has listed the following that help the learning process:

- Establish effective criteria for yourself.
- Measure your effectiveness.
- Identify your own learning needs.
- Plan your personal learning.
- Take advantage of learning opportunities.
- Review your own learning process.
- Listen to others.
- Accept help.
- Face unwelcome information.
- Take risks, and tolerate anxieties.
- Analyse what other successful performers do.
- Know yourself.
- Share information.

Honey and Mumford (1995) have also demonstrated that we each have differing 'attitudes' to learning:

- **Incidental learners** learn when shocked or jolted into a realization.
- **Intuitive learners** just learn somehow, but aren't quite sure how it happened.
- **Retrospective learners** learn by recalling and reflecting.

- **Prospective learners** plan to learn
- **Opportunistic learners** combine the last two attitudes.

This emphasis on 'conscious learning' is interesting, for it implies that maybe the best learners are simply forever awake and aware. Many participants in action learning programmes talk of the greater awareness and consciousness they now have of what is happening around them, and within themselves. To adapt the 'Johari Window' analogy: rather than becoming 'unconsciously competent' they are implying that they remain 'consciously competent' (see Figure 2.4).

As one participant wrote in a reflective document:

> What I am trying to do now is control which learning style I adopt through recognizing at a given point what is happening, and adopting a style that I feel is most appropriate to the situation. For example, at meetings where I am genuinely enthused by ideas and discussion, my activist and pragmatist roles dominate. I am consciously forcing myself to adopt a more reflective style in these situations. And I'm doing the same in my decision-making process back at work.

More important for action learning, however, is this notion of 'opportunistic' learning, for that is what action learners become – as witnessed by their remarks quoted in this book. They have begun to learn from a whole variety of opportunities. Life – and work – are their classroom:

> A wise person learns when he or she can. A fool learns when he or she must. (Duke of Wellington, paraphrased)

> To a great experience one thing is essential – an experiencing nature. (W. Bagehot)

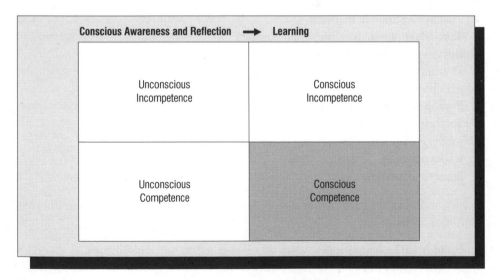

Figure 2.4　**Conscious competence**

> We are all surrounded by opportunities. But they only exist once seen. And they are only seen if they are looked for. (Edward De Bono, paraphrased)

Action learning makes people aware of their learning style, but also encourages people to become opportunistic learners. 'I have realized,' said one participant, 'that everything is data. I now expect to learn from any situation I'm in.'

By focusing on work-centred projects and action, action learning takes learning out of the classroom and into the workplace (or anywhere else, for that matter). In this way it opens our eyes to the fact that we can learn from anything, anywhere, and any time – by overhearing conversations, reading a book, taking time out to reflect, experimenting, observing some activity, and so on.

By becoming opportunistic learners, we also begin to gain insights into how and in what circumstances we learn best – a useful insight to have when we face new challenges or worries, for it means we can reproduce the circumstances which will help us learn faster and better in the future. And the faster we learn, the more effective we become. So if I discover that I learn best by being asked questions, I create circumstances where I will be asked. If I discover I learn best by listening to others, I again create those circumstances, and so on.

IS ACTION LEARNING SUITABLE FOR EVERYBODY?

As already pointed out, action learning is potentially for everyone and anyone – old or young, regardless of job, status, profession or role in life. But not everyone may be suitable for action learning. Action learning is very much a programme for those who want to explore, to investigate, for those who are inquisitive, for those who want to understand, to gain insights, to go on learning, and who are prepared to change.

On the other hand, those who avoid or choose not to come on such programmes may be the very people who stand to gain the most.

When participants were asked whether they thought everyone was suitable, their views were mixed:

> No, it's not for someone who is selfish and won't listen to others. He or she will pose problems. On the other hand, both they and the set may learn: the former to change and learn to listen and consider others; the latter to tackle someone like that, who may be like people they come across elsewhere and don't know how to deal with.

Some felt: 'You need a certain empathy with others.' Others thought it was not for those who are very self-opinionated, authoritarian and dismissive of others. The philosophy of action learning is about valuing everyone, learning to be tolerant, while still being intellectually rigorous and challenging. On the other hand, several participants pointed out, it could be an interesting experience for participants to be given the chance to 'tackle' such a person in the 'safe' environment of a set – and give the person being tackled some food for thought!

One participant felt: 'Some may find it difficult to participate in the process of the set, particularly if some members dominate. You need a good set adviser, otherwise the set will move to where the loudest noise is coming from.'

There will be those who have a strong preference for solutions and clear-cut answers, and for treating everything as a 'puzzle'. They may initially feel very unhappy with some of the more 'right-brained' activity that occurs in the set. But they may have their minds opened and stretched by such a programme.

And then there are those who genuinely prefer to work alone, who do so well, and who maybe should not be coerced into being different.

Interestingly, those participants who said they found the programme of limited use, and were unsure whether everyone would benefit from it, all pinpointed the way the set worked as being their stumbling block. It seems that this is the most difficult aspect of action learning for some – if not most – to grasp. It is also one of the main distinguishing features of action learning. (For more about the processes, and the how participants experienced them, see Chapter 5.)

TO CHOOSE OR NOT TO CHOOSE?

There might seem to be a risk of falling into a trap where those who go on action learning programmes are self-selected. This raises the question of whether participants should choose to go on such programmes or be able to choose not to. I would say that the right to choose is in line with the philosophy of action learning, and should therefore be built in to a programme. Those who choose not to, for whatever reason, may later be more willing when they see that participants are not eaten alive or mauled to pieces!

Joining an action learning programme presupposes a wish to – and a belief in, or at least a willingness to – test out the value of working in a more open, effective and constructive way with others than we are often wont to do, for a host of reasons, often allied with issues of authority, status, power, lack of confidence and fear.

It also presupposes that participants want to explore and investigate.

One participant on a mixed-company set (a senior manager in a quango) admitted that he had learnt little: 'I didn't really get involved. I felt I didn't want to. I could see others gaining and becoming enthusiastic. But it just wasn't me to be as open as the programme demanded, and which would have been the way to really gain from it.'

It is therefore important that people are given some information about the nature of an action learning programme, and are then given the option of not joining it if they feel strongly about it. However, there may be some benefit in the 'shock of the new'. One participant (an engineer, and now totally committed to action learning) described his first experiences of the set as being full of horror at the thought of having to talk about himself in front of a group of people, and was adamant he would do no such thing.

Someone who is coerced or not given this option can make the programme difficult for everyone else – although a great deal can be learnt by tackling and coping with a negative or disruptive member of a set. But it could in the end prove to be counter-productive and destroy any wider aim of the programme.

Thus, in action learning terms, this question is a typical 'problem', and not a puzzle!

TOO OLD TO LEARN?

For many people, learning stops at 18, or at most 21. 'We're too old to learn,' they say.

Are we ever too old to learn – and change? The answer has to be 'yes', if we shut our minds to the possibility. Learning demands a certain humility. Revans's statement that it is only when we recognize our own ignorance that we begin to learn implies that we need to overcome our own internal barriers – and those of others – if we are to continue learning.

Learning is our ticket to survival. Learning is fundamental to growth, adaptation, change and progress. By not learning, we remain as we are, we stay in the same place – which may, of course, be the most comfortable place to be. And it may, on reflection, also be the 'right' place for us to be at any one point in time – we remain there after considering alternatives, and not out of habit or fear. For to face up to the fact that maybe we could be – and might in the past have been – doing things differently often demands courage. Similarly, to admit that we do not know or understand something, that we need help and insights from others, can equally be a fearsome experience. What will people think of us? Will they laugh at us?

HOW DO YOU LEARN TO WORK IN AN ACTION LEARNING WAY, AND HOW DO YOU KNOW WHEN YOU'RE WORKING WELL?

True to its philosophy, you learn about action learning by doing it! This is the paradox of writing a book about action learning and the experiences of participants. Until you've experienced it, you won't really understand.

As for knowing when you're working well – you sense the difference, and you see how you're working differently. Gone are the general, often competitive discussions; gone is the advice and the interrupting. One member commented after just one meeting: 'We've become less competitive with each other – against each other – and we're working more effectively now with one another.'

There is also a new sense of achievement and satisfaction, a greater awareness, and for many, a release of new energy: 'You sense a greater awareness of everything. You find you're asking questions, concentrating on someone and their issue, totally focused and engrossed, and you no longer give advice.'

Other participants commented: 'You think about the responses you're given to questions – and you don't just accept them.' 'You look at what you're doing, thinking and feeling, and reflect on them all. It becomes a way of life outside the set as well.' 'You listen differently ... and you're more prepared to say what thoughts and feelings you have on hearing what others are saying.'

HOW DOES ACTION LEARNING DIFFER FROM OTHER ACTION OR EXPERIENTIAL PROGRAMMES?

There are other programmes which have much in common with action learning. The degree to which other approaches are sympathetic to action learning is outlined in Figure 2.5[6].

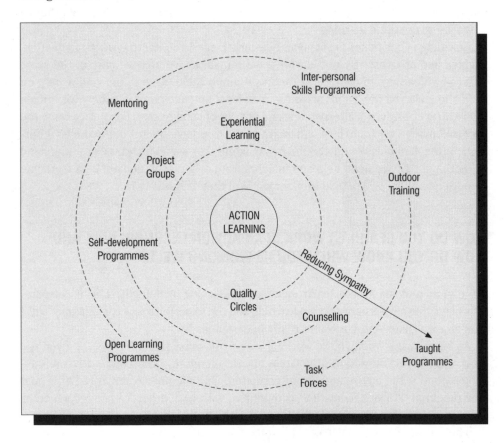

Figure 2.5 Sympathetic circles

Such approaches or programmes are all forms of experiential learning, and are highly complementary. Experiential learning is: 'the process that links education, work and personal development' (Kolb), and 'learning which arises from the first-hand experience of the learner' (Boud and Pascoe).

But action learning differs from other approaches/programmes in the following respects:

1. The focus is on the individual, and his or her learning and achievements (even when the aim of the programme is team-working or culture change).
2. The processes are different – in particular giving every participant airspace, and the questioning approach.
3. It emphasizes the underpinning values of honesty, respect for others, and taking responsibility.
4. It focuses on a real work-centred project.
5. It has a different time-span for its programmes.
6. Participants work with a set adviser skilled in process work, and in facilitating learning.

It is this combination of elements – and the rich brew that results, which is difficult to convey adequately in words – that participants have found so rewarding and useful (although by no means everyone finds it so, as this book will indicate). For participants, the differences were:

> ... the infrastructure of thinking and reflecting ... and the time and space for each individual – and the commitment that all this creates

> It's a programme where everyone is involved – the quiet and the vocal ones, the timid and the confident.

> ... working on a real project – not an imaginary one – and having to do something about it

> ... the emphasis on learning – all the time, not just at the end of the programme

> It's the discipline of the processes – of listening and of not giving advice.

> It involves the 'whole' person and who you are and what you value and want to be – not simply the 'role' person you are at work.

> Undoubtedly, other groups could help in achieving many of the benefits of action learning, but I'm not sure I'd have had the same confidence in their objectiveness or their level of understanding. Action learning really is different. It's about really listening ... and its underlying structure and common 'experiencing' by everyone present make the individuals want to participate more than in many other programmes. At work, for instance, we often listen, but we're really disinterested. At the pub, it's more mates chatting and giving advice. Neither of these happens in action learning. You have your own airspace – everyone concentrates on helping you, in the knowledge that their turn will come. It's the discipline that is powerful – you have to explain a problem or issue to the set, and in itself it's useful to have to articulate and get it into an order in your own mind ... and if you get lost, the set asks you to be more precise, or explain more. And it's really hard work.

For others, it was: '... unlike other courses where you're told what you'll learn, you're given outcomes to expect, and told what you'll be able to do after them. Here, the learning is much more up to you ... is your own individual learning.'

Going on to describe, rather than define, action learning, other participants said it was: 'like putting a mirror in front of you and confronting issues you'd prefer to ignore or avoid'. Another participant came at it from a different angle: 'It's like putting together your own programme. You find that in addition to your own project – the ostensible learning vehicle – you're simultaneously working on time management, empowerment, presentation skills, assertiveness ...'. Another agreed: 'It uses elements of lots of courses we've been on but never used.'

For another participant, it was '... about management development – and developing people generally', and:

> It's about professional development – and to be that it also has to be about personal development. You can't separate the two. To be professional you have to have competence to do a good job, meet new environments. It's not just a question of your knowledge and skills. So, put personal growth on top of these and you're doing more than relying simply on experience – which could simply look like twenty times one year's experience, rather than growth and change.

Some felt it offered a special 'spirit' – which they defined as being: 'not about finding answers to questions or problems, but taking the time and space to talk and think, and reflect on what you're being asked. It somehow releases you, gives you a sense of freedom.'

Others agreed: 'It's not about finding solutions to symptoms but about identifying the real problems.'

More graphically, a managing director of a small software company said it was: 'like shining a light into the corners – or lancing a boil that's been irritating you'.

SOME VISUAL IMAGES AND METAPHORS

Trying to unravel the experiences of action learning that participants spoke about felt like unravelling a complexly woven tapestry. But there were other images – both for participants and for me.

Metaphors were, for some, a way of trying to understand the process and to disentangle what they learnt, where, when and how. Images that participants drew on included: 'a big salad – you toss it around and come up with something that tastes good'; and 'a lentil loaf – deep, crunchy and long-lasting'. (Another participant was less flattering, and talked of 'knitting your own yoghurt'!)

Interestingly, the image of action learning as being an activity belonging to the 'alternative' society and closely resembling 1960s West Coast Californian 'experiments' cropped up only once, when a managing director of a small firm called action learning a 'new age activity'. He nevertheless attended all the meetings, and was very participative. His initial comments may well have been prompted by a need to protect himself.

A few other managers did admit that they grappled with the notion that anything that was 'supportive' and took place 'in a group' was going to be 'namby-pamby' and 'groupey-gropey'. One other participant – who has gone on to be one of action learning's most avid supporters – admitted: 'I was so scared of the idea when I first encountered it, I left it alone for two years.'

'Sitting in a balloon, and viewing the countryside below, with all the contours, rivers, trees,' was another version (not unlike the 'helicopter' image in popular use some years ago, but this time the balloon is a somewhat quieter means of transport, and one where those travelling in it are exposed to the elements). Another participant defined action learning as taking managers back again to the 'coal-face'. And as though combining these images, someone else described it as: 'like an archaeological excavation of a buried and forgotten city. The first find could be the only one, or with the right tools and attitude the whole city can be uncovered.'

Scaffolding – the means of moving up and down, horizontally, vertically or at different angles – was another vivid image: a means of moving around with flexibility and support.

One recurring image was derived from the theatre: the *commedia dell'arte*, in which actors in various roles and wearing masks were gradually able to drop them and reveal their true personas.

A number of men saw action learning as the 'feminization of management'. One went on to say: 'I'm not sure the action learning way of working is suitable in a more masculine environment which is aggressive, competitive, individualistic and ruthless.' The 'masculinity' was also to do with doing, and not talking, and with being crisp, clear and short-term. A 'feminine' organization, by contrast, was more caring, more teamwork-oriented, building on networking, and more 'democratic', where you were more likely to be listened to and valued. As one member put it: 'I learnt a great deal from the women in the set. They're much better at teamwork and sharing responsibility with others, and generally using others to help them arrive at a decision.'

My own metaphors – which emerged after just a few interviews with participants, and which continued to be applicable – were these.

Initially, a bowl of spaghetti: spaghetti, because every time I tried to separate one aspect of the action learning, it became entwined with other strands, and it was impossible to separate one from the other. If I pulled too hard, the strands snapped.

But the second – also culinary – image (I know not why!) was of a multi-layered chocolate cake. This image grew in strength (and layers!) as I realized the multi-layered complexity of action learning. I was also struck, though, that to achieve this richness, this complexity, several elements had to be present (see pages 9–10). Without them, the chocolate cake became a mere sponge cake, and the participants lost out on the breadth and depth that a well-managed action learning programme was able to offer.

A RECIPE FOR SUCCESSFUL ACTION LEARNING[7]

Ingredients:
6–8 people
Commitment
Trust
Concern
Time
Experience
Support
Challenge
Risk
Facilitation
Humour

Method:
Take a liberal slice of time, and mix thoroughly with the lifetime experience of several committed people. Sprinkle a generous helping of concern for others, and add enough trust to mould the mix until it gels firmly together. An added catalytic facilitator may help it to bind. Season with a little risk. Add support and challenge, whenever necessary.

Leave to simmer indefinitely, stirring regularly as you feed with a variety of problems. An occasional dash of humour will prevent the mix from sticking.

So what do you get? The opportunity:

- to focus on particular areas of your professional life and to discuss at a level which, for a variety of reasons, you cannot do at work
- to gain new perspectives on such areas, based on the experiences of others
- to develop and practice new skills in a relatively safe environment
- for reassurance that others have 'been there before'
- for friendship.

NOTES

[1] Reg Revans's books contain much that is useful for anyone interested in action learning: *The ABC of Action Learning* (Revans 1983, republished in 1998 by Lemos & Crane); *The Origins and Growth of Action Learning* (Revans 1982); he has also written articles included in *Action Learning in Practice* (Pedler 1997).

[2] Professor Tom Reeves, who asked me this question, wrote *Managing Effectively: Developing Yourself through Experience* (Reeves 1994), which takes individuals through a self-questioning approach, to try to simulate what a group in action learning would do.

[3] Vaclav Havel (1990) *Letters to Olga*, London: Faber and Faber.

[4] M. Ferguson (1982) *The Aquarian Conspiracy: Personal and Social Transformation in the 1980s*, London: Paladin.

[5] Isaiah Berlin (1969) *Four Essays on Liberty*, Oxford: Oxford University Press.

[6] Figure 2.5 is reproduced with kind permission of Jean Lawrence.

[7] Recipe devised by Dr Sheila Webb, Consultant in Public Health Medicine, 1992.

Part II

Action Learning in Practice

This part of this book deals with the practicalities of action learning:

- the set (Chapter 3)
- the action – projects and tasks (Chapter 4)
- the processes used in a set (Chapter 5)
- the set adviser (Chapter 6)
- the timespan (Chapter 7)
- the learning (Chapter 8).
- overcoming participants' reservations about action learning (Chapter 9)
- the future development of action learning, and its relevance to the learning organization (Chapter 10)
- setting up an action learning programme (Chapter 11).

Some of the chapters conclude with some case examples of action learning in action – brief sketches of when and how an action learning approach was used. They do not describe in any detail the outcomes, but are meant to highlight the wide variety of applications of action learning. (These case examples first appeared in my article 'Action learning in the UK' in *Performance Improvement Quarterly* (1998), vol. 11, no. 1, and are reproduced with their permission.)

3 The set

WHAT EXACTLY IS THE 'SET'?

The set is the small group of people who meet regularly during a programme, to work with each other. A set should consist of no more than six or seven people. If it is larger, people may opt out and not participate. The set should be:

- a helpful, questioning group
- a listening 'mirror'
- a resource group
- a support and challenge group
- a reflective group
- a learning group.

Set members act as a resource for one another, and as a 'support and challenge' group. Each member is in turn supported and challenged by the other set members as he or she tackles their project/task, and focuses on their learning. 'Comrades in adversity' is how Reg Revans described the set; others, such as Alan Mumford, have been more optimistic, calling them 'comrades in opportunity'.

HOW DOES A SET DIFFER FROM ANY OTHER GROUP OF PEOPLE GATHERED TOGETHER TO WORK?

The set differs in several ways, primarily because its task is different. The aim of the set is not to resolve issues together; it is to help each individual member resolve his or her own issues with the support and challenge of the rest. This will, of course, be modified somewhat if the set is working on a group project, but even then, each member should be allocated a mini-project, and hence the same process will apply for at least part of the meeting. At some point, the whole project will need to be addressed, and other processes will then be more effective.

A set also differs in the way it works. Instead of having a discussion around a table, as takes place in most groups, in a set each person has their own airspace, when the rest of the members focus on that person's issues or project, and work exclusively with him or her.

When a set is working, what takes place could be described as a dialogue with one person, rather than a discussion amongst a group. One participant, a police officer, was very clear how working in a set differed from other groups: 'You're not in competition, there are no threats, you want everyone to succeed, there are no prizes and you're all pulling in the same direction.' (For more on the processes used in the set, see Chapter 5.)

However, if the person who is presenting decides a discussion or a brainstorm would be useful, to hear others' insights and ideas – possibly before resuming the one-person format – then the set is free to do so. Sets are able to set their own agendas. Set advisers in such an instance will follow their own sense of how to respond (see page 138).

Set members are also committed to meeting regularly, with the same members attending, and with their focus firmly on their learning as well as their projects, and hence their actions.

The other major difference is in the constant attention to learning. At any one time, the learning may be focused on one person or – if it is appropriate – on the set as a whole. In time, members become attuned to thinking about their learning as they work together. At the outset, however, it is usually the set adviser who draws attention to it. (For more on the learning, see Chapter 8.)

Sets rarely appoint a chairperson or other roles, although at each meeting someone may agree to take some notes for the set – most likely on individual action plans before the next meeting, or issues of common interest that arose during the day – or simply keep an eye on time. A set will also not have an agenda, other than to make sure that, ideally, at a set meeting every member is given an opportunity to have their airspace.

Sets are groups which, if possible, are not joined by new members. A set becomes a cohesive group where trust and openness develop as members get to know each other. A new member disrupts this. It then takes time for the set to re-coalesce.

The set also differs from tutorial or seminar groups, in that it is the responsibility of the set members to work and find solutions. The set adviser is not a chairperson nor a teacher. He or she is there to help the work of the individuals and the set as a whole – by asking questions, or pointing out to the set what is happening and how it is working.

WHAT DO YOU GAIN FROM BEING IN A SET?

The set offers an opportunity for:

- time and space for your own reflections
- insights from others/with others
- different perspectives from others
- ideas with/from others
- others' experiences
- others' knowledge
- being questioned by others
- an opportunity to 'hear' yourself think – and respond
- support from others
- challenge by others
- sharing confusions with others
- sharing successes with others – and learning from them
- hearing yourself be helpful – and gaining in confidence.

A number of approaches are possible:

- The problem-presenter may describe his or her story/project, with the rest listening and asking questions.
- An individual may focus on a current quandary, or issue of concern or interest with the rest listening and asking probing questions.
- The set may discuss/brainstorm the individual's 'issue' – at his or her request only – while he/she listens.
- The set may focus on an issue of common interest or concern, and decide how it wants to work.
- The set may ask the set adviser to find an 'expert' on a particular topic related to their work, or may ask one of their own members to do a short input.

HOW DO YOU WORK IN A SET?

There are also a number of ways of relating to others when working with them, by being one of the following:[1]

- **prescriptive** – telling them what to do
- **informative** – simply passing on information
- **confrontational** – making them face up to something
- **catalytic** – asking questions to involve them, asking for their opinions
- **supportive** – showing care and concern for others
- **cathartic** – allowing feelings and emotions to emerge.

When working in a set, members have the opportunity to try out these various methods, and get feedback on the effect each has on the recipient. This – in addition to the emphasis throughout on asking questions (see pages 112–114) – is perhaps why many participants find that working in a set suggests to them new ways of managing.

Some people liken sets to quality circles. But several participants in programmes mentioned that they saw great differences, and were in fact planning to introduce an action learning way of working into their quality circles!

Before the set meeting – as with any other meeting – you need to ask yourself:

1. What do I want to work on today?
2. What do I want to achieve by the end of my airspace?
3. What will I do to make sure I achieve that?
4. What will I ask my fellow set members for?

At the end of their airspace, each participant will be given the opportunity to reflect on how they 'managed' their time, whether they got what they had hoped for, and if not, what they could have done differently. In this way, work within the set also becomes a focus for learning.

To get the most out of a set, you must be committed to:

- attending regularly
- giving everyone airspace
- giving everyone attention.

You should use the set to:

- ask for help/feedback
- share successes, mistakes, ideas
- be honest and open.

You should give feedback:

- Tell the set what you want/need.
- Tell the set what is helpful.
- Tell the set what isn't helpful.

You should involve:

- everyone
- the rational part of you
- the emotional part of you.

Above all, you should take responsibility, courage and risks.

It is also vital that confidentiality is maintained about what is said in the set. Only this way will participants feel free to be open and honest. You need to be able to trust the other set members, and it is only when we can be open and honest that we will address issues that will help us develop and learn.

In their supportive role, set members will be non-judgemental of others. A set thus becomes a place where people can be open and honest, about themselves and others, and give and receive honest feedback. Feedback is essential if development and change is to occur. In their challenging role, sets will explore the gaps and inconsistencies in a participant's story, or will challenge their beliefs and attitudes, and their thinking and actions – but still non-judgementally (see Chapter 5 for more on this).

One set member, a production manager with a major packaging company, created what he termed 'crude' categories for levels of openness in the set:

1. **The nudists** – those who are willing to expose both strengths and weaknesses to the set. The set is more important than the pride of the individual.
2. **The closets** – those who see the benefit of the open group, but only practise when it suits them. They keep their frankness in the closet for when they feel it is appropriate.
3. **The voyeurs** – those who want to share in the group experiences, but will only venture out when others have made the first move. They watch and join when the risks are low.
4. **The flashers** – those who seem uninterested in the ideas of group learning, yet occasionally provide flashes of inspiration which improve team performance.

ISN'T A SUPPORT GROUP RATHER 'SOFT'?

A support group which is nothing but supportive may well become a 'cocoon', and as such may not necessarily be very productive. On the other hand, cocoons are also places for development: without them, caterpillars could not become butterflies!

Support need not – in fact, *should* not – mean 'being in agreement' and sheltering. A set is rather, as several participants put it, 'a safe haven', somewhere to come in from the storm, to shelter temporarily, to take stock, regain energy and momentum.

As a support group, it is unlike any other group that most participants experience. At work, groups are not there for support, but to carry out a specific work-related task. Individuals in such groups are meant to be knowledgeable – and feel confident – in what they are talking about, take stances, and defend their viewpoints.

By contrast, for many a set is: 'the only place I can admit to not knowing, to having doubts, to feeling worried. You're not allowed to do that at work.' For others it is 'the only place and time I can be out of role', as one senior manager put it.

'By year two,' commented a participant on an 'academic' management programme using action learning, 'I needed my fix' ... it gave me clarity and energy. The discussions bring you conscious awareness, and it's the regularity which brings that energy and will to change, and learn.'

But this is not self-indulgence, as many participants were at pains to stress. And although a few of them talked of being 'hooked' and *needing* to talk to their set, they didn't see it as a drug, but something of importance. 'I found I was storing things up to tell the set,' admitted one person. Another laughed as she said that if she did something well at work, 'I'd think: The set would be proud of me.'

One participant was unabashed when he admitted:

> There's not been a time in the past seven years when I haven't been a member of a set. It's useful as a sounding board and it legitimizes the time we all need to stop and take stock. But we always say we haven't got time, and often we really don't as the pressures mount up. So, it's important to have that 'special' time. It's saved us time in the end because we didn't go down as may blind alleys as we would have done otherwise.

Another participant echoed a similar thought: 'You can, in a set, talk about your philosophy of life, as well as about your project. It's an opportunity to link things that are really linked for each of us as individuals but for which there is no room back at work.'

'It's a bit like having several mentors,' observed one member, 'something our managers should be doing, and aren't.'

What the set allows members to do is to talk, reflect, admit to emotions – something not done at work, and which may feel unnatural and scary to many. Best avoided! But when a group of people works closely together for a length of time, and members grow to trust each other, emotions of a more fragile nature will emerge. Doubts and fears will be talked about.

These doubts, fears and frustrations are not of great psychological dimensions, but ones that every normal, healthy human being experiences – even if they choose not to admit to them in certain company. Yet not talking about them doesn't make them disappear. Simply allowing them to emerge and be talked about – by making them legitimate – makes them less onerous, and less scary.

Potentially, there is a danger that someone may be experiencing deeper emotional problems. In such a case, the set adviser and the set themselves – not to mention the participant who is presenting these issues – needs to become aware of, and admit to the limits of their own competence to deal with these issues beyond a certain level.

Perhaps the greater danger, however, is that no emotions will be revealed and worked on, thereby severely limiting both each individual's and the set's potential for development and hence working more effectively and achieving better results in their projects. This again is where a professional and effective set adviser will enable and legitimize the expression of emotions in the (unlikely) event that someone in the set doesn't begin the process quite naturally.

THE NEED FOR CHALLENGE

Support without challenge, without questioning, without 'pushing' the participants to think, to take stock, to reflect, and take responsibility for themselves – this would indeed be 'soft'. 'Support' in the action learning sense means being non-judgemental, critiquing rather than criticizing, being available to give help and insights, and giving each participant the space and time to work through issues they are facing or are puzzled about in a 'safe' environment where they will not be criticized or held to account.

A set therefore provides a space where participants can also experiment with new ways of behaving, to see how comfortable they feel, and how they may become more effective back at work. 'The set was a useful sounding board. I would often arrive feeling persecuted and stressed , and left feeling good. The time and space to talk to others in a non-competitive environment would restore my own sanguinity and sense of perspective,' commented one participant:

> It's a place where you're challenged in a non-judgemental way. You realize your job isn't on the line, so you can admit to not knowing, to feeling worried – and just talking relieves the stress you feel. And by talking and being listened to you also get insights into what's causing the stress, and how to tackle or avoid it.

'It's difficult not to make the set sound like a crutch – but it isn't. It's more like an elastic band that stretches you,' summed up the experience of most participants.

Most participants *wanted* to be challenged and stretched. Those who weren't challenged commented on it: 'The set was too nice, they didn't challenge me, and they missed my confusion, because I gave off an aura of being and feeling OK.'

HOW MANY PEOPLE SHOULD THERE BE IN A SET?

The ideal number is five or six. If there are more, as in any other large group, it creates tensions and stresses that don't arise in smaller ones, because participants:

- may not have time to have their airspace at every meeting
- may not get enough space to be listened to, to think, to reflect, or simply to be quiet and sit silently
- may feel it won't matter if they don't turn up – they won't be missed
- may not want to be open and honest in front of a larger group
- may keep quiet because there are so many talking and asking questions already.

Having five or six people meet for a full day gives everyone time to tell their story at each session. If the meetings are shorter, this won't happen, which can raise some anxieties, and it means that some participants have to wait for a few meetings for their airspace. This in turn means that the cycle of action and learning may not occur. It is questionable whether such an arrangement is, strictly speaking, action learning, no matter how useful the discussion may be. But what's the follow-through? It is the process of having to do something and having to talk about what has been done and learnt – the 'revisiting' – that underlies the action learning process.

'Meetings are more productive when there are only five or six,' remarked one participant who had also experienced a set of nine members initially. 'Meetings have a different dynamic with fewer people, there's more contact, more space and time.' Another participant described how:

> our set was too big, so we've decided to break into two smaller ones. We think it will give us more of a chance to talk to one another, and we'll get to know each other better and go deeper into any issues ... in the bigger set if an emotional issue arises, you can't go into it sufficiently to help that person – it's a combination of too little time, too many people who each want space, and in a big group it's difficult to talk about one's problems anyway.

HOW IS THE MAKE-UP OF A SET DETERMINED?

The make-up of a set may be determined by a number of factors:

- whether the programme is an in-company or mixed-company one
- the objectives of the programme
- the specific issues participants want to address
- geography – it may not be feasible for regular meetings to take place if members have too far to travel.

Those planning and designing a programme need to consider carefully the aim of the programme:

- Is it to gather people from different functions, to enable them to work better together?
- Is it a career development programme? If so, a mix of people from different functions will add variety and different perspectives.
- Is it to resolve one department's issues? In this case, set members may all be from the same department.
- Is it to grapple with a common organizational issue that a group of people are facing, or where their insights would be helpful? If so, a set will consist of all concerned.
- Is it to ensure that people who have been on a taught course are applying the learning gained? If so, the set will consist of people from that course (and such sets could be in-company or mixed-company sets).
- Is it to expose people from one company to different ways of thinking and doing things by hearing the experiences of people from other organizations? If so, the set will be a mixed-company one.
- Is it to expose younger managers to a leadership programme, where they will focus on their 'development gaps' to prepare them for their next job moves? If so, set members will be selected after regular appraisals.

- Is it for the most senior people in an organization, who would feel more comfortable (initially, at least) in a set with no work colleagues; or maybe chief executives, who have no peers in their own organizations?

For more on projects and programmes, see Chapter 4.

HORIZONTAL-SLICE SETS

In most instances, set members will be made up of people who are of approximately the same level of responsibility. This is deemed to be important, because it means they can help each other more fully since, as one participant put it: 'They understand the issues you're tackling – may even have tackled similar ones to you.' The question is simply one of whether someone in a clerical grade, for instance, will have sufficient knowledge and insight to help a senior departmental manager resolve some of his or her work quandaries. Of course, it's possible they may, but it is an issue that needs to be considered.

This was borne out by one programme which was judged to be unsuccessful, in that participants felt they gained little and some individuals left the programme. The set members consisted of head teachers and departmental managers from medium-sized companies. In searching for reasons for failure, the set adviser found that the head teachers felt the managers didn't have the experience and hence the understanding of their problems and challenges. Their spheres of responsibility varied too much.

Another instance of a set which worked for some participants but not for others was described by a senior hospital manager who, with other colleagues from a variety of managerial roles, was in a set with consultants (the medical variety). He recalled that although it had been interesting, and he had gained from having to help the consultants understand aspects of management that they were encountering for the first time, he and the other managers felt they had gained less, because the consultants' level of knowledge about management was much more limited.

VERTICAL- OR DIAGONAL-SLICE SETS

Vertical-slice sets are those where members come from different levels of responsibility, but are within the same function or department. In diagonal-slice sets, members come from different levels of responsibility and from different functions and departments.

There have been many programmes with both vertical- and diagonal-slice sets. They have particular power – and relevance – where organizations talk of 'empowering' staff, of 'encouraging creativity', of 'creating a learning organization': fine words, but often pure rhetoric. Putting these ideals into practice requires some very pragmatic actions. One first step might be to 'experiment' by designing an action learning programme with vertical- or diagonal-slice sets to work together.

One company tackled their notion of empowering staff by doing this. The set included an older, senior manager, two young IT specialists, and the supervisor of a typing group. Their project was to consider how personal performance and team performance were currently assessed, to look at how people's achievements were recognized and rewarded, and following their findings, to devise a new appraisal system (which was implemented immediately). A second diagonal-slice set worked on cost-cutting and its implications, and a third one on improving training.

WHAT ARE THE ADVANTAGES AND DISADVANTAGES OF IN-COMPANY AND MIXED-COMPANY SETS?

The advantages of in-company sets are:

- the networking and inter-departmental contacts that are created
- the 'visibility' that such a programme gives participants
- the creation of a greater sense of cohesion within the organization, as people realize the benefits of working together
- a greater knowledge about the organization, all the functions within it, and the issues it is coping with.

> It was useful to have a cross-functional set. We never meet otherwise. We're separate fiefdoms. Or when we do meet it's within a structure and with tight time deadlines, so we never get to know each other.

Similarly, many participants felt that such gatherings allowed them to 'benchmark' themselves against others: 'It's often difficult to know how you compare with others – this is one way of checking out.'

The advantages of mixed-company sets are:

- seeing how different organizations tackle the same issues and problems
- feeling freer to discuss issues with strangers
- for very senior managers, the opportunity of sharing with peers.

> People in different companies have different perspectives, values, and understanding. Just hearing them is valuable. It challenges your preconceived notions that things have to be a certain way.

Said one manager: 'I feel that with a group of strangers you can be more open and honest ... and you have no hierarchies or difficult relationships to be concerned about.' Another talked of 'the release of being anonymous, with no one coming with preconceived notions of you or your role, so you have the space to be honest, and to experiment with different ways of working'.

'I'd always assumed that the way we did things was naturally the best. I've realized this isn't necessarily the case. In fact, I've taken away many very practical ideas on how to restructure our assessment procedures' – this from a personnel manager.

And for one participant from a blue-chip company, working with people from the public sector and realizing they had many insights and ideas he didn't have was 'a humbling experience'.

But one IT manager commented that such mixed-company sets, although very productive in many ways, were not suitable for certain purposes. For instance, if a company wanted to introduce cultural change, it would have to run an in-company programme.

A lecturer from the higher education sector remarked: 'The problems in my sector are the same as everyone else's in other organizations! That was reassuring. It meant we really could give each other insights and ideas that could be helpful, instead of repeating our own follies over and over again.'

Another manager from a large insurance company commented on the value he had derived from having in his set a manager from a small company: 'He simply brought a different, down-to-earth approach which was very refreshing.'

Conversely, a few participants thought that, fascinating though it was to work with people from other companies and get their perspectives and insights, 'You still have the problem of coming back into your own company and wanting to do things differently. It's the same re-entry problem you have when you attend any other "open" course.'

HOW DO YOU DECIDE WHICH TYPE OF SET IS BEST FOR YOUR PURPOSE?

There may be good reasons for not mixing people of different status levels. On in-company programmes, for instance, those in lower grades may feel intimidated, and think they have nothing of use to offer, whereas those in more senior positions may feel uneasy about exposing their doubts and fears in front of people in lower grades.

However, if a programme is being run in an organization that claims to be a 'learning company', with all its characteristics of openness, honesty, good communication, and so on, there would appear to be no reason for not having such vertical-slice sets. But I wonder how many organizations – their mission and values statements notwithstanding – are able to contemplate such groupings. (In fact, one of the issues now being widely discussed by those who have embraced an action learning way of working and learning is how to ensure that the whole organization begins to work naturally in this way, even after many programmes have been run.)

Sets are rarely made up on the basis of personality, skills or qualities, although some 'juggling' might occur to create a balance, say, of men and women, or to avoid having too many people from the same function (unless this serves a purpose). Where possible, a mix of abilities and styles of working is desirable.

'We had a good mix of experience – six to eight years of work on average, and a good mix of personalities,' commented one participant. By and large, it is the degree of randomness that adds a rich dimension to the learning.

WHY IS IT THAT SOME SETS FAIL TO GEL?

Sets, like other groups, create their own dynamics. It may be one member who upsets the energy in the set; it may be that the participants simply never feel totally at ease with one another. A few participants commented that they never felt comfortable: 'The chemistry didn't work, and we didn't get as close as I'd have wanted to, to feel free to really open out.'

A good set adviser will pick this up, and may raise it as an issue to be looked into and discussed – each participant offering their view and feelings on what is happening. This is an issue that is as 'real' as working on a project or task. It gives members an awareness that if a group isn't feeling comfortable, its work will be affected. One participant, who experienced a set working through this issue of not feeling comfortable, commented that she now feels free to comment on the processes in other groups she works with in her organization.

One or two participants also remarked that their sets had never become more than: 'a chat group, and we didn't get a lot out of it. People just went on talking, like anywhere else.' A good set adviser will intervene at such times, to ask the set to reflect on what is happening, and whether this is how they want to spend their time.

For those on in-company programmes, there will sometimes be an inclination to fall back into functional roles, wear those hats, and bring to the set the attitudes and beliefs that go with them. The set provides an ideal venue in which to explore the origins and validity of these.

Inevitably, office stories and gossip also occur, and fear of stories travelling back to the workplace may initially hold members back from being open and honest. This is one reason for stressing confidentiality. But many participants have pointed out that they learn a great deal from these stories. It gives them insights into other parts of the organization that they have little or no contact with.

Some sets don't gel because members don't attend regularly. Attending set meetings regularly is important – probably crucial. Attendance denotes commitment, for a start. If everyone is committed, this creates a working atmosphere. If some participants attend only intermittently, this conveys messages to the others about the importance the non-attending member attaches to them and the work they are doing.

Given that action learning centres on evolving personal stories, non-attendance also means that participants who miss meetings need to be updated, and the set loses a certain amount of its energy and time in having to bring them up to date.

Furthermore, the non-attending member also increasingly becomes a stranger who isn't present to help, support and simply 'be' with other set members as they tackle issues, move on, and develop. Such members may also lose out when their turn comes, because their non-attendance may be interpreted as undervaluing the set experiences, and by implication, the set members. Thus the set may well feel less committed to helping such a member – this creates confusing emotions for everyone, and may destroy the 'energy' of the set.

One set adviser said that she tells her set members that set meetings are an absolute priority, to be missed and interrupted only if the participant is called away by the chief executive or managing director!

If attendance isn't regular:

- You don't get to know the other set members, which may inhibit trust and openness.
- You miss out on others' stories, and it creates annoyance when they have to repeat what has been happening.
- Others may feel resentment, which may not be voiced, but could be shown in other ways.
- It indicates that you undervalue the set, and the work it's doing.
- You don't get the benefit of regular 'checks', and may increasingly see the set as irrelevant.

DO SETS ALWAYS WORK WITH A SET ADVISER?

In most instances they do – and initially, they really *need* to. The set adviser plays a useful role, helping the set to reflect and focus on learning, acting as a 'mirror' on what is happening, while also becoming involved in asking questions and working with each individual.

Initially, sets tend to be engrossed with the action, and forget their learning. One of the tasks of the set adviser is to adjust the focus.

After several meetings, the set adviser may no longer attend – but that is something to consider when designing the programme. Since one of the aims of every programme should be to help the participants grow to the point of being able to work and learn effectively without a set adviser, it is useful for a set to work, at some point, without one, and experience being 'alone', and what that feels like.

Sets that work without a set adviser often comment that they think they would have gained more with one. However, where sets are made up of experienced set members, there is less need for one, although there are many sets which continue to run for several years, and find the presence of a set adviser immensely useful.

Much will depend on the set, and of course, on the quality of the set adviser. (For more on the role of the set adviser, see Chapter 6.)

HOW DOES A SET AGREE ON HOW IT IS GOING TO WORK?

A number of aspects of how a set works are built into the action learning process itself. Airspace and the processes of questioning are basic to a good action learning programme. A set adviser will give guidance on these issues at the beginning of any programme – and remind participants when they forget.

However, there are other issues that the set members do need to be clear about, and talk about very early on, and where they need to create some ground rules.

As mentioned earlier, confidentiality is vital. One participant who admitted she 'hated the programme' explained that the main reason was that there was a 'spy in the camp' – by which she meant that what was said in the set was being passed on to her manager. As a result, she and other members of the set didn't feel free to be open, and to really 'work'. In another programme, a member discovered that the set adviser had discussed something she had said with her manager – this destroyed her confidence in the set.

Another important ground rule is that of being non-judgemental – which is important if members are to feel free to talk about a whole host of issues they may want to explore. Other ground rules may include not interrupting, having a timekeeper for each meeting, nominating someone to keep a note of every-one's action plans for follow-up at the next meetings, whether to permit smok-ing, not being late to meetings, not having telephone interruptions from the office, and so on.

Here are the ground rules that one set created for itself, along with its expecta-tions of the set adviser (worked out with him). These were hung on a wall at each set meeting, to remind members:

- Be honest and open – say what you mean, mean what you say.
- Stick to agreed schedule/plan.
- Practise positive listening.
- Be supportive and communicative.
- Give – and receive – constructive criticism and feedback positively.
- Respect confidentiality.
- Keep things in proportion.
- Let's have fun.
- In discussion, stick to the agreed issue.
- Come fully prepared to each meeting.
- Review the learning and the learning process – individually and together.

Because this set was working on a group project, they included a few additional items, such as:

- Ensure fair distribution of work.
- Manage the client.
- Review the future.

DO YOU NEED TO HAVE LEARNING AGREEMENTS AND CONTRACTS?

Views differ on the usefulness of having such agreements or contracts (the latter word has rigid, legalistic connotations of something that cannot be broken without penalties; 'agreement' feels more flexible).

Although it is important that each participant has a clear idea of what it is they hope to work on and achieve during the programme – and although these aims, together with a brief outline of how they will be achieved, can be encapsulated in words – the whole point of an action learning programme is that things move on and change. Often, participants come with one learning objective in mind, only to find within a meeting or two that it isn't the real issue that they need to work on.

One such example occurred in a set where one manager was focusing on his personal style and effectiveness – only to discover that deep down, he wanted a change of job.

Agreements and contracts may serve as a focus, but should be no more than reminders for learning – a means of keeping to one path and not straying too far afield.

The form of the learning agreement should be decided upon by the participant, the client, the participant's manager, and probably the development and training manager (particularly if the programme is based around personal and managerial development, possibly with a career move in mind). It should address the following questions:

- What do I want to be doing, or achieve? What do I want to make happen, or be doing differently?
- What do I hope to learn?
- How will I go about it? What spccific plans and actions are required? Who may be able to help? What resources do I need? Who may be opposed to it, and how will I tackle that?
- How will I know when I've got there? What will be happening? What evidence will there be that the goals are being achieved?

Agreements are not writ in stone. They are a focus for working and learning. Most participants find that in the course of a programme, they develop new ideas on what

71

they could be doing (actions), and who could help; and as they themselves develop, they are prepared to accept new ways of doing things. This results in their 'unanticipated' learning becoming as significant as anything they planned to gain (see Chapter 8 for more on learning).

WHERE DO SETS MEET?

This is not as trivial a question as may at first appear. Since the purpose of the set is to allow each member to work on his or her issue, and to have their airspace, such meetings should take place somewhere that is convenient for everyone. This can become an issue for mixed-company sets, or for in-company sets consisting of people scattered geographically.

Ideally, meetings should take place away from any of the participants' workplaces. This means there is less likelihood of members being called away to 'vital' meetings. The same goes for telephone calls.

A comfortable room, coffee, lunch and tea provided, and no disturbances make for sets that are able to concentrate on the task in hand: achieving their projects/tasks and their learning.

If the set is made up of people from different companies, they may meet at one another's workplaces, but the 'host' may risk feeling a sense of responsibility for the meeting's smooth running, and having less energy for the work of the set.

At the first set meeting, it is useful to arrange where and when the subsequent meetings are to take place. Trying to find mutually convenient dates in six busy people's diaries can otherwise become a nightmare! And once fixed, these dates should – as far as possible – remain fixed unless there is a crisis, or unless several members find great difficulty in meeting any of them.

HOW OFTEN DO SETS MEET, AND FOR HOW LONG?

Ideally, sets meet for a whole day once a month. Thus a programme planned to include six meetings would take six months – a good length of a time for a serious project to be undertaken and completed by participants.

Longer intervals risk making a programme seem to drag, and members losing their momentum and enthusiasm. If more than a month elapses between meetings, too much can happen for members to remember and recall for the set. It also leaves a long gap if there is an issue that members want to talk about with the set.

With a set of six members, ideally, a whole day is needed to allow every member to have their airspace. If set meetings last for less time – say three hours – this means that only two or three participants, at most, have time for airspace at any one meeting. Should any one member have an urgent issue, there would obviously be a 'negotiation' around the allocation of time.

If – as some sets do – they meet for only one or two hours, this can be problematic in action learning terms. If there is only time for one member to tell their story, other members may have to wait five months before their turn. Strictly speaking, this is not action learning: there is no action to be revisited and learnt from with the help of the set. True, individual members may be implementing their own action learning alone, away from the set, but again this falls short of real action learning.

The other possibility where short meetings are the only option is for everyone to have 15–20 minutes. This may sound like a long time, but all participants say that it is surprising how even an hour disappears without anyone realizing how time has flown.

However, in order to do any in-depth work, a problem-presenter needs more than a few minutes of the set's attention – up to an hour may be required if the issue is to be worked on in any depth, or if there is a major problem to be addressed. With less time, the work done is superficial, or time runs out before actions (and maybe solutions) can be addressed and planned.

If a set is working on a group project, the same issues arise. Within a group project, each member needs their airspace to tell the others how they are progressing on their mini-project.

WHAT HAPPENS IF I DON'T WANT TO PARTICIPATE ACTIVELY IN THE SET?

No one can force a set member to participate. Each participant in a programme takes responsibility for themselves and their learning – and hence their participation. Undoubtedly, the other set members, and the set adviser, would ask a non-participating member to explain what was stopping them, and would possibly also urge greater participation. Someone who decides not to participate – for whatever reason – may create problems for other set members; this would then be an issue for the set, and the set adviser, to work on. In the end, it is the individual participant who decides whether to participate or not.

Some participants did admit to not having participated much – out of choice, they claimed, although one or two said it was more out of shyness and diffidence. For one such member, the six-month programme was all too short: 'I was just beginning to come out of my shell, to feel confident enough to participate, when it came to an end.'

A number of participants said they didn't take part much because they felt uncomfortable with the set and its processes. They felt uneasy with other set members – 'the chemistry was wrong' – or simply didn't feel they wanted to share and be open:

> I didn't find it useful, and didn't use it to learn. I didn't want to use it and so didn't bring up my issues, though I listened to others. I admit that it was my choice and I think I'd have learnt more if I'd been willing to participate more.

Another echoed a similar thought: 'I didn't use the opportunities offered. But I'm not sure it would have made much difference, though it might have been useful to run things through with the set.' This particular marketing manager went on to explain that he had found working with people from different functions in the set very enlightening, and working on his project very useful and beneficial. In particular, it had given him confidence and visibility within his company, and these he felt were benefits enough.

In one set I worked with, a man decided to leave during the second meeting. What prompted his exit was another member recalling, in tears, an upsetting moment at work. Her tears and her speaking were controlled and fluent. However, the man felt this show of emotion was inappropriate.

On being questioned by the set, he admitted that he could not cope with others' emotions. If there was a chance that such emotions might surface again in the set, he preferred to leave there and then. And he did.

The others in the set were sad at this, for they felt he might have learnt something about his discomfort if he had chosen to stay and work on this.

Another set experienced a set member leaving after their third meeting. At previous meetings, he had always arrived late, would leave to make telephone calls or attend other meetings, and while in the set, he would aggressively challenge others, and vehemently justify all his own actions or statements. The set challenged him on these various issues, and in particular expressed unhappiness at his apparent lack of commitment to the set. In reply, he said he did not find the set helpful, and would prefer to leave.

They, in turn, expressed relief when he left: 'We think we'll now be able to work much better without these constant disruptions.'

THE VALUE OF WORKING IN A SET

One interesting finding from my experience is that, at the very outset of a programme, the project was usually seen as the 'learning vehicle', and the set was seen as 'just another group'. Participants therefore didn't give much thought to what they would learn from the group itself. A few mentioned that they had reservations about whether non-experts and 'mere managers' would be able to help them to learn anything.

However, many quickly commented on how much they had learnt from working in the set: in particular the insights they gained on how they worked with others, and how they behaved in other groups (see below). For this reason, a set can be a useful place to 'experiment' with different behaviours. So, if a participant is normally a dominant and talkative member of any group he or she works in, it might be useful to notice what it is like to remain more silent, and maybe listen more!

What also emerged is that much of set members' learning revolved around valuing others, changing the way they worked (for example, from being active to being more reflective), realizing the value of being supportive, growing in confidence. Participants mainly ascribed these unanticipated learnings to the set and its processes: it became a crucial learning vehicle.

REALIZING THE VALUE OF MIXING – AND WORKING CLOSELY – WITH COLLEAGUES FROM OTHER FUNCTIONS

Participants in in-company sets said they had come with preconceived notions about people from other departments and functions. Such mixed-functional sets allowed them to test out the extent to which these were based on fact or fiction, or alternatively, to begin to understand where the differences sprung from:

> You come with assumptions about people and the different parts of the organization they work in ... You label them, but then you see the different constraints they work under, and realize they're human too.

> It gave us the opportunity to learn about other parts of the organization – parts we'd never know about otherwise.

For another participant, it: 'cleared away the cobwebs – we heard everyone's story and began to build a more robust relationship which then fed back into our work'.

'You feel much more part of the company after such a programme,' commented one young woman. 'You begin to understand what it's all about, and that helps you feel more committed.'

For others, it was an eye-opener to see how very different the various parts of the organization were: 'Some departments were different animals almost. Some were more "feminine", open and caring, and more closely bonded than others. Where there was a strong male director, the culture was ruthless and aggressive,' observed one marketing manager after hearing his colleagues' stories.

Some went on to say: 'We're creating a network here, in our set – one we can call on later, when we have some issues to resolve. It will make that much easier, knowing there's someone you know and whom you can talk to openly. '

What such in-company programmes – and particularly those with group projects – also highlighted was the ability of a group of people to create major change within their organization, as one young lecturer at a college of further education pointed out:

> This was my first experience of working formally within a group to effect change with an organization. It was a very valuable experience, for it taught me how a small, focused group with very little individual power could effect powerful and far-reaching changes. The group has been very successful in its outcomes.

She went on to say:

> It also taught me how I can make a useful contribution to team effort. I also got to know a great deal about the institution I work in and it helped me clarify my role within it. Very importantly, it also showed me how the skills I realized I had could play a part in any organization I might want to work in. As a result, I was able to reframe my work experiences ... this produced a very new and interesting picture of my job, and it was a key factor in my getting a new job.

Another set (of research scientists) was able, after one such programme, to go as a cohesive body to their manager and instigate changes which each had tried but had been unable to introduce alone.

The result, all such in-company sets said, was to make them feel much more cohesive, more part of their company, more interested in what was happening, and better able to work with each other because they now understood one another's perspective.

BENEFITING FROM WORKING WITH 'NON-EXPERTS': VALUING EVERYONE

> I was amazed at how the non-experts in a given field can help you by asking intelligent questions – often very simple ones ... their lack of familiarity with my issue caused me to explain it from basics, and made me often think more laterally.

Having to explain things simply to colleagues from other departments – who would often ask very simple and straightforward questions – also gave the problem-presenters useful new insights, and often allowed them to see inconsistencies, gaps or anomalies that they hadn't spotted before.

A participant in a mixed-company set recalled: 'It was interesting – there was no one else in my set from finance (I'm in banking) – I was with someone from the NHS, computing, retail and telecommunications. I was able to help them spot what to me were glaring problems or gaps, and I had ideas on how things could be done differently ... They did the same for me.'

Interestingly, a personnel manager who found himself in a mixed-company, mixed-function set found that 'although one other member of the set was also from Personnel, I found the non-experts more helpful because it was in explaining to them what to me seemed so obvious that I often saw the flaws, or they would see something that I had missed because I was too close ... as was the other "expert" '.

For others, just having to explain to non-experts showed them the gaps in their thinking or reasoning, or gave them clues and insights they would not otherwise have gained – often simply by hearing themselves talk out loud: 'As you talk out loud, you start saying things that you didn't know were even in your mind. It's something to do with talking out loud. The same doesn't happen if you're merely thinking quietly to yourself.'

On the other hand, a few people felt it a drawback to have to go back to basics – they felt it wasted time, and said they would have preferred single-function sets. One IT specialist particularly felt this. But then he added that he had found it immensely useful to work in the mixed-company set he was a member of, and to listen in particular to the dilemmas of a general manager of a small building firm. 'It gave me a totally new perspective on many matters,' he commented. It seems there is no clear rule!

Working with non-experts also had wider ramifications, for as members began to realize that they were able – as non-experts – to help the other set members, they gained confidence in themselves.

THE VALUE OF WORKING IN A SUPPORT GROUP: SHARING, AND HELPING OTHERS

When they first embark on action learning, few participants think of sharing as something that offers them the opportunity to learn:

> At the outset I was very competitive and action- and results-oriented ... and very isolated. It's helped me work differently. I began to talk to others, it made me more professional at work. In the set, I'd watch the dominant personalities and realize they're not necessarily always right, and when others were given – or rather, took – space to speak, we all became more creative. I've transferred this back to work.

Sharing also brings out the diversity that exists among people, and with it the realization that: 'It is this diversity which is the richness.' As another manager put it: 'One of the most fundamental discoveries for me was the valuable resources that existed in our set ... an eye-opener for what exists in other groups.'

'It is this emergence of ideas, thoughts and insights when working with others that makes the set so powerful,' mused some more philosophically minded participants. One or two wondered if they could have achieved the same benefits on their own. 'You should be able to do action learning on your own,' one of them thought. On the other hand, many drew attention to the fact that the set itself is what triggers off new ways of thinking and new perspectives, 'bringing out things in you that you didn't even know were there'. 'The more you share, the more you get back. You learn from others if you're prepared to share.'

But it's not just the telling of one's story, and hearing those of others in return:

> It's more what they caused me to think about – either because they were asking themselves questions, making comments, describing their experiences – and I'd find myself thinking and asking myself questions ... I did this particularly when I had the 'space' to do so – often after I'd been the focus of attention, and when it was someone else's turn ... when the spotlight was off me. At times it's difficult in that space to take in fully what has been happening, or what you've been offered by the others.

Many participants I spoke to said how surprised they were that they learnt as they helped others: 'Hearing your ideas accepted and valued by others meant you began to apply them yourself. But they only emerged because of the others talking about their issues – you'd never have had similar thoughts or ideas about yourself.'

The more pragmatic managers commented on how the sharing – the hearing of others' stories – also made them realize that there many different styles of management – and that you need to vary your own approach as well: 'You can't be caring all the time. You have to manage different people in your team differently – but all equally and fairly.'

A 'FEMININE' PROCESS

A number of participants – notably the men – described this sharing as the 'feminization' of work: 'I learnt a great deal from the women in the set – they're better at teamwork and sharing responsibilities with others, and generally using others to help arrive at decisions.' Another admitted: 'I've never liked – or been – a macho manager. I can now be effective, and it all occurs in a manner which is relaxed, informal, collegiate and collective.'

A third manager – this time a woman – recalled how she had for some years felt uneasy at the 'style' of managing that was expected of her: 'It felt unnatural to me – to be authoritarian, a disciplinarian, someone with all the answers.' Her experience of action learning, she said, gave her 'permission' to adopt her own style and be, as with the previous participant, more collective in her approach – though without relinquishing her ultimate responsibility for decisions taken.

A few other participants felt that action learning itself was a 'feminizing' process, because it emphasized sharing and collaboration rather than individualism and competitiveness. 'It's about sensitizing you, making you more "feminine",' said another man, but he added forcefully: 'But it's not soft, it's not opting for an easy life, and it makes you more self-reliant and decision-oriented.' A senior executive remarked that a good many more senior managers were probably in need of this 'sensitizing' process.

THE BENEFITS OF INCREASED CONFIDENCE

For most participants, this sharing with others – the openness and honesty – revealed that: 'we all share the same problems, regardless of organization, function or even project. No matter how we defined what we were working on in this programme, in the end we all landed up with the same fundamental problem – of how to relate to and work with other people.'

One young woman described how she had become more confident: 'I'd been timid and mousey before. I'm not really sure how it happened that I changed. The set were supportive of me, gave me space. But as I saw I was able to help others, I realized I couldn't be talking complete rubbish. I heard myself say: "Take your own advice, then, and apply it to yourself." '

The safety of the set offered some participants a chance to experiment with new ways of behaving or new approaches back at work. One revealed: 'I'd practise with the set how I would approach my manager, until I felt comfortable and they thought it was fine.'

Support in the set thus legitimizes asking for help. It also enables participants to admit to not knowing, or feeling vulnerable. And the discovery that both activities are 'OK', and nowhere near as fearful and threatening as they had imagined, made it possible for them to do so back at work, and to be, as many put it, 'my own natural self'.

'I now have the confidence to say I don't feel confident,' said one man. 'I feel it's all right to admit I don't know something,' was a comment many made.

Quite simply, as one manager said: 'You realize that you're not alone in your worries and concerns, or alone to resolve them.'

In one set I facilitated, one manager – a deputy branch manager of a building society – was on the programme to help him develop more confidence in himself, for it was preventing him from gaining his next promotion. It was also stopping him from gaining sales experience which he needed for that new post. But there seemed little point in pushing him, or in sending him on yet another course on how to be a good salesperson.

In the set, he admitted to being shy. During the first meeting he talked very little, except to say that he was not good at 'small talk' nor at being 'outgoing, like salesmen need to be'. But as the set began to work, it soon became obvious that whenever he spoke, the set listened with particular attention. Everything he said made sense. Slowly, he took on a leadership role. Then he was given feedback by the set on how they perceived him. At the third meeting, he agreed with the set that he was feeling more confident and thought he might try phoning one or two potential clients whom he knew, and invite them out to lunch. He still might not be able to sell, but he did now feel able to talk to them about their financial interests in a quiet, business-like way. With the encouragement of the set, he agreed to 'take a leap'.

When he reported back at the next meeting, he was completely overwhelmed. It had been easier than he had imagined: he had found both men very willing to simply talk about financial matters, and both expressed interest in the services the branch could offer them. Two potential new clients!

He used the next two set meetings to discuss what he could do next, but was realizing that he could sell simply by being his own natural self – that he could remain in character, and didn't have to pretend he was something that he wasn't.

He continued to build up his confidence, and by the end of the programme he could even show financial gains he had made for the branch. His participation in the set meetings was now total, and he was generally considered by the other set members to be the most capable of the group. A few months after the programme, he was promoted to branch manager.

HAVING TO TAKE RESPONSIBILITY FOR YOURSELF

Being a group that both supports and shares, a set also has expectations of each and every member:

> The set forces you take responsibility, they have expectations of you at every meeting ... On one occasion when I hadn't done what I'd said I would, and came up with some excuses, the set simply told me they were disappointed in me.

> You're made to face up to things because the set asks you and pushes you gently. You're forced to face your weaknesses – maybe it's just giving presentations, and you're avoiding it all the time.

The discipline of having to report back at every meeting also creates a sense of responsibility: 'You know your turn will come, so it forces you to act, to prepare yourself ... it's helped me be more prepared now for meetings back at work.'

Members also develop a sense of responsibility for others – wanting them to work, learn and succeed – and are serious about helping them. One woman, newly appointed to a managerial post and unsure about how to work with her boss, hesitated about 'taking action, assertively', and so, after several meetings, her set colleagues decided to frog-march her to his office and force the meeting. Another set – in an academic institution – remembered how they had 'pushed one member who didn't seem to be getting on with finding a project. It felt uncomfortable at the time, but he later told us he needed that pressure.'

This can also be threatening, though, as several participants mentioned: 'Your colleagues won't let you hide, they make you confront issues you don't want to. But you don't half feel better once you've talked about them.'

Having themselves experienced the relief of talking, many participants were attempting to adopt a similar openness back at work, and trying to persuade their staff to be more open and honest – usually by being so themselves, and thus becoming a model.

Taking responsibility, getting a sense of achievement, gaining in competence and confidence – this heady combination leaves many participants energized and enthused by the end of each meeting: 'I'd come tired and deflated, and at the end of the meetings I was ready to face all the issues that had been worrying me before.' 'I always came away fired with energy and confidence. The next two or three days at work are full of vitality and positive thinking,' was how another experienced it. Others commented that between meetings, or even after the set was no longer meeting, a phone call to another set member could revitalize flagging spirits or confidence.

If only for this result, set meetings seem to be a good thing!

REALIZING THE VALUE OF BEING HONEST

Being honest with themselves and others is not, many participants admitted, what they were good at. Are any of us? But working with the same group of people over time, observing the ground rules, being supported 'in sickness and health' – in mistakes as well as successes – and in giving and receiving honest feedback: this all helped participants to become more honest, and to value this development:

> The set helped me be more honest with myself – particularly admitting to my emotions, and seeing them as a valid part of the picture. So, if I genuinely feel frightened, threatened, hassled, that's part of the equation that needs to be looked at – either alone or with others.

Another member admitted to being frightened to admit to anger at work: 'There is a code which says you don't show your emotions. So we tried it out – in the set – to role-play, and help me show anger. '

'I really valued the challenging, the honesty and the feedback – as opposed to the constrained response that you get from colleagues at work,' said a young telecommunications manager.

'It's given me confidence in myself – that I have something to offer (my father always said, 'You can do better'), and action learning has confirmed that,' said one middle-aged manager.

For many, this openness and trust that builds up in the set is: 'emotionally releasing. You begin to understand why you react in certain ways, and it helps to control, and not sublimate, those feelings and express them in an appropriate way.'

'I wish we could have an atmosphere like this at work,' sighed another manager. 'I've always wanted – sought – this type of gathering at work, but never managed to achieve it – you need to structure it into work.'

However, being open and honest does not always come easily. One participant recalled in her reflective document: 'The set had talked about the need to be open and honest, but I found that in reality they weren't – they just said they wanted to be.' Then, during the course of a discussion, she discovered that other set members were not learning much, and her view – which she shared with the set – was that they might if they were prepared to be more open and honest with themselves and each other. Her document continues:

> I was concerned that I had opened up and raised this issue, and that others seemingly didn't share my views about the importance of learning, and how to get there. I felt alone, and left the meeting frustrated, and wondering if there was any benefit to continuing on the programme. I felt let down.
>
> I begrudgingly attended the next meeting. Everyone seemed more relaxed, which had the opposite effect on me, and the more I listened, the more I realized I would have to say

something about my feelings, otherwise I wouldn't be able to continue. Again, I felt nervous as this was the second time I'd raised the issue of feelings. The set responded silently and then diffidently ... but later they admitted that what I'd said had made it easier for them to talk to one another, and work constructively, simply because I'd drawn attention to these issues ... and it had freed them up to admit to some of their feelings.

THREE CASE EXAMPLES

A PERSONAL SUCCESS PROGRAMME IN A LARGE INSURANCE COMPANY

In this Personal Success Programme for high-potential first line managers, personal growth and success were the goals. The set met every six to eight weeks, for an evening and a day, over 12–18 months.

Each participant had a learning contract, and 'success' was measured by differences in how they handled their current job, how they managed in a different job, and by the skills learnt and awareness developed. No specific 'projects' were used, but each participant came to talk about ongoing issues at work. The programme had senior management sponsors, but they tended to keep a low profile.

There were difficulties in introducing action learning, because although the culture espoused the notions of being open, supportive and creative – empowering staff – the organization found these ideas difficult to cope with in practice. The head of Training and Development said: 'The pace of the development of the individuals outstrips the organization's ability to develop ... inadequate options are offered to people, and they leave ... The culture is quite conservative, risk-averse and formal ... all we can do is to make small waves.'

The same company had also run a management programme for first line managers in Customer Service, coming into a new role. Their common 'project' was 'improving customer service', where each participant shared with the set members how he or she was progressing. Each had a learning contract, and any 'taught' input was at the participants' request, to help them with issues they were facing. The programme ran for a year, meeting for one day every eight weeks, with a facilitator. Evaluation of 'success' included 360-degree evaluation (where a participant's boss, colleagues and staff all give feedback).

TWO SENIOR MANAGER LEADERSHIP PROGRAMMES

A water company running a leadership programme for a mix of senior, middle and young managers has built in action learning as an integral part of their programme. Lasting for 15 months, there are three days of 'taught' modules every three months; in between, sets of eight meet to work on a problem of corporate importance, identified by senior sponsors (from the board), to give participants a broader business awareness. The set, acting as consultants, may have a hand in implementing their proposals.

Sets meet as often as they wish, for as long as they wish, with a set adviser for the first two meetings, and then at the discretion of the set members. At each 'taught' module, each set reports on its progress.

> Action learning as an integral part of a programme ensures that participants have an opportunity to begin using the ideas they learn during the 'input' days, and participating actively in their own learning ... if they don't have this opportunity, there is no guarantee they will change ... Having set advisers is important in our culture, which is dominated by engineers who are task-focused, but rarely stop to reflect and focus on their learning.

A pharmaceutical company has created an international leadership programme for 1 500 middle and senior managers. The programme consists of three three-day workshops – on learning and leadership, on businesses and personal change, and on project management and team-working. Linked in with these workshops are action learning sets, which also serve as syndicates at the workshop days.

The sets, consisting of diagonal slices of people from different functions, meet in between the workshops, and each participant brings to the set an ongoing work problem or issue to talk about and resolve.

Sets work with set advisers for the first two or three meetings (each of about half a day), when they learn the processes of set meetings – based around questioning – and are reminded of the need to stop, reflect and focus on what they are learning.

The feedback has pronounced action learning as 'magical' and 'wonderful'. It is the notion of space and time to reflect which has really excited participants: 'It's legal, and it's OK!'

NOTES

[1] Adapted from J. Heron (1977) *Dimensions of Facilitator Style*, Human Potential Research Project, University of Surrey.

4 The action: projects and tasks

The action – be it a project or task – is the ostensible vehicle for learning. I say ostensible, for although it is crucial that every participant undertake 'action' in some form, it is not the sole means of learning. Learning, as we shall see, occurs from all the elements that make up an action learning programme.

Reg Revans's helpful distinction between 'puzzles' and 'problems' (see page 6) is a guide to how to choose a project/task to work on. Problems are useful; puzzles are not.

ARE THERE DIFFERENT TYPES OF PROGRAMMES, AND HENCE PROJECTS?

Broadly speaking, programmes – and hence the projects that are worked on – fall into two categories: in-company ones, or mixed-company ones (see pages 22–24). Within this distinction, projects may be individual or group ones.

Revans postulated that there are four main variations (see Figure 4.1). Of the four variations that Revans defined, the least likely to run – for logistic, and 'intelligence' reasons – are those where participants work on projects in a company which has no relationship with their own. There are, however, programmes with participants from different businesses which, although separate, belong to the same parent company.

In-company programmes are the most common, and may be run for people in all functions and from all levels of responsibility.

Mixed-company programmes are more likely to be attended by more senior people who have fewer, if any, peers within their own organization. Alternatively, programmes may consist of people who have attended an external course which has an action learning component built in, to help individuals to put into practice – back at work – what they have learnt on the course.

The projects thus undertaken will vary depending on whether:

	Familiar	Setting	Unfamiliar
Familiar	Both familiar		Task familiar Setting unfamiliar
Task			
Unfamiliar	Task unfamiliar Setting familiar		Both unfamiliar

Figure 4.1 Types of projects

- they will be carried out in the participant's own department, and hence sphere of knowledge
- they will be something that is completely outside a participant's normal activities and functions, and possibly even in another company
- they are individual or group ones.

Determining which projects to choose will depend to a large extent on the aims of a programme.

WHICH ARE BETTER: INDIVIDUAL OR GROUP PROJECTS?

In the majority of action learning programmes, participants undertake individual projects. However, there are instances where a group project better meets the aim of a programme, for instance where the task requires inputs from several individuals (such as creating a new appraisal scheme, see page 66, or reorganizing a workshop, see page 105), or where the objective is team-building.

Those who have experienced working on both group and individual projects sometimes say they gained more by working on an individual project. It allowed them to focus on their own learning needs in greater depth, and they felt a greater sense of commitment. But well-focused mini-projects within a group project should ensure that each participant achieves both action and learning

Thus, both individual and group projects should be two-pronged and focused on:

- an important work-based task that a participant undertakes, where action and implementation is required (not a purely research-based project)
- identified personal developmental needs.

WHY IS IT IMPORTANT TO HAVE A PROJECT?

It is one of the fundamental beliefs of action learning that we learn best by undertaking some action, which we then reflect on and learn from.

The main reason for having a project or task is that it gives us a focus that is real and important, and that means something to us. It creates a 'hook' on which to test out or hang our stored-up knowledge, and it provides evidence of actions and behaviours, which are a means of measuring how much we have really learnt.

As one manager pointed out: 'The benefit of learning by doing, i.e. having a project, is that it ties the learning into something relevant. There are a great many things which I learnt as isolated facts, but they only have curiosity value until I can find ways of applying them. Learning by doing takes care of that, and the experience provides a much more indelible memory.'

The main way of learning is by revisiting the action we take, and in the light of insights or lessons learnt, planning how to undertake the next steps in the project. This is how, on an action learning programme, participants are able to monitor their progress over a period, witness their own development, learn from mistakes, experiment, and hear how others are progressing. It is by having such a project – such a focus – that participants learn 'purposefully'.

A project also allows participants to see what they have achieved and how they are developing and changing themselves in the process. It is by having this focus that they are able to go around the learning cycle (see pages 39–40) and to create of it a spiral – in other words, move on. So a project also gives participants a starting point for their journey of discovery and development.

One participant who wasn't pushed to identify a project – or even other tasks to work on – commented: 'I felt much less involved in what others were saying. I think I learnt less than I would have if I'd had a project.' A female member of a set which throughout its life addressed only one participant's project, with the other set members acting merely as supports (which I do not believe to be real action learning), commented: 'I felt uninvolved, quite bored in fact, and don't think I learnt anything.'

Without a project/task, there is thus a danger that the participants will be less committed, and that their learning will have little focus and become merely a string of interesting thoughts. There is also a danger that the set meetings will become simply another discussion group, or will begin to veer towards being what some have termed a 'therapy group'. It is the project that keeps the action and the learning focused.

WHAT CONSTITUTES 'ACTION'?

A project/task could be focused on an organizational/departmental or section issue/need that a participant is working on or is 'given'. This issue may be either new, and hence a challenge, or perennial and troublesome, requiring investigation and a possible resolution (for examples of projects, see below).

For participants in more senior managerial roles, the issues may be quandaries, irritations or opportunities with wide ramifications – such as how to resolve a problem of career change, how to deal with a hostile board team member, how to cope with a difficult colleague, how to get agreement with team colleagues on an issue, how to manage change, how to create a better relationship with a customer or supplier, and so on.

The project/task could be a developmental issue – qualities, competences or behaviours that a participant wants or needs to develop or improve, such as questions arising from a career development or a change of direction.

The essence of a project/task is that it must be something that participants can get their teeth into, will find a challenge, want to or are able to resolve, that is important to their organization, and within their sphere of responsibility and authority to do something about – to implement, that they can report back to the next set meeting and, importantly, will learn from.

Above all, the project needs to be something that the participant can tell as 'my story' – something they are involved with, and which allows them to use the pronoun 'I' when talking about it (rather than the telling of 'history', where the focus is more likely to be on others, and 'them').

It needs to be something work-focused and important, which a participant is:

- responsible for
- able to do something about
- able (ideally) to implement.

A work-focused project can be defined as:

I will undertake X so that Y, which means that I'll learn Z.

A development-focused project can be defined as:

I want to develop X, so I will choose Y as a means, which means I'll learn Z.

You should apply the following questions to a project/task:

- What am I trying to achieve?
- What's stopping me?
- What can I do about it?
- How will I know when I've achieved what I set out to? (What will be different? What will be happening?)

The project/task should be something which fits into the time frame of the programme. However, it should not be a case study or research project, nor consultancy work, unless this is the specified learning need. Desk or book research and study into causes of a problem would not constitute an action learning project, for the simple reason that there is no *action*. Nor is action learning concerned with finding quick solutions. It aims to go beyond symptoms to fundamental issues and real problems. Action learning thereby 'reaches those parts that other programmes don't reach' precisely because it doesn't go for the quick fix – instant answers to immediate problems.

Knowing that the set will request evidence at the next meeting is a great motivator for everyone. It acts as a goad to do something, and not procrastinate or find excuses, as many participants found. But for many participants, what was more important – what made action learning different – was its discipline: the constant revisiting of an issue, to work on it publicly until it was resolved. 'It's the returning to a project, the follow-up of the story at the next meeting of what you did or didn't do, what happened, with what results, and what you may need to do next. That is what makes it so useful and valuable,' said one manager.

Tasks and other short-term issues may thus be resolved over the space of two meetings. Longer-term projects, on the other hand, would normally be chosen to last approximately the length of the programme.

Issues addressed in projects might include:

- managing a particular change
- empowering staff
- introducing new assessment programmes
- implementing 'Investors in People'
- introducing total quality programmes
- improving communications throughout the company
- streamlining work processes and procedures
- developing middle managers' potential
- modifying a paperwork system to enable managers to spend more time with sales staff
- changing from an autocratic to a facilitative style of managing
- reorganizing a production line
- tackling absenteeism on a night shift
- improving management performance
- establishing field communications for engineers on the road
- increasing the profitability of a small engineering firm
- creating equal opportunities for women or other disadvantaged groups
- creating and building up a new role and its responsibilities
- establishing a communications system for sales people on the road.

I came on the programme looking for the answer to a business problem: low profitability. Carrying out the project demonstrated to me that low profitability was not the problem. It was merely a symptom of other problems which have their roots both within me [the MD] as person, and outside in the marketplace.

As a result of the research and reflection I have done, I have developed a system model which illustrates just what this business actually does, and how it relates to me, our staff, our customers and society. One result of this is that I am now more aware of the importance of issues external to the firm, and I now try to spend time considering what we should be doing and less time monitoring how well we did what we chose to do.

CREATING, RATHER THAN PROBLEM-SOLVING

Although participants may come to an action learning programme and focus initially on problems, if they first establish what they want to achieve, and what outcomes they are looking for, working on their projects will be a more forward-looking exercise.

Robert Fritz makes a clear distinction between 'creating' – which he defines (in line with the dictionary) as bringing something into being which does not exist at present, and problem-solving – which he sees as moving away from, or eliminating something which we want to avoid: 'In the tradition of the arts, it is well known that creating is not problem-solving ... Problem-solving does not enable [people] to create what they want and often perpetuates what they do not want' (Fritz 1994).[1]

Applying this thinking to action learning projects forces the participants to ask: 'What do I want to create?', which gives them a forward-looking, results- and benefits-oriented slant, which may completely alter the approach taken in a project:

Evidence of the learning is that something has been created, put in place, or is now being done differently and successfully, and that the participant has gained something from the exercise.

A branch manager in a major building society brought as his project 'my own development as a manager'. His assignment was to work on it by focusing on various everyday managerial tasks. He had been on a number of courses about management, but his performance – and that of his branch – was still proving to be a worry: 'All the courses I've attended and articles I've read have given me the theory, but I still don't really seem to be able to put them into practice effectively.'

One area that he and his 'client' identified – in order to improve performance – was staff motivation. He worked on this issue, drawing on the support and insights generated at the set meetings. This practical approach resulted in him arriving at the third set meeting and announcing thoughtfully: 'I've realized that the problem isn't about motivating my staff. It's about motivating myself.'

CAN YOU CHANGE PROJECT IN MID-PROGRAMME?

There may be a number of reasons for changing a project in mid-programme. Participants may find that their project does not last the length of a programme, or for some reason they cannot continue on it. In both these instances, it is perfectly acceptable to move on to another project. Sometimes a project as originally defined simply proves to be too large a task to undertake, and it makes sense to focus on one aspect of it.

The only caveat is that a participant shouldn't back out of a project because he or she is simply finding it too demanding in developmental terms.

Programmes for younger participants or those in middle-management roles tend to be project-based because it is felt that they provide a more challenging and focused learning opportunity. However, as many pointed out, although they worked initially, and probably for most of the time, on their projects, 'Later, we also brought our daily problems ... or we'd talk about other issues that concerned us, such as the company culture, which discouraged the asking of questions.'

More senior managers' 'projects' often tend to be their ongoing issues and quandaries. One commented: 'We'd each work on the issue of the moment that concerned us. Sometimes as you hear others talk you realize you have a similar issue as well, and then when your turn comes, it tumbles out. It's not always necessary to come with the same issue at each meeting.'

WHO CHOOSES THE PROJECTS OR IDENTIFIES THE TASKS?

Ideally, a joint decision will be reached between the participant, his or her manager, the client for the programme (see below), and probably also the personnel and/or the training/development department. However, everyone involved must remember that a prime focus is the participant's learning needs, which he or she will address by working on a suitable and important project.

The choice of project will therefore emerge from:

- **the participant him or herself** – possibly based on an annual assessment that has pinpointed certain areas or skills that he or she needs to develop in order to progress and develop their career; a project is then identified that will enable that participant to tackle and develop issues that will give him or her the opportunity to develop the specified skills or qualities
- **the participant's client** – the person in the organization who is 'backing' him or her, and to whom the participant will finally report on their achievements (see pages 94–95 for a fuller description of the client and their role), who may have a project they would like the participant to work on

91

- **the participant and his/her manager** – together, they may identify a project within their department/section that needs working on and that would provide the learning opportunities for the participant (such a project may also arise after a participant has attended a course or workshop).

There may be some obvious issues that the organization needs to work on, and that participants on an action learning programme would also benefit from working on. The only danger here – as one programme I investigated discovered – was that the participants saw this as the hijacking of their programme by senior managers, for their own pet projects, with little attention paid to the participants' learning objectives: 'Our project was imposed – and when we didn't seem to be getting results, we began to get negative vibes from managers. But the problem for us was that we were learning, even though visibly we weren't achieving on those projects.'

The widespread issue of introducing and managing 'change' – be it within their own work roles, or the wider subject of culture change and introducing new ways of working, aimed at involving and valuing staff – in itself opens out ideal projects for participants on an action learning programme to work on and study their own changing role and changing behaviour, as well as introducing change that will affect others.

In the last two instances, group projects are a useful means of achieving the desired twin goals of action and learning.

SETS CHOOSING

One set of young managers was given a choice of projects – in fact, a choice of whether to work on a group project or whether to undertake individual ones. They opted for the former, because one of the aims of the programme was to give them the opportunity of working in a team – something they didn't encounter in their everyday work:

> Many of us work pretty much alone in our jobs [in retailing], so it's good to work with others for a change. We also wanted to compare our different styles of managing, and learn more about the business overall. We each work in different segments of our business. There's a feeling in the company that we should all know more about the 'whole' and not just our bits of it. So this was an ideal opportunity.

This group worked as consultants to their marketing director, since 'gaining consultancy skills' was one of the objectives of the programme.

Another set in a local authority which had been brought together to develop teamwork was invited to choose a project which would be of relevance to them all, and which they would feel comfortable working on. Each member suggested a project chosen from their own work environment, and the set then chose which they felt most appropriate, and one from which they would all benefit. The project they eventually opted for was concerned with establishing good communications between three geographically separated offices.

At their first meeting, the set decided that the initial challenge would be to identify some of the problems with the current system and to sell the idea of improving the communications to B's (the problem-holder's) three offices. Set members went to B's offices, interviewed his staff, and collected views on problems and how to resolve them. Thus, even before the second set meeting, a new telephone procedure had been suggested and created, to get around the problem of permanently engaged phones.

The second challenge – which was discussed at the second set meeting – was how to create more regular and higher-quality meetings between B and his scattered staff: 'I wasn't seeing them regularly, so we decided on fixing dates and times for me to see staff. We also decided it would be helpful if I visited locations informally, just to talk to people and hear their problems and their ideas for resolving them.'

Following this meeting, B met with one group of his staff (traffic wardens) who had been 'marginalized' before, and by adopting an action learning approach to the meeting, he came away with a mass of ideas on how to improve communication between the wardens and the community, in particular how to co-operate with old age pensioners on their permits and other rules about parking.

'I learnt,' said B, 'that there are lots of good ideas out there if you give people a chance to talk! It's helped me to delegate more to my staff.'

The set meetings continued to produce ideas, and at each meeting B reported back on progress. For B, the benefit of working with the set as opposed to going it alone ('I don't think I'd have found the time to work on this issue if I'd had to do it alone,' he admitted) was:

> the opportunity to talk through my ideas with others, but most importantly to draw on their experiences and what they had been doing in their various, very different departments. I was also concerned about implementing new ideas and how my staff would react. Would this all be seen as a flash in the pan? So, talking things through was helpful. I began to appreciate my team back at work much more, and we began to talk more openly, even about feelings! I began to realize how much I was able to affect people. I'd also had a fear of making formal presentations – and having to do one for senior managers on the set's work and what we'd achieved has given me confidence to do so. I gave a presentation to thirty people the other day!

These set members gained in many ways:

> It's mind-blowing. I'm in my first managerial job, and I'm realizing through this project that people can do so much if you give them the opportunity. I'm soaking things up like a sponge – it's the exposure to others' experiences which is so useful.

> Hearing others' stories has made me realize there are different styles of management. I've also learnt from the mistakes of others!

> It's the making of contacts with colleagues – the networking – that's been so valuable. The length of the programme has been crucial – so much better than the short sharp shock of other courses. You realize that you can't achieve things immediately.

I chose the role of 'chair' of the group deliberately – I know I'm good at that. But what I've learnt is to distinguish between being a manager and a leader – and it's helped me work with my own group back at work.

They all commented how they were now making much greater use of cross-departmental/sectional/functional groups to work on new proposals and everyday issues of concern.

PARTICIPANTS' MANAGERS NEED TO BE INVOLVED

This may seem obvious, but it is worth reiterating why they should be involved:

- A participant's project is likely to be focused in the participant's area of work. The manager may thus be the source of some interesting ideas as to what could constitute the project.
- The manager will be losing the participant and his or her time for something like a day a month at set meetings, and for other stretches of time as he or she focuses on the project.
- Development of staff is one of a manager's prime responsibilities. He or she is the person most likely to know about a participant's learning and developmental needs.
- Because the programme is about learning, it is likely that a participant may make some 'mistakes', and the manager must realize that making mistakes (not major financial or system mistakes, of course) is part of learning.
- If the project is about work outside the participant's immediate area of work, it will take him or her away from everyday issues for some of their time, and the manager needs to understand this.

EVERY PROJECT NEEDS A 'CLIENT'

A client is a senior manager whom the participant will report to on his/her project and learning. A client is rarely a participant's manager, because a line relationship can impose other constraints, and may not allow both parties to be as open as they need to be about any problems.

Reg Revans coined a very useful catch-phrase to remind people that they are not alone when working on projects – or indeed at any time when they are attempting to do something. He reminds us to identify someone (or some people) who:

- **knows** what it is we are trying to do or accomplish
- **cares** about what we are undertaking, is concerned that it should succeed
- **can** do something to help us – who has some power, influence or authority.

The client is that person who 'knows, cares and can' – someone who understands the nature of the programme, thinks it is important, and can be influential in making sure that the participants gain access wherever they need to, and that the programme is given high visibility and acceptance. He or she is the champion of the programme.

Clients are also indispensable allies for the person (often a training and development manager) who has introduced the programme in the first place.

IS 'IMPLEMENTING' ESSENTIAL IN A PROGRAMME?

'Implementing' means carrying out ideas and recommendations – seeing them through from start to finish. Producing reports and recommendations only to leave it to someone else to work out the implementation phase is the easy option. Being required to implement prevents the set from resembling a think-tank or debating group – for, intellectually stimulating or emotionally releasing as such groups might be, without implementation, nothing actually changes.

Furthermore, unless a participant puts into effect the developmental projects or tasks they are focusing on, and reports back to this effect, we have no evidence that they can do something differently or better, and therefore no indication of whether any learning or development is taking place: 'The doing triggers off different experiences, thoughts and feelings ... and so a new learning. If we're to learn to be managers, rather than consultants, we need to handle implementation,' observed one participant. She went on to describe how implementation had given her an insight: 'I learnt what was practical, what was bearable and what was acceptable ... and I am more aware that next time I make proposals, I need to consider those on the receiving end much more!'

One hospital manager recalled:

> I came up with a proposal of how to involve various managers and consultants in our hospital in a new approach to gaining new business from local GPs. However, it was rejected as being too long, people were not interested. Yet it was crucial to our survival that we act. So I tried a different tack. I identified a few individuals who were in favour of my plan, and informally we began working together. We acquired some new clients and extra business that way, and when it looked as though my idea had some validity, the other managers and consultants began to show interest. So implementation was crucial for me to gain acceptance of the plan. It's taught me to be flexible and to have various strategies, not just one, for implementing proposals.

On the other hand, many programmes do offer participants a great deal of learning without that final stage. Those young managers who had set out to 'learn about being consultants' learnt from performing that same function for their client. Others in similar positions learnt a great deal about handling people, handling data, negotiating, and a host of other useful skills.

So, in instances where sets meet for too short a time for everyone to have airspace to work on their project, or in a learning community, it is important to ensure that at the end of each meeting, everyone formulates their next action plans, even if these are based only on insights they have gained while hearing others talk about *their* projects.

One participant summed up what many others felt: 'Implementing is not necessarily integral. The whole experience is important. and you still learn even if your project isn't implemented.'

A PRACTICAL EXAMPLE[2]

A large dairy farm (at that time part of the Dartington Trust) was coping with cut milk quotas, and searching for means to improve its profitability. The farm workers, the manager felt, would undoubtedly have some useful ideas.

An action learning programme involving the seven farm workers and running over a few winter months produced some excellent money-saving ideas, including:

- a costing exercise by the farm mechanic on the farm-owned combine harvester (which led to the decision to scrap it)
- a scheme by the herdsmen to reduce the milking parlours from three to two
- an investigation of feedstuffs by the relief herdsman (an ex-student from an agricultural college).

At the set's request, the farm manager attended the last half-hour of every set meeting.

DOES A PROJECT HAVE TO BE BASED ON SOMETHING IN A PARTICIPANT'S OWN DEPARTMENT OR SECTION?

No. Whether it is will depend on how the programme is conceived (see Figure 4.1, page 86). The main criterion is that it should be something he or she can learn from which is also of importance to the section or department in question.

Working on another department's problems isn't always the greatest motivator, as one set pointed out. They were workshop-based engineers, and their project involved establishing effective field communications for their engineers on the road:

Although we had a lot of useful ideas, we didn't see that we would have the benefits, and so we weren't very motivated. Had I been a field engineer with all the frustrations, I would have gained more ... It would have motivated me to think more.

The aim of this particular programme was to bring about more in-company teamwork. On the surface, allocating sets projects that are of use to others looks an ideal way of achieving this aim. But at another level, it may fail to generate sufficient enthusiasm. As a continuation of the programme, the set was subsequently allocated a project within their own section, with very different results (see page 105).

This brings us back to Revans's point: we are most motivated to learn when we are tackling an issue close to our own hearts and work.

WHAT ARE THE DIMENSIONS OF A PROJECT?

Much has been written on project management, and this is not the place to go into details, although some knowledge of project management is clearly helpful when working on some – if not all – projects undertaken in action learning programmes.

Many projects cross departmental or functional boundaries, and obviously, most projects will cross personal boundaries and impinge in some way on others. Thus managing projects requires skills of persuasion and influencing. Project managers need to develop an understanding of others' roles and needs, and need to be good at co-ordinating activities. In particular, they need to pay particular attention to the question of how to carry out these inter-personal/functional/departmental aspects of a project, and not simply focus on the 'what'.

In their book *Take the Lead*, Boddy and Buchanan (1992) list the four basic themes or elements present in varying proportions in most projects, no matter how they may be initially defined (and many of the projects they studied sound uncannily like the type of projects undertaken in action learning). Each will involve, to some degree, each of the following:

- **Tasks** – developing a new product or service, quality improvement
- **Structures** – rearranging departmental functions and responsibilities, changing communication and co-ordination channels, changing the culture and management style, introducing new job evaluation or payment systems
- **Technology** – changes in physical plant and equipment, introducing new computer systems, changes in plant or office location
- **People** – changes in working arrangements of individuals and groups, attitude change, team-working, programmes to enhance skills and performance.

As the authors point out: 'In some change projects one element is clearly dominant ... Successful change management requires attention to all four elements ... Effective project management means looking beyond the most visible features of a change.' The following, they suggest, always need to be addressed:

- how tasks may change, and what impact this may have
- how staff will be affected, and what their response may be
- how roles and duties may change, and what this may mean
- how the culture may be affected or may need to change
- how working relationships may alter
- how authority may be affected.

They remind 'project managers' to pay attention to both old and new information sources, to co-ordinate and network more than ever, and to be aware of the need to help people with learning and attitude changes they may be required to make.

So, to implement a successful project, the authors argue, more is needed than simply an ability to analyse and suggest structured methods of implementation: 'The change in emphasis ... is to place more reliance on the acquisition and use of a range of interpersonal skills.' Of the inter-personal skills needed, they mention in particular:

- communicating
- negotiating
- team-building
- involving and building good relations with everyone who may be affected, to create a sense of ownership in them.

They also talk of the need to manage in four directions: up (senior managers), down (staff) and across (their team, and others involved across other boundaries). They need to identify who has an interest in the project – who are the key figures (which resembles Revans's 'Who knows, cares and can?').

When a project is undertaken within an action learning programme, these inter-personal skills receive a great deal of emphasis and encouragement.

CREATING A 'STORY'

In addition to working on and talking about their project/task – what I call the project's 'history' – in set meetings, participants need to focus equally on what I call their personal 'story' (see Figure 4.2).

When working on the project's 'history', participants will be exploring:

- what the problems/issues are
- what outcomes are being sought
- what resources are/will be available
- who will be involved
- what processes are being/can be used.

When focusing on their personal 'story', participants will be exploring their:

- own role
- commitment to the task
- understanding of the organization's needs
- own self-development, and how it will affect others
- values, and what's important to them
- ways of working with/relating to others
- own needs and motivations.

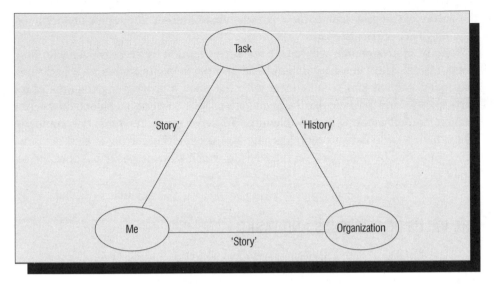

Figure 4.2   Focusing on your 'story'

HOW CAN I MAKE SURE I WILL GET THE TIME TO WORK ON MY PROJECT?

If the participant's manager isn't kept fully involved, or at least fully informed, then he or she is – quite rightly – going to feel put out. A well-run programme will have involved participants' managers in early discussions, and stressed the importance of the programme.

Where a manager remains unhappy, the participant's client may be able to help, as may the training or management development department, or whoever is the instigator of the programme as a whole.

As for giving the participant 'time off' – this becomes less of a problem if the task or project is part of the participant's own work or is something the manager can identify as being important to his or her section/department, or the participant's own development.

Even so, there may still be problems as pressure at work mounts and everyone takes on more tasks and more responsibilities, with the same finite amount of time in which to do them.

WHAT HAPPENS IF I CAN'T FIND A PROJECT?

This fear is frequently voiced by participants at the outset of a programme. Sometimes it is difficult to pinpoint a project until the participants know more about the nature of the programme, for it is somewhat different from other programmes they may have participated in.

A well-run programme will have been set in motion by an organizer who first alerts clients, the personnel department, the participants themselves and their managers, emphasizing to all concerned what such a programme requires of its participants – and in particular the need for a project to work on. Hence the participant is not left alone with this dilemma. To avoid such problems, one company which makes wide use of action learning was considering having a 'bank' of projects, submitted by managers, on the basis of which suitable participants would be found.

THE VALUE OF PROJECTS AND TASKS

Obviously, the aim of the programme, the choice of projects and whether the project should be tackled on a group or individual basis all have a bearing on how much participants learn and gain.

My research revealed that participants who had individual projects, or who had well-defined mini-projects within larger group projects, learnt and gained more in terms of breadth and depth of insights – as witnessed by their comments. A number of participants who had experienced more than one type of programme remarked: 'Individual projects allow you to do more personal, deeper learning.'

The quality of the set adviser, and how often the set was reminded that learning was as important as action, also appeared to influence what and how much participants learnt. One set, tackling a group project without the benefit of a set adviser, commented: 'We haven't done a lot of conscious learning. Maybe we'll do it at the end.' However, another – with a set adviser always present – commented: 'We haven't really stopped to look at how we worked as a team, although we've learnt a lot from the project itself.'

UNDERSTANDING THE COMPLEXITIES IN AN ORGANIZATION

There are many gains, but in particular, participants commented on a greater insight and understanding of their own – and (in mixed-company sets) others' – organizations, and hearing about others' projects, which broadens participants' horizons, giving them broader insights into organizational issues and problems, particularly those of people in different functions: 'You begin to understand the constraints people face – for instance, Finance and Personnel have different issues to grapple with, and hence bring different perspectives.'

By examining everyone's projects – particularly on in-company programmes – participants begin to see how they and their department are part of a larger entity, begin to see how bits of the jigsaw puzzle fit together: 'I know a great deal more about the company now – and begin to feel much more part of it,' said one young marketing manager.

This cohesion is enhanced when participants discover that people in different departments can help them with their projects – that their insights and questions are useful and make sense: 'I was really amazed at how people from other functions were able to help me – simply by asking intelligent questions which made me stop and think.'

Coupled with this is the realization that, as one engineer put it: 'No matter how we defined our projects and what they were seemingly about, in the end they all came down to the same problems: relationships with others – be they your boss, your colleagues or your staff.'

'The fact that everyone else has problems – not just me – was comforting,' was a frequent comment.

One set of engineers who worked on a project for another engineering section gained a greater realization that: 'We are a collective – we now understand better how we are interconnected with the field engineers, and that our overall profitability depends on all of us working together.'

In mixed-company programmes, there is an added dimension of comparing how different organizations tackle different issues – or even the same issue – differently. For one participant, this latter experience was, as he put it, 'a humbling experience'. Coming from a blue-chip company, he had always assumed that the way things were done in his company was the best and the only way. Now he saw this was not necessarily so.

IT OPENS UP NETWORKS AND INTER-DEPARTMENTAL CONTACTS

'It was a ticket – a licence to investigate ... a door-opener to people.' And once the project has opened doors, participants realize that what has lain hidden behind them is not as awesome or frightening as they had imagined.

One young manager was in some dread of visiting the finance director: 'I needed to see him as part of my project. My manager suggested this. I spent 35 minutes with him, and he told me not to hesitate if I needed to ask him anything again. I'd somehow not expected such an open approach to me. You begin to see senior managers as approachable human beings.'

'I realized,' said another, younger manager, 'that just a little bit of knowledge and research can give you major insights – and definitely enough to go and talk to others as a basis for discussion. You don't have to be an expert before you go and ask others for something.'

Some discovered that they knew as much as anyone, and had equally valid insights: 'I had no need to be in awe of people,' said one research scientist, who continued: 'Before, the Marketing Department intimidated me. Now, no longer.'

Many participants mentioned that the project had achieved more than teaching them the value of using others; it had given them contacts throughout the company which would be of use in other circumstances back at work. Each contacted person knew a host of other people, and this would expand their own network: 'I was amazed at how helpful people were – willing to help and give you their time. I hadn't expected that. I had always thought they would think I was wasting their time. I think people actually like helping you.'

'Working on my project with the help of others made me realize that there is always someone I can talk to if I need to. Before, I'd bottle up stress, problems and worries. Not any longer,' was another comment.

One took his experience of such networking – and the help he had received on his project from set members from widely differing backgrounds – a step further: 'In any project team, I now have a better mix of people, with different skills and styles of working. The differences – of knowledge and perspective – are a strength.'

Where the programme had a high profile within the organization, it gave the participants themselves a high profile, too (something not to be sneezed at): 'You meet people you'd never have the opportunity to meet. They get to know you, too. It gives you much wider horizons and understanding of the organization – and it gives others a chance to assess you.'

Working on projects had thus legitimized for them the viability of approaching others in the future – whether to ask questions or simply to go up to people and introduce themselves – and in the process, to build up their own useful network of contacts for the future.

IT INSTILS A DISCIPLINED WAY OF TACKLING PROJECTS, EVEN BACK AT WORK

The 'discipline' that many participants talked about consisted of several elements. Firstly, there was the discipline of having to create a plan of action, to work out who could help, and build up a network of contacts for information or insights; next came making sure they had the authority to do what they were proposing, and being clear about the final goal, and lastly, building in evaluation stages as the project progressed. These and many other aspects of working in a systematic way on their project they found immensely helpful.

What primarily created this discipline was working under the microscopic gaze of others, who were also able to help formulate the various steps and stages – either from their own past experience, or simply because they were similarly involved in working systematically, and hence listened to the unfolding story of a project and could see where the gaps were.

The other main aspect of discipline was the constant revisiting of each participant's project, at consecutive set meetings, to see what stage it had reached.

As one participant said: 'It gave me some methods and systems ... a structured approach to any assignment: how and where to look for help and resources, collecting evidence, being clear about the problem; making sure you have criteria for measuring or evaluating what you're doing; having strategies for coping and managing. Before, I'd be running at 90 m.p.h. and getting nowhere.'

Another ticked off the necessary steps point by point: 'Be clear about the problem – ask questions; establish your criteria for assessing/measuring your work; have strategies for coping and improving; and always collect evidence; and get feedback.'

Another observed: 'Once you have an idea, make it tangible. Have a plan of action, create networks of people who can help you, check out the literature, ensure you have the authority to do what you want to do, hold meetings with others.'

Many alluded to the fact that this discipline was an amalgam of having, in their mind's eye or on paper, a 'learning cycle' – which they adapted into a 'working cycle'. Thus, rather than rushing from idea to action, they built in extra stages, considered more options, worked out different scenarios, and allowed for frequent assessment. Many also talked of building in thinking and reflection time.

Several also commented that they had become aware of the notion of 'task' and 'process' – and the value of stopping to consider the latter: 'Before, I'd simply focus on what I wanted to achieve – but how I was going to was not something I spent too much time thinking about. I never, for instance, stopped to think about my decision process. Now I set goals, consider options for getting there, flag up issues I need to consider further.'

Thus, for one manager, action learning invited: 'a certain caution in what I do. I'm less inclined to give an instant decision or answer. I prepare my ground more, think, go away, come back.'

IT GIVES PARTICIPANTS RESPONSIBILITY FOR COMPLETING A PROJECT AND MANAGING ALL THE ELEMENTS

For many participants, this was the first time they had tackled a major project and had responsibility for it. It was this feeling of ownership of a project that impressed many: 'Ownership of an issue, the responsibility to carry it out, and the authority to do so, plus real personal commitment to it. You need all three for something to really happen.' It was their experience of what ownership could result in that made many aware that their own staff would also benefit by being given ownership.

Another participant commented that his manager's confidence in him had been increased by the way he approached his project. As a result, he was given an increased budgetary control, and more responsibility generally.

A young member of a set laughed when she recounted how her manager felt he was learning by listening to her and being party to her thinking as she tackled her project – a small-scale practical one concerned with creating a logging system to ensure that all phone calls to the department were received and dealt with effectively, and monitoring the whole process's effectiveness.

In another project, a client told the set – who were consulting him on a major marketing project – that he had learnt and gained considerably by working with them.

A manager talked of how the project had given him insights into the art of managing: 'In the project, you become aware of your responsibility to take control and make judgements and take decisions on what's important, and have the confidence to manage others and not allow emotions to over-rule you and intervene ... a step in the direction of maturity. '

Where implementation was an integral part of projects, and where in addition those projects were based in their own departments, participants felt more commitment. Such factors definitely provide an impetus and sense of energy to set projects. But implementation added an extra dimension to the sense of responsibility, for the fruits of the project need to be seen as being, as one participant put it, 'practical, usable and bearable':

> If you don't implement, you have pie-in-the-sky ideas of what you want to do. But you change these if you are responsible for implementing. And it makes you more aware, the next time you suggest something be done in a different way.

For those working on individual projects, implementation was not always built-in. For one participant, however, it was crucial that it should be:

> I came to learn how to communicate better. I'm also a 'theoretist', and weak on doing things – I'm not a 'concluder' or a 'producer'. So being forced to produce and conclude was good for me. Our department had a bad reputation, so I set out to improve our communications with other departments through a whole host of initiatives. It's made me very conscious of the need to have good channels of communication in a company.

Many also talked of having to learn to negotiate, to compromise, to take others much more into account. Where implementation was not part of their brief, some participants talked of a sense of frustration at not knowing whether all their hard work would ever see the light of day.

BETTER TEAMWORKING

The team benefits of focusing on implementation are clear from the following account:

> As part of the company's strategy to build better team-working, our engineering workshop was put into a set to resolve our own day-to-day problems. Focusing on our own areas of work was a second bite of the cherry – in the first part of this programme we'd worked on problems in other areas of the company. But working on our own work gave us more enthusiasm because it was left up to us. We decided we needed to be more efficient and improve our turnaround time for repairs.
>
> We work on the repairs of a variety of telecommunication products. We identified what everyone does, what are the problems and where bottlenecks existed. By working

together we managed to create a system for what happens when a repair job comes in, channel phone calls through one person, and establish a system for ordering spare parts and handing work out (before, our manager did this). And we physically reorganized the layout of the workshop to make it more efficient.

What we've achieved is a cycle turnaround that has been reduced from ninety days to five days! Our next step is to reduce the five days to two days.

I volunteered to be the 'leader' because I was interested and saw it as an opportunity to learn and grow. I'd also been one of the people who was always backbiting, so I decided here was an opportunity to do something rather than just complaining. It was a frustrating project at times, and it took much longer than I'd anticipated.

The result of working together is that now people are more willing to co-operate with one another, to share their expertise with one another ... and to use the phone! Morale has definitely improved. There's more of an understanding that we survive collectively and not individually, and people are more willing to stay on after hours without claiming overtime. They're also coming up with ideas for what else we could be doing differently – that wouldn't have happened two years ago.

Yes, there are still some cynics who think the whole programme and team-building effort is a great con, but gradually they're coming round. But one of the lads has for many years been consistently 'sick' three or four times a year, and now the others are realizing that it affects their workload, and have begun to tackle him and point out what he is doing. We're taking more responsibility collectively.

Much of our initiative was made possible by the attitude of our manager. He's learnt much about the workshop and how it works, he understands our problems and now gives us the opportunity to put things right. I'm not sure we'd have managed to achieve so much without him – with a more autocratic manager.

What it's made me realize is that such a programme is about giving people the power, and improving the workplace. And after all, it's the workpeople who know more about the workplace than their managers. I've learnt to take initiative (not just to gripe!), I've become more assertive, and much freer to be honest and open with managers, and listen to them more. Before, I simply regarded their decisions as being destructive. I just hope that in the future I'll continue to go to managers and explain the impact of any decisions they take.

FOUR CASE EXAMPLES

TWO DEVELOPMENTAL PROGRAMMES

A unique use of action learning, now into its sixth year, is where the action learning follows a week's experiential behavioural programme on managerial effectiveness, with both junior and senior managers in different functions, and from a variety of companies.

Following this week, during which participants get to know each other well, become very empathetic, learn to listen in a very active way and understand 'the words and the music', they are invited to meet as a set, and to bring – to work on – their own everyday life issues and concerns at work, and their understanding of themselves as managers. They contract with the set adviser for three meetings, after which the contract is revisited.

Another developmental programme – this time for human resource personnel – both in-company and consultants – has now been meeting for nearly a year, with six set members coming together for about six hours every six to eight weeks. All are interested in using action learning in their work, and the issues they work on are real business issues: how to operate as human resource specialists in their own organizations, or how to operate as independent human resource consultants.

TRANSFORMING PROJECT ENGINEERS INTO MANAGERS

A few years ago, with the privatization of water boards in England and Wales, one group of project engineers, who were to become managers of small servicing businesses, came together into two action learning sets, to study together their new role in an entirely new business. As their common project they took their new roles, and worked individually, at each set meeting, on how each was managing and learning. In a few instances, two or three participants joined to work together on issues that they had a particular interest in. They worked with a set adviser throughout.

Half-way through the programme, once they had begun to understand their new role, and to realize what they needed to know, they themselves devised a week-long programme, with the help of a training manager, and invited people who they felt had the appropriate knowledge to help them understand their new businesses.

A LEADERSHIP PROGRAMME FOR THE SHOP FLOOR[3]

A food and drinks company decided that first line managers and supervisors were the right people for their leadership programme. Each participant, after discussions with their line manager, offered four problems he or she was currently tackling and which needed to change, in order to show tangible improved results. Participants had access to open learning materials, which they discussed at set meetings, and – at work – applied the ideas they had been introduced to. Workshops during the programme also included presentation skills, time management and project management. Each set met with a set adviser present.

'The honesty and speed with which they challenged problems, questioned themselves and tested theories surprised the set facilitators,' was one comment. By the end of the twelve-month programme, most of the participants had exceeded their performance targets.

NOTES

[1] Robert Fritz's ideas are developed in *The Path of Least Resistance* (1989) and *Creating* (1991).
[2] My thanks to Alec Lewis for sharing this with me.
[3] This programme is described in more detail in Meehan and Jarvis (1996).

5 The processes in the set

The processes of a set are very different from processes in other groups. Participants coming on an action learning programme certainly had no anticipation of learning anything special by working in the group, other than simply 'helping' other members to achieve their projects. The processes are thus one of the 'eye-opening' elements of a programme, and are, for me, one of the main keys to effective action learning.

What is also interesting is that these process skills are some of the basic communication skills that everyone needs to learn if they are to work effectively with others – colleagues, staff or 'bosses', customers or suppliers. Once tried out, they become 'obvious': 'I was excited by its common sense,' said more than one participant.

WHAT HAPPENS IN A SET MEETING? WHAT ARE THE SET PROCESSES?

There are a number of fundamental processes that occur and need to be observed (and some avoided) if the set is to gain the real benefits of working with action learning:

- airspace – allowing time and space for everyone to work on their project individually, recalling and reporting back, and working on the next 'phase' or issue
- asking helpful and challenging questions – but not seeking answers
- listening 'actively'
- giving feedback and sharing insights
- focusing on learning as much as on action
- reflecting – and maybe responding
- allowing time and space for silences
- not judging or giving advice; not telling anecdotes (unless they are helpful); not offering solutions
- finding a formula for sharing ideas.

AIRSPACE

Airspace is the time during which one participant, the problem-presenter, tells the other members where he or she has got to since the last meeting. They tell a continuation of a 'story' – which other members get to know well, and become involved in.

The value of action learning is that this airspace gives you an opportunity to focus on:

- your story, and not just a history of a series of events (for more on your 'story', see pages 98–99)
- your experiences, and not just facts and figures
- your anecdotes, and not just a progression of events
- what you felt like, and not just what was happening
- your metaphors (to help you understand), and not just the facts.

Participants often find that it's both enlightening and therapeutic to tell their story, and to hear themselves recall and recount:

> As you explain things to the set, you hear your own inconsistencies, the missing elements, the illogicalities. But you need to do it out loud.

> If you only consider 'internally', in your own thoughts, your mind can lead you down all sorts of pathways. But somehow as you speak, your voice can give you away. And others are listening, and can spot the flaws, where the gaps are, and will pursue you down the alleys you are following. Eventually, the trick is to learn to do this yourself, though having others listen will always add an extra dimension.

Having their own time and space was something most participants said they had hardly ever experienced before. Normally, there are interruptions, the hijacking of your issue and space by others – the noisiest and those good with words. But the imposition of a discipline created a sense of confidence in those being listened to: 'I didn't realize how powerful – but also how unnerving – it was to be the focus of everyone's attention, to have their undivided attention. It felt wonderful!'

At the outset, though, several participants said they feared that their issue/story/problem/quandary wouldn't be of sufficient interest to the rest of the set, 'but then the realization that what you have to say is of interest, of relevance to others, that they are interested, and that they are learning from the interaction makes you feel good and gives you confidence'.

Thus, in a set meeting, the 'conch' is passed around to everyone. But such airspace is not a five-minute affair: 'I thought we'd resolved my issue within a few minutes, but when we started working in an action learning way, I realized that we had only scratched the surface,' said one young nurse-manager.

Most participants were surprised at how it took at least an hour to get to the bottom of an issue, quandary or problem – often redefining *en route* what the real problem was – and then work through how to tackle it: 'That's one of the advantages of airspace ... that you feel you're not taking up people's time, that it is legitimate to work through to the origins of an issue.'

During a participant's airspace, it is the task of the others to help by asking questions that will clarify issues: to 'shine a torch into the corners', and to unfold all the components of the ongoing story – the events and thoughts and feelings and insights.

Airspace is important for the learning: we each need the opportunity to be prompted, and to reflect on, that learning. Holding on to this airspace is important, for it means that the set has a 'dialogue' with one person at a time, rather than having a 'discussion', as in other gatherings.

With the focus on one person, others do not have the opportunity to go off on tangents that interest them, do not hijack the airspace to tell their own stories, or shift the set's focus onto them (unless they have asked the presenter if that would be useful), nor do they begin to hold conversations with one another, unless the presenter asks them to (see below).

In other words, the problem-presenter is in charge of his or her own airspace.

Some useful statements for a problem-presenter include:

- 'I'd like to explore ...'
- 'I'm wondering whether ...'
- 'I'm not sure if ...'
- 'I'm uncertain about ...'
- 'I can't decide whether ...'
- 'I'm puzzled by ...'
- 'I'm confused by ...'

BEING AN EFFECTIVE SET MEMBER

In a useful article, 'Action learning: Reflections on becoming a set member', Beaty, Bourner and Frost (1993) describe how to be an effective set member.

Helpful behaviour by set members includes:

- listening and attending
- learning not to interrupt
- conveying interest and empathy
- being supportive
- challenging
- asking helpful questions
- being clear that what they are about to say/asking and considering whether it is helpful to the presenter
- providing information where required
- offering insights and ideas (at the right time and in the right way).

Helpful behaviour by problem-presenters includes:

- preparing for meetings
- being clear in their own mind about what they want to achieve from their air-space, and what they will do to ensure this, as well as what they will ask of the set
- structuring their time
- telling the set what they want, and pointing out to the set what isn't helpful.

USE OF LANGUAGE

Several participants commented on the emphasis in action learning on the use of the pronoun 'I'. It is usually the set adviser who first points out that saying 'one' or 'you' distances us from what we're saying.

We need to say 'I' to develop a sense of ownership of the actions, thoughts or feelings we're talking about. And many participants remarked that it felt more honest – and empowering – to:

- use 'I' with the active form of a verb, rather than the passive of the verb – 'I sent my report late', acknowledging responsibility, in contrast with the passivity of 'My report arrived late.'
- substitute 'I' for 'you' or the ubiquitous 'one' – saying 'I often feel ...' as opposed to 'One/you often feel(s) ...'.

How we use language both reflects, and has an impact on, how we 'see' things. Here are a few instances of how changing words may well alter how we perceive things, and what we do and learn:

- verb tenses – using the present, often with a generalization, implies permanence (and a hint of no change possible), as in 'You always say ...', as opposed to 'You said ...', where it is a one-off event
- recycling nouns back into verbs – for instance, saying 'I'm trying to motivate X' instead of 'I'm dealing with X's lack of motivation' creates an action
- using verbal forms rather than adjectives to describe something – 'I didn't manage to ...' leaves more room for improvement than 'I'm useless at ...'.

ASKING HELPFUL AND CHALLENGING QUESTIONS

Helpful and challenging questions are the key to working in a set. By asking questions, we hand responsibility back to the 'problem-owner'. But their aim is not necessarily, nor always, to elicit answers. Sometimes their aim is rather to help the presenter to think, reflect, and maybe respond. And questions need to be asked in the right spirit – not aggressively.

Most participants find that it is helpful if the questioners preface their questions with an indication of what they are after:

- **to clarify** – 'Are you saying that ...?'
- **to try to understand** – 'Could you explain so-and-so a bit more ...?'
- **to follow through a train of thought** – 'You said a moment ago that ... If that's the case, what would happen if ...?'
- **to mirror** – 'So what you're saying is ...?'
- **to open up new avenues** – 'Have you explored/thought of ...?' or 'Would ... be of any help?'
- **to challenge** – 'What do you feel most uncomfortable about?' or 'What do you feel most challenged by?'
- **to elicit honesty** – 'Do you feel you're making any impact – and if not, what can you do about it?'
- **to unpeel layers, to dig deeper** – 'And then what happened ...?'
- **to check out** – 'Are we asking helpful questions?' or 'What haven't we helped you with yet?'

And then there are the pseudo-questions – those comments, reflections and feedback by other set members on what they are hearing, such as 'It seems as though ...' – which draw people out further, and are also useful, provided they contain no element of censoring or judging the presenter.

One participant gave an example of some of the questions the set adviser had asked her when she commented that she was having problems working with a colleague: 'He asked me questions such as "When you speak to X, what do you think her views are?" and "How did she respond?", or when I told of an exchange we'd had, "How would you feel if she had said that to you?", and so on. Questions like these expose you to a different level of thinking, a different slant altogether.'

WORKING WITH QUESTIONS

Asking questions, as many discovered, is not that easy: 'I'd never realized how difficult it is to formulate really helpful questions.' 'The secret is to get people talking, so saying "I don't understand", "Tell me more" or "You seem to be glossing over ..." encourages them to say more.'

One participant said he structured the sequence of his questions, beginning with the 'what' and 'who' questions, to begin to form a picture, followed by the 'whys' to clarify the story; only then would he progress to the 'what' and 'how' questions, directed at what actions or interventions were possible or appropriate.

Questions may sometimes evoke a defensive response in the presenter. The set can address this either by asking why the presenter is feeling defensive – which in turn might open up something that needs to be explored further – or, if this defensiveness results from a questioner probing too aggressively, the set may point this out (give feedback) to the questioner. If this is pursued, the questioner will in turn learn something about him or herself.

It is sometimes difficult not to bombard the presenter with questions: 'I began to feel I needed to protect myself from all the questions that were being fired at me, with no time to stop and think,' said one participant, echoing the comments of many others.

This bombarding often happens when the set is still inexperienced and new to action learning. With time, things change. Set members learn to listen to the questions others are asking, listen also to how the presenter is working on them, and learn to wait before they ask their question, which could take the presenter down a different track.

Bombarding may provide an opportunity for a set adviser to intervene – to ask the set what is happening. Such a question makes the set aware of group processes that apply not only to working in a set, but in any other group. In this way, the processes of the set provide a learning opportunity about interactions for everyone in the set.

LISTENING ACTIVELY

Listening is one of our least developed skills. Yet it is potentially one of the most important.

We *think* we listen, but often we only hear part of what is said, or we hear at a superficial level; we fail to make connections or see contradictions between what is being said and what was said a short time ago. Alternatively, we shut out things we don't want to hear; or we become so engrossed with what we want to say next that we miss what is being said. Likewise, we also don't always 'listen' to the non-verbal signals – the body language, the tone of voice.

When we listen actively to another person, we follow precisely what they are saying, and create a picture of the scenario in our mind, so we can notice where the gaps and spaces are, where the information is incomplete or puzzling, where something is being glossed over. But listening is not something that most of us are good at: 'I think visually, almost spatially – and I've applied that to my more general thinking – and listening! If I can see issues in a picture form that helps me analyse them. I can now also see myself as part of that picture and where I fit in,' said one participant who worked in the Design Department of a large company.

If we listen actively, we are also more likely to hear what is *not* being said; we become aware of the 'thought bubbles' that contain a subtext which isn't being shared: 'One member of our set said he was keen to run some action learning programmes, but kept delaying doing anything about it, finding excuses in the pressure of work everyone was under. Eventually we realized that his subtext was: "I don't think my staff could cope with this level of thinking and questioning; they're not capable of it." But he didn't want to say so openly.'

It is the responsibility of a presenter to tell other set members if they are misinterpreting what he or she is saying. In this way, set members get feedback about their own skills – or lack of them. The set adviser will probably also comment if non-listening seems to be a trait of one person, or even of the set. What is valuable about this is that behaviour exhibited in the set is often the same that occurs elsewhere. If set members can learn to listen differently in the set, they are likely to transfer it back to work.

By extension, being listened to, without interruptions, is a luxury few of us have experienced. After one set meeting, a participant said, almost with tears in her eyes, that it was the first time in her life that she felt she had been really listened to.

GIVING FEEDBACK AND SHARING INSIGHTS

A useful function of the set is giving feedback, or sharing insights. As the person with airspace is working on the issue they have brought, other members may begin to have insights about what he or she appears to be doing – or not doing – both in the set and back at work. They may also begin to notice the person's manner, tone of voice, or energy level. They may begin to voice – silently to themselves – agreements or disagreements, unease, or many other feelings or thoughts.

It is useful to share these with the person who has airspace. It may highlight for them something they were aware of but were hoping to avoid talking about. And learning – or perhaps gaining the courage – to give such feedback is useful for other set members.

Many of us are afraid of giving honest feedback. We bite our tongues and hold back, only to gripe later – normally to someone unconnected with the event! We stop ourselves because we don't know what the reaction will be: will the person be angry or hurt? Feedback may lead to a negative reaction, so it's a question both of how it's given and received.

Every manager needs to give feedback, and the set provides an opportunity to learn to give and also to receive it. Set members may give feedback to a presenter on how he or she appears, or what they are doing or saying. And the person giving the feedback will in turn get feedback on whether it was done in a helpful manner.

Being given feedback, both positive and negative, may be difficult. As the receiver, we need to learn to listen to it, think about it and respond, rather than reacting instantly – something that the time and space in the set allow members to start doing.

Feelings of doubt, anxiety or lack of confidence, as well as excitement and energy, exist in the sets, particularly at the beginning of a programme, as many participants recalled (see pages 170–174). They mirror the feelings we have elsewhere, but to which we often don't admit. Yet they colour how we are and what we do. They are powerful agents. Recognizing them, and simply admitting to them out loud, often proves not to be as worrying as the *idea* of doing so, and may loosen the hold they have on us.

Insights and feedback from other set members prove useful. If they share their feelings, this confirms that we are all human, after all! The courage gained from such sharing makes it easier to acknowledge, understand and genuinely take such feelings into account back at work. It is just one way in which the set can be used as an 'experimental bubble'.

FOCUSING ON LEARNING AND CHANGING

Stopping to think and be aware of what each member is learning is a crucial process. This may take place as someone is working in their airspace, or at a specifically allotted time during the set meeting. It may simply take the form of the set adviser asking questions such as: 'So what insights did you gain from that?' or 'What will you do differently next time?' As set members become more accustomed to such questions, they also begin to ask them, without prompting, and share responses with the other set members.

One of the main roles of the set adviser is to remind the set that they are there to *learn*, and not simply to 'act'. As one set recalled, their set adviser 'used to drip-feed the question "So what have you learnt from that?" until it became second nature for us to ask ourselves and each other the same question'.

The learning has to do not only with work each person is doing on their project, it also concerns what is happening in the set, and how members work together. As one young manager pointed out: 'You start out with a project, but end up learning so much about yourself.'

This constant emphasis on becoming aware, learning and changing is probably one of the fundamental ways in which a set differs from other groups. 'It's about change ... and changing. Changing how you see things and interpret them, how you do things ... and seeing others change – and seeing how you get to this position of "change" through becoming more aware, open and honest,' was how one participant described the learning. Others agreed: 'It's about learning to do things differently and becoming sure that what you're doing is effective – through listening to others, telling others, asking yourself and others questions, admitting you're unsure ... learning from your interaction with others and their responses, becoming aware of your inner irritations and how they affect what you do or say ... all of this is open for examination.' (For more on learning, see Chapter 8).

Opportunities to learn also occur away from the project and the set, back at work. To help set members become aware of this learning, the set adviser may suggest a moment for reflecting, at the beginning of every meeting, on the time that has elapsed since the previous meeting, and the experiences members have had.

REFLECTING

Reflecting can mean one of two things. The first is reflecting back or mirroring back to the presenter what he or she is saying, or what feelings they are conveying: 'So you're saying ...' or 'You sound angry.' This helps the presenter hear what they have said, which is maybe what they didn't mean to convey, and also gives them the opportunity to say more. 'Hearing back' in this way can be helpful.

Reflecting also has another more contemplative meaning. It's something many of us don't do, either because we 'don't have the time' or because 'it isn't in my nature'. In this sense, reflecting is the process of recalling events, feelings, actions and thoughts, and being honest in assessing them – 'shining a torch on them', as one manager described it.

Set members can help one another – and themselves – to understand various ideas and concepts that are talked about but often not put under a microscope, by reflecting in this more contemplative way: maybe about such issues as 'What is the job of a manager?' or 'What exactly does motivation mean?' or 'What do you mean by quality?'

One set recalled reflecting – together – on such issues as commitment, trust and honesty. Another remembered reflecting on the notion of leadership. The purpose of such reflection is to clarify everyone's thinking, and throw light on why people – or indeed the set members themselves – behave or respond in particular ways.

One could almost claim that without such reflecting, we don't learn or change; we simply repeat what we have always done. If we are truly to learn and change, we need to reflect on our actions, or those of others. But this alone isn't sufficient. We also need to reflect on what we thought, said and felt, as well as on what we didn't do or say. And it may be useful to reflect on what others did and said, or what they didn't do or say – possibly even on what they might have been feeling. In this way, we begin to gain a fuller picture, and may begin to understand better what actions, interactions and relationships are about.

It is at this stage that reflecting with others becomes a true dialogue with them. This obviously takes time, and there are occasions when this is inappropriate, such as when decisions have to be taken quickly. 'Activists' will particularly feel uneasy about spending time reflecting, when they could be doing something. But as one participant realized: 'There's more to learning than simply action.' And another said: 'You need to build in an infrastructure of thinking – action on its own isn't enough – it's merely another project group.'

In an action learning programme, the processes give each participant this time to think and question themselves (and others) and reflect. The processes virtually demand it. And working in a set with others who have different inclinations, or are good at reflecting, can demonstrate to those who are not so inclined, by nature, the benefits of reflection. But, as one young IT manager pointed out ruefully: 'The trouble is that I now realize the value of stopping to think, but there is no space allocated for thinking time on our work sheets.'

Nevertheless, once it becomes a habit, reflection ceases to be something that happens only at certain stages in a learning process, as defined in the learning spirals. It begins to take place all the time; to become almost like a silent inner voice (or an imp sitting on your shoulder!) that whispers questions to you, such as 'So why are you avoiding so-and so?' or 'Why did you react like that?' or 'So what insights did you gain from that?' (See Figure 2.2.)

SILENCE

Silence can be – and is – interpreted in differing ways. It may be seen as a person having nothing to say, feeling intimidated, or thinking. It may also simply be allowing oneself the space just to 'be' – to not think for a while, to stop the mad rush of ideas and thoughts, and let some deeper consciousness take over.

Through simply stopping – being still and silent, even without consciously thinking – we find that the insights, answers or whatever we are searching for emerge into our consciousness. 'I'll sleep on that' – a common enough phrase – taps into that other consciousness, that bit of us that 'knows' or remembers but that we seldom allow to emerge. How often do we try to remember something, and then say: 'If I stop thinking about it, I'll remember'?

Silence could be valuable for many reasons. One experienced action learner commented that the set she was currently working in – as a member – had a lot of silences: 'The silence is to do with people thinking, puzzling, or simply letting what's been said sink in. I often babble, and one of the set members then says to me: "What do you feel like now? What do you need?" '

'It's disconcerting when you finish saying what you have to say, and there is an expectant silence … the group obviously think you have more to say. It then forces you to say and reveal more, and say things you've not said before. It forces you to take that extra step … simply the expectation of others that there is more to follow,' commented a banker.

But silence can make people feel very uncomfortable, so they try to overcome this by filling in the silences. They may crack a joke, move physically, or break into it in other ways. Much may depend on how long such a silence lasts: there are comfortable silences and uncomfortable ones. This is another instance where a set adviser might decide to intervene and comment on the silence, or ask members what they were doing and feeling during it.

NO JUDGEMENT, NO ADVICE, NO SOLUTIONS

It is vital not to pass judgement if, as we have seen, the set members are to feel comfortable with each other, and feel free to discuss issues that may make them feel vulnerable.

On the other hand, not judging does not mean not challenging; nor does it mean agreeing with what is being said. It is the form and tone of voice that are adopted that mark the difference.

'Advice,' someone once said, 'is profoundly pleasurable to the giver.' This would be good enough reason for stopping before we give it. What are our motives? Is it to give help, or to make ourselves look and feel good?

But there are other reasons for not giving advice. Firstly, we are never in a position to do so, for we are not the other person, and probably do not fully understand them and their set of circumstances, nor the full extent of the issue they are working on. We often begin a piece of advice with the spoken or unspoken phrase 'If I were you', to which the only response is: 'You're not me ...'.

Furthermore, and importantly, advice does not make the receiver work on the issue in the same depth that he or she has to when asked to consider options or ideas.

Not giving solutions touches on a slightly different aspect. We as helpers often leap in with solutions before the real problem as been identified. Solutions, like advice, make us, the giver, feel good and useful. But it also creates a 'Yes, but ...' or 'No, because ...' relationship with the presenter. 'Why don't you do so-and-so?' can turn into a game of verbal 'ping-pong': 'No, I can't, because ...'.

What's worse, the givers end up feeling angry or resentful that here they are, offering so much, and still the presenter is hesitating. However, hesitation may be a clue that the presented problem is not the real issue; deep down, the presenter knows this, and their hesitance may signal that they are struggling to get to the bottom of things but need help.

Interestingly, it is frequently at such moments that honest feedback to the presenter – possibly about how they appear, or their tone of voice – can open out new avenues to explore. One set recalled how their set adviser had intervened when the set was becoming frustrated that all their good ideas seemed to be getting nowhere. She commented to the presenter: 'You don't seem to have much energy or enthusiasm for the task you've set yourself', which penetrated to the real issue!

Some presenters sound very convincing when they come to a set meeting with a clearly defined, well thought out, logical problem. The group may thus easily be seduced into accepting this, and be tempted then to launch into possible solutions. In fact, even the most confident presenters are sometimes unaware of what the real issue is that they're tackling; what they are looking at may be either symptoms, or second-stage problems which simply disappear once the real problem has been identified and worked on. As one participant said: 'In action learning, we don't seek solutions but rather the real issues. If we solve symptoms, we merely bury the problem.'

The managing director of a small software company on a programme linked to a distance learning MBA came to a set meeting wanting to discuss some issues from a workbook on personal development.

He began by focusing in on a particular exercise, and the set gleefully followed him into it and began offering advice on how to do it, and what else to read. But this didn't seem to resolve the MD's queries. So he persisted, and eventually, by asking questions rather than offering solutions, the set managed to draw out of him that what lay beneath his questions was a more fundamental one: whether he was the right person to continue running his company. He had created it, built it up, and it was now running well, yet he felt that he was the wrong person to be at the helm. He wanted more excitement, uncertainty and risk. In fact, what he probably liked doing most of all was setting up new ventures.

The initially presented issue was therefore not the one that needed exploring. At the end of that meeting, he told the set: 'Your advice at the beginning was useless, your anecdotes were boring, but your questions really helped me.'

FINDING A FORMULA TO SHARE EXPERIENCES AND IDEAS

Participants come to a programme with a mass of useful insights and experiences. This is one of the strengths of such programmes. Set members also feel they want to 'help': 'I felt so useless not being able to give X help and solutions,' is something participants often say at the beginning of action learning programmes.

Most people would admit that supplying a solution makes them feel good. And in many instances – particularly if the presenter has genuinely run out of ideas after trying everything he or she can think of – it is helpful to be offered fresh ideas. On the other hand, it may be that the reason there are no solutions in sight is that the wrong issue is being pursued.

In our efforts to help, we often leap in with solutions to problems and issues we as yet do not fully understand. It's as though solutions are more important than finding out the root of the problem.

It is also quite common for sets to be seduced by a presenter's request for solutions, often at the beginning of a session, and well before the whole issue has been presented. The tell-tale request often comes in the form: 'I'd like the set to give me their ideas on how to ...'. One way of countering this is to toss the question back and ask the presenter what he or she has already done or thought of, and building on the responses.

Reformulating suggestions into 'Have you thought of ...?' can be a useful way of triggering off thoughts in a presenter's mind. However, set members need to avoid the temptation of following up this good, straightforward question with embellishments such as: 'For instance, if you were to ...'.

Alternatively, a set member may say to the problem-presenter that he or she has had an experience or done something which may be helpful, and ask whether it would be useful to describe it. Again, this formula gives the presenter the opportunity to accept or refuse (preferring to use some other process), and thereby take responsibility for the next stage. The presenter also has the option of stopping the story being told if they don't consider it to be helpful. On the other hand, it may trigger some good new ideas.

Another option is for the presenter to ask the set to brainstorm for a few minutes while he or she listens, before returning to the format of airspace.

WHAT'S SO VALUABLE ABOUT QUESTIONS?

The major difference between asking questions in action learning, and asking them in most other settings is that in action learning, questions aren't seeking answers. Rather, they are seeking to help someone go deeper, understand, respond to what is being asked, give it thought. They are not a quest for solutions; they are an opportunity to explore. To use a metaphor: asking questions is rather like peeling back the layers of an onion skin.

'The value of being asked questions is that they made me think,' is a comment frequently made by set members.

It is often helpful if set members preface their questions with the reason for, or intention behind it, such as: 'I haven't quite followed what you meant by ... Do you ...?' or 'I feel there may be other avenues to follow. Have you ...?' 'You seem to be ... What about ...?' The questions are often ones the presenter hasn't thought of, or maybe doesn't want to ask him/herself – maybe ones they are afraid of asking.

As the presenter hears themself respond to questions, they may hear inconsistencies; alternatively, as they begin to talk out loud, they often find that they begin to develop insights, ideas or explanations that didn't occur to them while simply thinking silently to themselves. The very act of talking out loud is creative.

Moreover, it is not only the presenter who is helped by the questions. As set members ask questions – and see them being considered seriously – it also gives them confidence in their ability to listen, understand, and ask effective and relevant questions. This can result in them beginning to behave differently at work: for instance, asking questions in meetings, or asking their boss questions they have previously been nervous of asking.

When a question of theirs helps someone else, it can make them think: 'That was a good question, I ought to ask myself that question, too.' And hearing others' questions is instructive. 'I'd never have thought of asking that question,' is a comment set members often make.

Questions uncover what we don't know. Only then do we know what we need to pursue further in order to know. As one hospital manager said: 'Identifying what you don't know is a first step to beginning to learn.' This echoes Revans, who has said on so many occasions: 'We only begin to learn when we become aware of what we don't know.'

But in some organizational cultures, questions are not encouraged. One set voiced their concern at this – for the culture in their organization was one of 'Don't ask, just do as I tell you.' On the other hand, some of these beliefs may be based on fear of what might happen when you do ask questions – as one participant recounted: 'I've learnt to question my managers, and they don't, as I'd assumed, bite your head off. In fact, they treat me with more respect.'

This questioning device has its origins – for the Western world – in Socratic dialogue. But unlike this older form, action learning questioning is softened because it takes place within a set which has ground rules which exclude judgement, which preclude questioners vying to show how clever they are and how much they know, and which stress being supportive while also being challenging: 'I enjoy the intellectual stimulation that this work gives me,' was one comment.

Thus the intention is to help, indeed *make* the other person think. The intention is not to arrive at a truth or to develop an intellectual debate, regardless of how stimulating that might be. That can take place in the bar after the meeting!

CHOOSING HELPFUL QUESTIONS

Helpful questions are those that open up doors in the mind. They are designed to get the presenter to think more deeply, to test their beliefs and assumptions, to really explain what they mean, to explore why they do certain things, avoid others, and so on.

Open questions are more helpful than closed ones. Questions that encourage the presenter to consider the 'hows' and 'whys' were particularly commented on by several sets. They were, they said, in many ways more powerful – and action-oriented – than the 'what' questions, and were often ones that they hadn't thought through.

There is, of course, a time when each of these questions is helpful. Questioners need to be aware that 'why' questions in particular can sometimes put people on the spot, depending on the tone of voice in which they ask! If their tone expresses horror, it could make the presenter unnecessarily uncomfortable. On the other hand, such 'why' questions could be helpful challenging questions. But it may be that instead of asking 'Why did you do X?', it might be more helpful to ask: 'What did you hope to achieve by doing X?' or 'What prompted X?' or 'How did you think X would help ...?'

Other examples of helpful questions include:

- **questions that begin with 'how', 'what' and 'why'**
- **precision questions:**
  - 'What exactly ...?'
  - 'How exactly ...?'
  - 'Bigger than/more than ...?'
  - 'Everyone?'
  - 'Always?'
- **powerful questions** (when a presenter says 'I can't.'):
  - 'What's stopping you ...?'
  - 'What would happen if you ...?'
- **reflective questions** (mirror back what presenter seems to be saying):
  - 'So you're saying ...?'
  - 'You seem ...?'
  - 'What's at the back of your mind?'
- **'idea' questions** (without spelling out the details!):
  - 'Would ... be of any use?'
  - 'Have you thought of ...?'
- **project-focused questions:**
  - 'What problems does that cause?'
  - 'In what way is that a problem?'
  - 'What isn't happening now?'
  - 'What do you want to be different?'
  - 'How would you like X to respond?'
  - 'How do think that Y needs to be changed/altered?'
  - 'What would you like to do – ideally?'
  - 'How do you feel about that?'
  - 'Who have you consulted/talked to?'
  - 'Who else might you talk to?'
  - 'How does the other person/department see the issue?'
  - 'How will you go about it?'
  - 'In what way will that help?'
  - 'Who else can you involve/get to back you?'
- **feelings-focused questions:**
  - 'How are you feeling about this?'
  - 'Do you feel confident?'
  - 'What worries you most?'
  - 'What excites you most?'
  - 'Are you being honest with yourself?'
- **questions about the set's processes:**
  - 'What else would you find helpful?'

- 'How can we help you?'
- 'Are we getting away from your question?'
- 'Are we being helpful?'
- 'What are we doing here, now?'
- 'What are we doing at the moment?'
- 'Why haven't we tackled ...?'
- 'What have we learnt?'

It can also be useful to use statements expressing feelings, such as: 'I feel uncomfortable/confused/angry/helpless.'

CAN'T YOU REFLECT AND LEARN ON YOUR OWN? WHY DO YOU HAVE TO DO IT IN THE SET MEETINGS?

Yes, you can reflect on your own. The advantage of doing it with the set is that we are forced to do so, and can't escape by claiming we have no time, or feel it might be more comfortable next time, or maybe it wouldn't be all that useful anyway ...

We can reflect on our own, but the value of doing it with others is that none of us has a monopoly on good or helpful questions, insights and perspectives. Working with others increases the scope of our reflection and learning.

Participants recognize that ultimately they must learn to reflect without the help of the set, but this is not to deny the benefit of coming back to the set for an injection of others' insights and perspectives.

Undertaking this reflection and learning on one's own also means we do so silently – yet many participants said that having to express things out loud caused them to say things that had not occurred to them before.

In the process of carrying out the research for this book, and writing it, I found that although I did not meet with a set, I 'talked to' my word-processor! The very act of writing down a stream of consciousness often resulted in ideas and insights emerging that I had not had while thinking about what I was going to write.

Thus, writing – the equivalent of speaking – had the same effect of bringing into the open new ideas and insights, and an element of creativity.

Perhaps it has something to do with emptying the brain of one mass of data, to enable it to create more? Maybe the producing of words – on screen or out loud – is akin to an artist or musician learning by trial and error, by creating something that is then modified, added to, and so on.

WHY IS IT SO IMPORTANT FOR SET MEMBERS TO REPORT WHAT THEY HAVE DONE, OR WHAT HAS HAPPENED SINCE THE LAST SET MEETING?

Reporting back creates a rigour. It means that everyone is expected to achieve something between meetings, and the expectations of others are a strong goad. But the rhythm of having to do it is also important. It creates momentum.

Reporting back is also a way of looking at the evidence of what you've done and learnt. And it's a means of seeing – and getting others to give you feedback on – how you're developing and changing, what you're doing differently, and what you still haven't mastered. It's a form of benchmarking.

'It makes you think – and act' and 'It makes you reflect on what you've done, what you've achieved, what you're going to do next. It keeps up a momentum,' were just two comments from participants on the usefulness of reporting back.

Several participants remarked on: 'the discipline of that hour, and needing to do my homework – either some action, or plan, and report on what I'd done. The expectation of others focuses the mind!'

To another set, it was the reporting back, and hence the creation of a thread in the story, that was critical: 'Without it, you're just another talking group.' One manager said that for him, the reporting back was the key to action learning: it's what made the difference between action learning and any other form of talking, sharing or discussing.

HOW DO THE PROCESSES HELP PEOPLE TO FEEL EMPOWERED?

The set, and its processes, illustrate behaviours which are capable of creating an environment where individuals – if they wish – can empower themselves:

- Airspace gives people a chance to talk and be listened to, and build up their confidence to speak up elsewhere.
- The discipline of listening to others shows respect for their views.
- Asking effective and helpful questions, as well as realizing the value of asking *simple* questions, gives people the confidence to speak up and ask questions elsewhere.
- The focus on learning stresses the importance of admitting to both successes and mistakes, using both as points for personal growth, and a sense of achievement.

Likewise, the values which underpin action learning – respect for others, valuing differences, being honest – are the same ones that are fundamental to giving people a sense of their own worth. Thus the democratic processes of action learning enable people to feel empowered. If all of these are transferred back into work, it creates a climate where people become empowered.

ARE THERE ANY TAUGHT ELEMENTS?

Some programmes have taught inputs (known in action learning as P – Programmed Knowledge); others don't. The taught inputs may be either directly related to the programme and the learning that participants are hoping to gain, or they may be mini-inputs – often at the request of participants – which focus on issues they want to know more about, and enable them to gain the most from action learning.

'We had short inputs on transactional analysis,[1] information-gathering and the Kolb Learning Cycle, which were very helpful,' said one group of young graduates for whom action learning was part of their 'induction' programme. Other sets mentioned mind maps,[2] SWOT,[3] and force-field analysis,[4] and one set, where participants were taking part in a company leadership programme, requested a short input on negotiating skills.

Some programmes – depending on their objectives – also incorporate other taught elements related to team-working (including outdoor programmes) or communication, or more functional inputs relating to business strategy, marketing and finance. There are also subjects which lend themselves ideally to having action learning incorporated with them, such as project management.

Several participants who had attended a previous week-long management development programme said they couldn't imagine attending an action learning programme 'cold', without that previous input.

A number of programmes are built on previous courses, and are considered to be a consolidation of them: a chance to try out, to see which of the taught elements is useful and applicable, where and when, and offering a unique opportunity to share experiences and insights, and ask further questions.

Increasingly, action learning is becoming incorporated into management courses offered at universities and in distance learning programmes. Participants gain knowledge from lectures or workbooks (in the latter instance) and meet for action learning days, where the emphasis is on applying the learning to real-life instances/projects. Sets work like any other non-academic sets. (For a list of management courses using action learning as an integral part of their programmes see page 26.)

THE VALUE OF EXPERIENCING THE PROCESSES

From initially assuming the set will simply be dedicated to helping each other learn, participants begin to value the processes themselves as some of the most important elements of action learning – and a high point in their own learning:

> Using action learning processes has been dramatic. I am beginning to change my whole approach to interactions – even at home! I have recognized why in the past I have found others so frustrating ... When I've wanted to discuss a problem, they give me their solutions!

Working in the set gave participants a taste of what it might be like to work in such productive groups back at work. They also welcomed the opportunity to study the group and its processes – all part of the emphasis on learning: 'I've learnt several transferable skills by working in the set: how to listen and focus on questions, how to facilitate and act as a mentor, and how to present – you find you're presenting to the set in a mini way all the time.'

LISTENING IS VITAL

Learning to listen had a number of beneficial side-effects. Pragmatists realized: 'You learn from others' mistakes' and 'It's by listening to others that I began to ask myself questions about what I was doing and thinking.' 'I've learnt to listen to others, and through that listening to challenge and ask myself why I don't think of doing so-and-so, or why I hadn't considered questions they were considering.' And because, as one manager put it: 'Experiences – like dreams – need interpreting', one person's reflections or insights expressed out aloud gave others – if they listened – food for thought.

Action learning's emphasis on listening also has other interesting knock-on effects: 'I've realized we're not all singing from the same hymn sheet – it's useful for a manager to know that!' said a young woman. And many commented on the experience of being listened to – and how that improved not only communication, but also confidence: 'Being listened to builds up your self-esteem and confidence.'

However, as several pointed out, listening is not an easy task – although we assume it is: 'Listening is a task that requires a lot of practice. Complete listening is about comprehension, not just recall ... and comprehension is also about empathy, and being non-judgemental ... and trying to understand, and burying your biases ...'.

A number mentioned how productive it was to have an opportunity to challenge, and not be met with resistance, anger or defensiveness.

Several managers were planning to transfer some of the set's ways of working back to their work environment. Two or three were planning to turn their staff 'teams' into sets. 'After all,' said one of them, 'each of my staff is an expert in her own field. I can hardly play the autocratic manager with them!'

'You realize that by changing behaviour you can change a culture,' pondered another manager. 'The processes have given me a template of how people can work together effectively. You sense the atmosphere when a group is working well – and I don't mean agreeing with one another. They're listening to each other, and you know because you see how what they say relates to what the previous person said. Silences are OK, and the body language tells you a lot. And, importantly, disagreements are approached constructively.'

Many felt they were now more effective at other meetings in their workplace, and one even commented: 'I feel it's legitimate to comment on the processes in meetings – and not simply address comments to the chair on the agenda!'

One woman commented: 'The ground rules we have in the set have made me realize that we assume we have common ground rules back at work, when we don't.'

SHARING WITH OTHERS

Invariably, set members were amazed that it was possible to learn so much by focusing on others' stories: 'You learn from others. You hear and see what they do, and you see yourself often doing the same thing! So you begin to resolve both your own and others' issues simultaneously.'

Many made the jump from realizing how much they had gained personally – by being given the time and space to talk and by hearing others do the same – to the relevance of applying such a process back at work: 'After all, those doing the jobs know most about them. We ignore them and their ideas at our peril.'

For others, the ability to share was emotionally very releasing: 'You begin to understand why you react in certain ways, and it helps to control (not sublimate) those feelings and express them in an appropriate way.' It was observing her questions being listened – and responded – to that marked a major step in improving the self-esteem of one young woman: 'Much more beneficial than an assertiveness course,' she laughed.

HONESTY IN COMMUNICATING

There are five levels of communicating:

- **Level 5** – ritual and cliché: surface communicating only, giving nothing of oneself
- **Level 4** – reporting facts: sharing information, communicating at a superficial level
- **Level 3** – ideas and judgement: taking risks, revealing bits of oneself
- **Level 2** – feelings and emotions: building on Level 3, giving more of your real self, understanding and living with differences
- **Level 1** – peak, 'open' communication: harmony with others, empathy with them, though not necessarily agreeing with them.

Most participants in action learning find that they move from Level 5 to Levels 2 and 1, because the trust and confidence developed in the set create circumstances where it's OK – and beneficial – to be at Level 2 or 1.

One woman was strikingly honest about what she learnt from just one episode in her set:

> I'm very self-confident and also competitive. I'm also a high contributor: I suppose, in a way, because I feel responsibility for a group I'm working in. So I gave my 'all' to the set. But I'm also quite perceptive about processes – so I was able to tell the set that I usually

do babble and talk. One day, I joked that the set gave me the 'licence' to talk. At the next meeting, the joke back-fired on me, when someone commented 'jokingly' about how much I talked ... and they laughed – but more at me than with me. I sat and said nothing for the whole afternoon, part self-pity, part tantrum. Nor did anyone say anything to me. I didn't help the person with 'airspace', and wrote, after that meeting, in my diary: 'Am I being over-precious? Have I joked at others? Do I talk too much?'

At the next meeting, one of the people who'd laughed commented that she felt she'd contributed to the meeting last time because I'd given her the space to do so.

So my question to myself then was: 'Is silence the most I have to offer?' I felt odd for a while, and then realized that I could sit silently, and that would be OK. I just made one or two quiet points to the person whose airspace it was, and some time later he told me that my comments had changed the way he tackled his project – i.e. it was my quiet, reflective insights that had been more helpful than my talkative self.

What I also learnt was that by being too polished in telling them about how my project was going, I was leaving nothing for them to explore with me, which left them feeling inadequate. I decided for the next meeting I would be casual, and I purposefully experimented with being less prepared than I was comfortable with. I apologized for not being prepared, and I felt really uncomfortable and inadequate. But the set told me later that they felt more able to help me, and in fact we all felt that we had jointly worked very well together to help me reach some decisions. And they felt the working together was brilliant, and they gained from it.

What I learnt was that if I appeared too competent, I inhibited others – and that could apply at work, and not only in a set. And it was quite painful learning for me, for I was contemplating – inside myself – issues of pride, arrogance and a questioning of my motives.

IT'S OK NOT TO KNOW

Mastering the technique of asking questions in itself brought unexpected insights. Almost every participant I spoke to said something along the lines of: 'It's extraordinary how what you think is the problem often isn't – the questioning reveals the real one!'

Whereas in the past they might have been afraid to ask certain types of questions, participants found that action learning changed their perceptions: 'Ignorance is OK. I'm allowed to not know things. We're often so afraid of asking questions in case people think us stupid.' This new-found freedom to say 'I don't know' without feeling stupid or guilty gave many participants the courage to be honest back at work, too. 'Why pretend?' some of them said. 'Asking questions isn't a sign of stupidity.' Instead, questioning was seen as a constructive action when they didn't know or understand something: 'Asking questions simply means I'm seeking explanations or more information.'

LEARNING TO TACKLE 'DIFFICULT' PEOPLE AND SITUATIONS

Although not everyone had encountered difficult set members, those who did tackle them felt they had really made significant progress, and gained in self-confidence. The reason there were few opportunities for this was probably due to the self-selec-

tion that most programmes operate (in fact, one of the criticisms that some participants levelled at their programmes was that they did not help them to work with the
politics of an organization, including certain categories of difficult people).

One set I spoke to did have the opportunity – and learnt from it. But the person
who probably learnt most was the young man in question. Very bright and aggressive in manner, he kept his set in thrall for just one set meeting. He interrupted,
talked most and loudest, always had a comment or observation, and turned every
discussion around either to what he was doing or what he thought. The set adviser
decided at the first meeting not to interfere with what was happening, waiting to see
if the set would respond.

During the second meeting, one young woman took the initiative. She told him
she found it impossible to work with him in the group, and itemized what she found
disruptive in his behaviour. One other woman added her comments, too. The man
thus confronted began to explain and justify his behaviour, but failed to modify it to
any great degree. However, at the next meeting there was a sufficient change in his
behaviour for the set to be able to work well and constructively on everyone's project. However, his airspace continued to be taken up with how bright he was, followed by disparaging remarks about all around him at work.

At the fourth meeting, he was unusually silent, which others remarked on. He
responded by saying he had thought about the previous meeting, felt he had learnt
a lot by working with the set, and would like to share this with them at the following meeting. At the fifth meeting, he told the set how he felt he had changed, and
that he was now a much happier person. He felt his behaviour sprang from a sense
of insecurity, and – for all his noise – from lack of confidence. He was aware of how
his behaviour caused problems and was disruptive – both at work and at home. He'd
done a lot of thinking, had talked to his manager, and was moving to a new job which
they both felt he would be more suited to – dealing more with ideas and concepts,
and less with the practical, day-to-day issues which brought him face-to-face with
people all the time.

STOPPING TO THINK AND REFLECT, AND BECOMING MORE AWARE

Many managers are action-oriented; indeed, most roles emphasize action to the point
that stopping to think and reflect is seen in some quarters as not working. Many participants commented on this, particularly after they had experienced this 'time for
thinking and reflecting' that the set offers: 'I've learnt that action isn't the only way of
learning. You can learn when there is little action,' laughed one active manager. Another
said: 'At work, we're achievers of activity. Here, you can legitimately look at the reverse
of this: the thinking that is needed for any activity to be ultimately effective.'

The questioning approach was a first step for many in the direction of reflecting.
Questions often raised issues they hadn't considered. Or feedback from set mem-

bers prompted a looking inwards: 'The set gets you to try and look objectively at what you're doing or thinking ... and you often find that you are part of the problem you have described ... we're all so good at blaming others.'

Becoming more aware – aware of everything – was something most participants alluded to: awareness of people's behaviour and beginning to understand what it meant; sensitivity to what people were really saying; awareness of undercurrents; awareness of their own impact on others, and vice versa; listening, and not just hearing; acknowledging the existence and validity of feelings, and an awareness that openness and honesty produced results where closed-mindedness and game-playing were ultimately destructive. Many struggled to put these insights into coherent sentences and phrases: 'I'm just more aware – conscious – of what goes on around me,' said one man. Others talked of acknowledging feelings, being honest, being conscious of having insights, picking up people's discomforts.

This awareness also related to learning: 'I've learnt that there is learning to be done and that it's dynamic. Back at work, when staff say, "I'm learning," I now automatically ask: "What are you learning?" ' Another participant had realized: 'Everything is data from which I can learn.' Others remarked how it was now second nature to them to stop and reflect on what they were learning – going around a learning cycle in their minds.

TRANSFERRING THE 'NEW ME' BACK TO WORK

Transferring their new-found sense of being empowered back at work on a daily basis often proved difficult for participants – 'It can be all too easy to fall back into old habits', 'I can't do X; my manager won't let me', 'I haven't got the time' – even occasionally falling back into muttering: 'That's not the way we do things around here.'

One young woman was quite open and honest:

> One of the men in our set was very domineering. I felt able – after some time – to tell him that I didn't like what he was doing and that it was difficult to work with him. At the time I felt I had been rude to him – simply pointing this out! But he acknowledged what I said. So I felt pleased that I'd plucked up the courage to tell him because in fact it changed the way we worked in the set from then on, and we became much more conscious of processes. But I still find it difficult to say something like that back in the 'real' world. But at least I've begun to sometimes say what I feel about a person's behaviour. I've begun to separate out process from 'content'.

Another manager talked of 'the problems of transferring some of the me in the set to the me back at work. It'll take time. I've established a personal style over the past twenty years, and it's difficult to change that. What'll others say, how will they react? They still see the old me and expect me to do certain things in certain ways ...'.

'Maybe we need reminding,' said several participants, 'Maybe we need regular injections of being in a set ...'.

THREE CASE EXAMPLES

OPPORTUNITIES IN LOCAL GOVERNMENT

A major city authority

Picture a large, hierarchical, command-oriented, tradition-bound and paternal-istic local authority, in a rapidly changing world. Introducing action learning as a means of helping people cope with major changes in technology and legis-lation was a difficult and slow process. The training manager (new to the authority) adopted a process of influencing senior managers, working with a group of them who expressed interest in management development, and ensuring that most training programmes run had an element of action learning squeezed in somewhere. From these brief experiences came several requests, notably from engineers and environmental health officers, stated as wanting to have more 'practical' programmes: 'We don't want to be lectured at.'

New legislation had placed an onus on the environmental health officers to ensure that caterers of all description (from local cafes to exclusive hotels) understood and implemented the new regulations. Their task was to create an effective change in behaviour that would last, rather than simply the communi-cation of a bunch of facts.

Their five-day programmes, run on three full days and four half-days, over four months, began with a one-day workshop on learning styles and commu-nication skills. Thereafter, each participant worked on an individual 'project', focusing on how he or she would help their customers understand and imple-ment the new laws – what events they would plan and run. Set meetings, with a set adviser, consisted of feedback to the group on each 'plan'.

Local government managers in a deprived inner city

The local authority in one of Britain's poorest inner cities designed a pro-gramme for both top and middle managers in the authority, to alter the way they delivered their services, becoming more customer-focused, and chang-ing dramatically how they worked, even exploring whether what they were doing was what was needed by the community: 'We turned over every stone.' They wanted to explore where people's energy, excitement and enthusiasm lay, and harness that to the work of the authority.

The programme for the fifty middle managers – with the aim of breaking them out of their old-style, bureaucratic way of thinking and working – was designed to transform them into facilitators and change agents: 'Incremental change was not enough. We needed a blitz.' The three strands of the pro-gramme included 'taught' modules on project management, how to persuade people, working with teams, and so on. The second strand was to work on a service improvement project – which they would implement; and the third was action learning sets, with four participants – all from different sectors – meeting for four hours, with a facilitator, to explore both their projects and ongoing work issues.

At the time of writing, a third of the projects have been implemented, another third are almost ready to go, and the last ones are still being worked on. Participants have, it is reported, changed their everyday style of working, have broken down hierarchies, and have grown in confidence.

A PERSONAL DEVELOPMENT PROGRAMME

This programme had the explicit aim of being 'developmental'. It started out with the belief that 'action learning is about developing a sense of authority and identity in an organization ... breaking free from defensive routines'. Participants in the sets were told that they would be encouraged to work on their 'anxieties and stresses'.

In spite of its developmental character, this programme was explicit about focusing on real business issues, building in opportunities to develop insights into how the organization worked. This programme, like many others, was integrated with two short workshop modules.

NOTES

[1] A way of showing how our ways of addressing and treating people affects their responses, and vice versa.

[2] A diagrammatic way of creating a 'list', or developing an idea, which also allows you to draw connections between items.

[3] Listing Strengths, Weaknesses, Opportunities and Threats in any given situation/project.

[4] Listing, in two columns, the forces in favour of, or supporting an idea, decision or plan of action, and those forces opposed to it.

6 The set adviser

The set adviser – the facilitator to a set, who helps the participants with their learning – was not a role envisaged by Reg Revans. Nevertheless, it is an important role, but one that differs in many respects from the roles of a tutor or counsellor. For the set adviser is not a tutor, a lecturer, a chairperson, a group leader or an assessor/evaluator of the set members.

It is crucial the role of set adviser is played competently and professionally. For most programmes and participants, the set adviser provides the key to awareness of the learning. A good set adviser will make sure that participants stop, reflect and consider their learning. A less competent one will merely focus on actions.

The task of the set adviser, together with set members as they gain more confidence, is to keep a balance between the project and the learning, but also to remind members to keep a balance between action and self-development at work – not to lose their awareness of the learning possibilities when caught up in daily affairs.

Finally, the set adviser is responsible for creating an environment conducive to learning – comfortable surroundings, coffee and tea breaks laid on – in which participants are unencumbered by other problems such as telephone interruptions, or being called out to other meetings.

WHAT IS THE TASK OF THE SET ADVISER?

The main task of a set adviser is to encourage the set – and each individual within it – to look, listen, question, think, understand and learn. In this sense, the set adviser is part of the set.

The set adviser works with the set to help each participant focus on what he/she is achieving, or finding difficult, gaining and learning from the programme, and – importantly – now doing differently.

135

As far as the whole set is concerned, the set adviser helps it to focus on the processes it is employing as it works, and on the learning from them – identifying which processes are helpful and which are not, and the implications of this.

A set adviser will keep a finger on the pulse of what is happening, and will intervene when he or she feels that there is an issue – someone's learning, or the set's processes – that is worth focusing on and analysing. For instance, if one member is talking so much that no one else can get a word in edgeways, a set adviser may comment skilfully on this (if no one within the set has yet done so).

A set adviser's tasks are thus:

- to help set members focus on appropriate projects or tasks that they bring, and to work on them with the help and encouragement of other set members
- to make set members consciously aware of everything they do, say, think and feel
- to draw attention to the continuous learning opportunities that exist both within and outside the set
- to maintain the very specific processes in the set, which enable all this work and learning to take place
- to model effective behaviour and language which results in constructive working and learning in the set, and to help set members understand and adopt both.

A good set adviser will also encourage participants to become aware of their learning on a number of scores:

- gaining new knowledge and information
- reasoning differently
- behaving differently
- becoming more aware
- gaining greater understanding of themselves and their motives
- altering beliefs and values
- questioning assumptions
- acknowledging feelings and their impact.

HOW DOES A SET ADVISER WORK?

He or she uses a variety of means to remind members of the importance of learning:

- Participants may be asked to reflect on what they are learning as they recount their stories.
- Following each member's presentation, the set adviser may ask both the presenter and the set to reflect on the interaction and what they each noticed and learnt.

- At the end of each meeting, the set may be invited to reflect on what they have learnt, and share it with the others. A similar approach is often helpful at the beginning of meetings, to help members focus on what they have learnt while away from the set.

As one participant said: 'The learning outside the set is often due to reflection points brought up in the set.' Another said: 'I live on what I'm learning in the set.'

Some useful set adviser questions and comments include:

- 'Are we being helpful?'
- 'Can we stop for a moment and check on how we are doing?'
- 'How do you feel about what is going here?'
- 'Could you turn that comment into a question?'
- 'Should we check on the ground rules?'
- 'Did you hear what Y said to you?'
- 'I am hearing ...?'
- 'I am not hearing ...?'
- 'How can we make this set more effective?'
- 'What does that mean?'
- 'Can I suggest you use the first-person "I", rather than "you" or "one"?'
- 'You've told us about your problems; how about your successes?'
- 'The set seems stuck; shall we stop and talk about what seems difficult?'

Some set advisers help members focus on learning by asking them, say after three meetings, to think about what they are doing differently back at work, and what difference that is making. Asking them to tell others forces everyone to be explicit. As one participant put it: 'Working within the set forces you to exercise your brain.'

The set adviser will also acknowledge and legitimize the fact that there are emotions bubbling around. Some participants may feel that it is inappropriate to voice emotions. By voicing his or her own first – modelling – the set adviser begins to free them of inhibitions, though of course this won't necessarily release them from the fear of what might happen if they do express an emotion.

Furthermore, as the 'outsider', the set adviser can also ask the simple, 'idiot' questions that set members may not think – or want – to ask. These often test beliefs and assumptions, or feelings.

CAN ANYONE BE A SET ADVISER?

In principle, yes, if they feel drawn to the role. But it does take certain skills and qualities, and most set advisers have either been set members, or are experienced facilitators. If managers are used as set advisers, it is important that they have some training.

One set I interviewed was facilitated by a manager who had spent half a day learning about being a set adviser, and the set were not impressed with his performance!

A set adviser's qualities should include:

- the ability to be non-judgemental, and accepting and allowing others to be themselves
- a genuine belief in the potential of everyone, respecting them and trying to understand them
- a commitment to helping people learn and develop, and offering them the 'power' to do so and take responsibility for themselves
- patience – the ability to allow people to do and learn things in their own time and at their own speed
- an enquiring, inquisitive mind that seeks to understand
- personal, intellectual and emotional integrity, openness and honesty.

The set adviser's skills include:

- using any occurrence in the set – a problem presented, a statement made or behaviour exhibited – as an opportunity for learning
- balancing being involved with the set with keeping an eye on what is happening in the set
- expressing appropriately his/her feelings or thoughts
- listening, and hearing what is being said and how, and noticing what is not said or expressed
- understanding group processes and the roles being played, and noticing norms, beliefs, fantasies or taboos created by the group
- working sympathetically and with understanding with set members who are reluctant to participate or unhappy with the processes
- knowing which facilitative style to use at any one time in the life of the set, and with whom (see page 59)
- choosing when to express feelings or act on intuition, rather than relying solely on analysis and logic.

'It took me a while to realize the set adviser was not going to teach us anything,' commented one participant, echoing what many others said. This inevitably causes frustration, at times anger, in some participants. For others, it is liberating!

The role of the set adviser is to judge – perhaps 'sense' is a better word – how best to help participants to learn. For instance, will they learn best when pushed or cradled? Will harsh confrontation bring more results, or is a gentler, more supportive approach more likely to encourage development and change? Each individual reacts to different goads: a set adviser has to make sensitive assessments.

It is elements such as this that set members will also become aware of. Such an assessment is indispensable to anyone who is a manager, for it relates directly to the question of how to motivate staff. This is just another example of how working in an action learning set has obvious benefits for relationships back at work.

The set adviser will also take decisions on whether and when to intervene if he/she feels that emotions, values, beliefs and other fundamental issues are being glossed over. Often, a good adviser will act almost intuitively, picking up vital clues, listening intently, or becoming aware of body language. A set adviser's unease may very well be shared by set members, who do not want, or do not know how, to confront it. David Casey examines the role of the set adviser in two useful articles: 'The role of the set adviser' (Casey 1997a) and 'The shell of your understanding' (Casey 1997b).

SOME GUIDELINES

It takes time and requires some form of training to develop the skills of an effective set adviser. Some people take to the role naturally; others find it more difficult. The role has close affinities with that of a mentor, and also has many parallels with the role of a good manager who enables and empowers his or her staff, gives them responsibility, and develops them – indeed, observing the set adviser caused a number of managers to rethink their roles as managers (see page 145–146).

Here are some guidelines for set advisers:

- Ensure that as set members work on their projects they tell their own personal 'story', rather than recount only the general 'history' of the situation they are working on (see pages 98–99).
- Be aware of/reflect back/ask questions about the presenter's thoughts and feelings, as well as their actions.
- Be aware of your own thoughts and feelings, and feed them back to the presenter or set.
- Suspend your judgement, put aside your reactions and try to get inside a speaker's frame of mind and context.
- Pick up generalizations, and ask for specific evidence.
- Point out untested assumptions and beliefs.
- Check out beliefs versus truths.
- When appropriate, comment on the processes you are observing – and those that are missing.
- Make members aware of the value of distinguishing between content and process.
- Remind members of their responsibility to manage their airspace and time.
- Maybe suggest different ways of exploring – by 'drawing' on a flipchart, creating a mind map, or by brainstorming (briefly).
- Be a constant reminder of the learning opportunities both within and outside the set.
- Do not feel you have to constantly participate actively. Silence is fine!

It is quite normal for set advisers to experience doubts and quandaries. Some of these might include:

- 'Did I intervene enough?'
- 'Did I time my interventions well?'
- 'Did I say too much, and not allow members to learn from one another?'
- 'How come I missed ...?'
- 'I don't think we worked sufficiently on ...'
- 'Did we spend enough time reflecting and gaining insights?'
- 'Was I too hard on X?'
- 'Did I push Y sufficiently?'
- 'Are my biases evident?'
- 'Do I treat set members differently – and why?'
- 'Did I stick to asking questions, or fall into the trap of offering solutions?'

Set advisers themselves often join sets of set advisers to work on their own issues and tackle these misgivings.

DO YOU NEED TO HAVE A SET ADVISER?

Most people who have participated in action learning programmes find the presence of a set adviser helpful, for some of the reasons outlined above. 'You definitely need one in the early stages,' was the general consensus, 'to help, to guide, to remind you of the processes. But later, as the set learns how to work effectively, and to focus on the learning as well as their actions, a set adviser may be less necessary. Maybe you can invite them in for particular meetings.'

A set adviser is in a sense a non-involved, outside, objective voice, able to see what is happening, able to intervene when he or she deems it necessary, able to bring the set back on track if they begin to side-track from their own tasks and learning.

One set recalled: 'When we complained that we were stuck and weren't getting anything out of the set, the set adviser asked us to list how we felt about that, and what we thought was causing it. That opened us out, and we began to work better. On another occasion, when again we felt our learning had stopped, he got us to draw a graph to express how we saw our learning up to that point, and note down how we had been learning. That again released us and moved us on.'

Others talked of their set advisers 'keeping us on track, pulling us back when we went off at tangents, or became involved in wider discussions'.

'If the set adviser isn't good, or isn't present,' remarked those with that experience, 'the temptation is to concentrate on the tasks [the projects] and forget about watching our processes and our learning. That misses entirely the point of action learning.'

One set was of the opinion that it had worked well on the group project, and had learnt a great deal about the issue they were working on. However, they were less sure of their learning about the 'ostensible' purpose of the programme, team-working: 'You can operate without a set adviser, but I don't think we necessarily challenged each other enough when we were alone. Maybe we need that catalyst. We found ourselves falling into suggestion/advisory roles ... and anger was not expressed.'

SETS WORKING ALONE

The task of every good set adviser is to work themselves out of a job, as set members gain similar expertise. Frequently, set advisers will contract with a set that after three or four meetings they will review their role. Where a programme has been arranged to run for, say, six months, the set adviser will continue for this time. But if a programme is subsequently continued, the set may not need the set adviser any more, or may ask them to attend at intervals.

Sets I interviewed who had worked without set advisers were in two minds. One – a mature set consisting of experienced action learners – felt a set adviser was unnecessary. But two other sets who also worked without set advisers were both of the opinion that they would have gained – and learnt – more with one.

Many programmes which may have started out with an experienced set adviser continue with people who have experienced action learning as participants, and who feel drawn to the role of acting as set advisers. Because the role of set adviser is seen by many participants as an 'alternative' way of managing (see below), this has many added advantages. However, when deciding to use internal people, it is useful – and particularly helpful – for those new to the role to themselves be part of an action learning set of new set advisers, whose tasks/projects are to work on how they tackle this new role!

IS THE ADVISER A SPECIALIST OR EXPERT IN ANY PARTICULAR FIELD?

Yes, the best set advisers are skilled in observing and highlighting processes, including the process of learning. They observe how a group is working together, listen, see and sense what is happening, and then express this to the set – frequently in the form of a question! What they are thus doing is distinguishing clearly between tasks and processes.

One participant, whose set adviser turned out to be knowledgeable in the field of marketing, but less so in facilitating, said: 'I would have preferred a set adviser who understood more about processes ... I'd have learnt more. There was little distinction between him and a tutor.'

In demonstrating helpful processes, set advisers model particular behaviours that they judge to be useful and effective. Simultaneously, they are adopting the action learning practice of handing back to the set responsibility for what they are doing, and giving them the 'power' to do something about it. So, when asked direct questions by the set, a set adviser may decide that giving a direct answer isn't helpful. Instead, they may suggest that the set work on the question.

However, many participants admitted that initially there was confusion – even anger – over the role that the set adviser adopted. As one member commented: 'The set adviser didn't direct or tell us what to do, he sat there ... I found it all very disturbing. You're used to having tutors who point you in a direction ... and here was something different that I didn't understand ... until I realized what she was doing ... getting us to take responsibility and power, and learn by doing so.'

HOW MUCH DOES A SET ADVISER INTERVENE?

At the beginning of a programme, as set members become accustomed to working in this novel way, a set adviser may intervene quite a lot, to remind the set what their task is – to help each of their individual members learn – even when the programme is about team-working.

But as a set gains more experience and learns about the processes of action learning, and how to behave in a supportive, challenging yet non-judgemental way, the set adviser will probably intervene less.

The set adviser is also a *member* of the set, in the sense that he or she will participate – when appropriate (without taking over from the set!) – in the asking of questions. But at the same time, the set adviser tries to keep a watchful eye on what is happening.

Some sets had different experiences – not always, in their view, productive. One set which had two set advisers over the period of the programme compared them:

> One became quite involved with us. He knew a lot about our 'task' [a set project] and our work environment, and got us to ask questions we'd never thought of asking. He also checked how we felt we were doing as a team. But he tackled individual issues outside the set in private. The second adviser, by contrast, kept a distance – even sat outside the group – and commented only on processes.

Neither was entirely satisfactory, they felt.

In another set, participants were concerned that their adviser had become too involved with them – almost part of the set – and thus less helpful, because: 'He tended to agree too much with us' and 'He talked too much.'

One of the traps new set advisers sometimes fall into is not distinguishing sufficiently clearly between individual learning and group learning, and emphasizing the latter at the cost of the former. Both are important, but the idea of airspace for work means mainly focusing on the one person's learning. This may of course involve looking at how the set helped or hindered the process – a learning opportunity for the set or individuals within it.

WHAT DO YOU DO IF YOU HAVE A 'BAD' SET ADVISER?

The best response to this question is: 'Use it as a learning opportunity.' However, this would probably need courage and skill (and is something that sets working with a *good* set adviser would learn to do!).

Unfortunately, it can and does happen that set advisers are not helpful. This may be because they do not understand what action learning is about, or because they have had no training or experience in this form of facilitation, which is very different from being a tutor, or running a seminar.

To gain the full benefit of action learning, participants need – and deserve – to have a good set adviser. The programme organizer is responsible for choosing set advisers, and it is to that person that participants unhappy with their set adviser should turn.

But participants need to be clear about what exactly they are unhappy about. If they want the set adviser to hold their hand, and the latter refuses, this may not be grounds for changing a set adviser – especially since he or she may have the set's best interests at heart.

One participant recalled one set member who talked all the time, 'hogging the time': 'The set adviser did nothing. We weren't sure how to tackle this man – was it OK to tell him what he was doing? Eventually, two of us did. I'm pleased I took the risk – it helped us work better as a set, and I learnt that giving that sort of feedback isn't as terrifying as I'd thought.' She thus learnt a lesson she might not have had if the set adviser had taken up the issue first.

There are also, sadly, instances of unprofessional behaviour by set advisers – such as being judgemental, picking on individual members, and being abrasive and dismissive. One set talked of their set adviser doing nothing as: 'screaming matches took place in the set, he didn't intervene, he did nothing ... and we also felt powerless to react ... all very confusing'.

Yet another had experienced a set adviser who was: 'critical, condescending and aggressive. We didn't trust him at all. We lost one member because of him, and another withdrew and didn't attend regularly. He picked on us, and we became victims. It puts you off learning.' No one in this set tackled the set adviser, either. They did not feel able to do so, did not feel they had skills to do so. It never occurred to them that they could *do* something – or even that it was their responsibility (if only to themselves!) to do something about it: a situation remarkably similar to many that people find back at work, and feel similarly powerless to intervene in – a common case of actual or perceived powerlessness!

143

One set talked of a set adviser not observing the confidentiality ground rule, which limited the work done in that set.

Relationships with set advisers can be difficult territory to negotiate, and any unhappiness, complaints and queries should be raised first with the set adviser in question, and then with the programme organizer. This is a learning opportunity for the set and for the set adviser.

Above all, a set adviser should avoid:

- giving advice
- interrupting (unless there is a learning point to be made)
- pressing their point
- insisting they are right, or refusing to admit they made a mistake
- being defensive
- making fun of set members
- being critical or judgemental
- looking bored
- cracking too many jokes
- talking too much
- taking sides
- reporting to people outside the set what happens in set meetings.

THE VALUE OF WORKING WITH A SET ADVISER

MAKING US AWARE OF HELPFUL PROCESSES

> Our set adviser 'taught' me to listen and analyse, to question and encourage others to say more, to help them – and the others – understand ... She did this by modelling that approach.

> I found that her suggestion to ask 'how' and 'why' questions, rather than 'what' questions was most helpful. We don't focus enough on how we're going to carry out all the plans we keep talking about. It's made me realize that so many of our problems are concerned with how we work with others, and gain their commitment and support. The 'how' questions force you to consider this.

'I thought I asked questions and gave the other person the opportunity to answer, but the set adviser pointed out that in fact I tried to give advice hidden in pseudo-questions,' laughed one participant.

Another participant said the set adviser: 'steered the dialogue in the sense of seeing the positives of the differences between people, because differences make you look at your own and other people's assumptions'.

'The set adviser,' remarked another, 'would often pull us up if we began to blame others for what was happening. We'd be reminded that we also had a choice – to go along with something or not; to do something or not; to respond or keep quiet.'

A member of another set remembered: 'The set adviser pushed us but rarely gave us answers, just went on asking questions – to get us, of course, to reflect and find our own answers. Even of our own behaviour in the set – he'd ask, 'What's happening here now?', which throws you at first; then you learn to look at the processes: who's angry, who's dominating, who's listening, who's running away ... It makes you so much more aware of what happens back at work, in meetings or teams.'

Building on this, one young woman said she now felt freer to comment on what was happening in groups or meetings she went to – something she would certainly not have done before.

A GOOD SET ADVISER CAN MAKE YOU AWARE OF LEARNING, ANYWHERE, ANY TIME

One set described how their set adviser drip-fed the question all the time: 'So what have you learnt from that?' It became like an ever-present echo. Each of them now asked themselves that question almost subconsciously, no matter what they were doing or what was happening:

> I found one of the most useful questions she asked was the 'meta' questions: not simply 'What are you doing differently now?' but '... and what difference is that making?'. Asking that question makes you aware of how you impact on others, and how your changed behaviour will change others, too. I was on a leadership programme, and it made me aware of how to give people space to empower themselves. She quoted one phrase which has stayed with me since then: 'Leadership is about making other people powerful!'

Others said it was their set adviser who got them to 'plumb the depths', either by his or her comments or questions: 'Unpeeling the onion skins – persisting with questions that made me think – that was really helpful. The rest of us seemed to be happy with many superficial answers.'

Another member talked of his set adviser 'teaching' them to listen, analyse, question, encourage others to say more, help them understand, challenge statements and give support, through modelling those processes herself. Not all sets are so lucky.

A ROLE MODEL FOR 'MANAGING' AND CONSULTING

A number of participants also commented on the role of the set adviser as being one model for managers to follow: 'Coaching and mentoring is part of every manager's job. By learning to work as an effective set member, by using a good set adviser as a model, you're learning the processes you need for mentoring and coaching as a line manager,' was the realization of one participant.

Others went further, beyond coaching and mentoring to everyday managing:

> I used the set adviser and his way of 'managing' us, the set, as a model for managing. The format of the set with a set adviser has given me a new way of working. I see my role as being a 'set adviser' to my team, wanting them to achieve their potential, and not feeling

threatened by it ... I try and adopt the way our set adviser worked, using questions in a quiet way, and dropping in the occasional 'pearls of wisdom'.

Another participant had similar thoughts: 'Our set adviser kept us to our learning agendas ... he didn't teach, but he'd ask us what we'd learnt from various things we mentioned or talked about. I've tried it with my staff, and find I'm increasingly using the set adviser as a model.'

One participant, a consultant, made the connection that, for her: 'Facilitating – something we as set members learnt to do – is in fact the best form of consulting.'

Our set adviser could have so easily have taken over and directed us when we were floundering – or been judgemental ... or simply not known how to cope. Instead, he allowed us to empower ourselves.

The lesson in being empowered was not lost on some managers who, back at work, were following a similar model with their own staff, as well as colleagues: 'We're having to change our role at work, but with no clear-cut ideas of what that could be,' said one IT manager in an oil company. 'I've been working with my staff and colleagues, and have adopted a role similar to that of a set adviser: I ask people what they want to contribute, and don't impose my own views.'

THREE CASE EXAMPLES

TEAM-WORKING IN HOSPITALS

The various sectors of the health service have been running action learning programmes for many years. These vary from programmes for senior managers from various health authorities meeting to support and challenge one another on strategic plans and decisions, to hospital managers grappling with everyday managerial questions and problems, to nurses, doctors, other professionals and managers meeting to work at understanding better one another's work, priorities and needs, and the overall business of the hospital, with the aim of achieving a better service for their common customer – the patient.

Such hospital projects typically include customer care, outpatient design and cost management – all with clear, measurable deliverables. Tasks, teams and processes are thus equally addressed as the different professionals and administrative staff work together in the same set, hearing and beginning to understand each others' different perspectives.

Introducing a new questioning culture

In one such programme, focused on introducing a new culture, a hospital stated specifically that it wished to 'expose itself to a questioning approach from its managers ... and to encourage managers within it to responsibly question the status quo'. It wanted to create multi-disciplinary working and improved teamwork, to create a sense of confidence in individuals, engender a more business-like approach to implementing operational policies, and to empower staff to contribute to change. Action learning, it was felt, could best help staff to themselves create such a new culture, since its very processes and philosophy mirrored what the hospital wanted to achieve. The sets worked throughout with set advisers.

A 'live issues' programme

To help managers and professionals in the health service cope with issues arising in an ever-changing environment, a local health authority ran a multi-disciplinary programme for managers, doctor-managers and nurse-managers. Each was not only managing their own internal staff and managing their own budgets, but having increasing contact, and close working relationships, with outside bodies.

The programme aimed to help the participants work on their new roles and tasks. They each brought their 'live issues' to each set meeting, and when that issue seemed resolved, they brought another one. Questions from other participants helped them see links and themes, as well as patterns in their own work and behaviours: 'There is a different level of discussion when we're involved in collaborative work ... more of a dialogue than a discussion.'

DEVELOPING QUALITY LEADERSHIP

The idea behind this programme, also run in a health authority, was to get managers and medical staff to talk to one another, not about one another. Participants, all from different hospitals within the authority, held very senior positions and had many roles, which they at times found difficult to handle coherently in the turbulent world they worked in. The participants felt a sense of comfort in the set, which had agreed total confidentiality on what took place within it.

One of the major issues they thus felt free to talk about – and these sets often worked more as discussion groups – was the nature of management, their own assumptions, their various approaches to it, and how each of them saw themselves as managers. 'I want to make sense of what happened yesterday,' was a common opening statement.

7   Time

An action learning programme takes longer than most other programmes or courses – except for academically based courses. Why? Can it all happen in a shorter time-frame? Time is money, so can people really be released for so long from their everyday work?

TAKING TIME

One of the key advantages of action learning is precisely that it is not a short course, but a programme spread over a number of months – or longer. Some may argue that this is impractical, that there simply isn't the time. At this point, I am usually reminded of the Frenchman who said: 'We never have any time to stop and think now. But we always find the time later to stop and put things right when they've gone wrong.' In other words, we do have the time, but we choose how we're going to use it.

In a world of instant coffee, microwave ovens, push-button entertainment on TV, anything that takes just a little bit longer is viewed as suspect.

Comments from participants on action learning programmes indicate that it is precisely the element of time that is so crucial. By spending more time, we give ourselves the chance to learn, we gain understanding, we consolidate and 'internalize'. Learning is never instant. It is because of the time spent in recalling, reflecting, thinking about subsequent actions and next steps, testing out, reflecting again, and so on, becoming aware and continuing on a learning spiral, that we consolidate and anchor our learning. It is this stress on recalling, revisiting and reflecting – what so many participants referred to as the 'discipline' of action learning – that we only experience over time:

> You need energy, motivation and commitment to persist with action learning. Don't give up early – even if you're dubious and feel it's of limited value. Time is crucial. You become like a sponge – gradually saturated – and then you need more time before it begins to drip out, and you realize what's been happening, and what you're gaining.

149

WHY DOES A PROGRAMME TAKE SO LONG?

One reason is that learning takes time. It is never instant. We may assimilate ideas or new skills quite quickly, but consolidating them – making sure we really have understood, mastered them and can apply them effectively – takes longer. We only know this by testing things out, and by subsequently taking the time to recall and revisit both the mistakes and the successes, and reflect and learn – going around a learning cycle, which over time becomes a learning spiral. If it's behaviour or attitude change that is being looked for, these do not develop overnight.

Time is also needed for each member, in their airspace, to really 'unpack' their project, their questions, their uncertainties. As one woman put it: 'You think you've solved a problem in five minutes, but if you spend more time, you realize you haven't. You've only scratched the surface. After an hour and a half we began to feel we were really getting somewhere.'

Time is also tied in with continuity: the repetition of sets and set meetings, and the discipline of going round a learning cycle (or spiral). Once isn't sufficient. One participant was adamant: 'You need to spend a year doing it. A week is not the same, you need the longer period.' One reason is that in order to learn new things, we often need to first unlearn what we have been doing for years.

Yet another reason why action learning programmes take longer than most is because they are project-based. To work on a real project within an organization and manage it through its various stages takes time. And to gain full benefit from action learning, each participant needs to go around a learning cycle more than once – they need to report back at least two or three times, to feel they are moving forward with their learning, let alone their actions.

IS THERE AN IDEAL LENGTH?

No. However, if a programme is too short, the learning will be more superficial. Less than three months is probably not useful.

The frequency and length of the meetings is crucial. Ideally, sets should meet for a full day once a month, allowing each set member up to an hour's airspace at each meeting – which takes time. A programme lasting three months allows for only three meetings, so there may not be enough time for everyone to revisit their actions and their learning. This will be exacerbated if the set meets for only two or three hours, because the amount of airspace will have to be radically curtailed, either by reducing the amount of time allocated to each set member or by limiting airspace to one or two participants per meeting.

Most programmes last between six and twelve months. Some, however, have been known to go on for several years. The set adviser will normally contract with the set or the organizer of the programme to work with a set for, say, six meetings. Thereafter, the contract can be renegotiated.

Those sets that continue for longer usually do so from the participants' choice. Those most likely to last that long are made up of very senior managers – chief executives and managing directors. They, in turn, are less likely to be able to meet once a month, because of their pressure of work and responsibilities. Instead, such groups tend to meet every two or three months – often for an evening and the following day.

Continuing with a set – which, as many point out, is the only time they have for themselves, and is the only place where they can drop their masks and share their questions and anxieties with others – is invaluable.

One managing director who has been a member of a set for some ten years – although some of the members have changed over that period – said it provided him with the mirror he needed to help him reflect on decisions he was facing, issues he was dealing with, and was a time to tap into accumulated knowledge and experience of other very senior managers with no axe to grind.

HOW DO YOU PERSUADE OR CONVINCE YOUR MANAGER TO LET YOU HAVE SO MUCH 'TIME OFF'?

As discussed in Chapter 4, participants' managers need to be involved very early on, and must be party to the selection of a task or project. If that project is focused on an issue of relevance or importance to that person's job, or to the section/department he or she works in, the manager is likely to feel more willing to allow 'time off'.

The way to convince an employer or manager is to explain why it takes so long and, perhaps more importantly, to point out the benefits and the tangible results.

It is essential that the programme has the support and backing of a senior manager (the 'client'), because this will ease any tension with a participant's immediate boss. Once the importance of the programme to the organization is stressed, participants should have fewer problems with their managers.

Having suffered at the hands of their managers, a number of participants felt very strongly about the need for managers and clients to be involved in the early stages of any programme: 'You must have the commitment from managers to the programme – otherwise you risk being hassled by them. The day of a set meeting, my manager would, almost like clockwork, come up with an important meeting that I had to attend, or other things that I had to do that day. It made things very difficult for me.'

THE VALUE OF TIME

'Action learning sows seeds that take time to germinate,' said one veteran of action learning.

REFLECTION TAKES TIME

Many participants commented on their realization that the act of reflection was not something instantaneous. Ideas took time to germinate – often insights would come at times seemingly unconnected with what was happening in the programme.

'Time and reflection go hand in hand,' as one participant remarked. 'Reflection isn't the instant thoughts you have. It's a longer, deeper process, and insights may occur at times which have nothing ostensibly to do with the set or programme.' Another commented: 'Action learning makes you think – but that doesn't happen quickly either. It takes time. The questions often dam up old routes of thinking, and it takes time to go down the new ones.'

LEARNING TAKES TIME

Referring to the benefits of an action learning programme over and above, or following on from, book learning or taught learning, one participant on an academically based programme commented: 'I came to accept the concepts [of action learning] early on, but it took time to see the real benefits, and to know how to do it". Much of that was because, at first, I kept wanting books and experts to be around, and it takes time to get used to doing all the questioning and learning yourself!'

As a corollary to this, many remarked that action learning programmes are particularly useful when participants are trying to 'consolidate' knowledge acquired on more traditional taught courses, where the subject matter, such as management, has to be applied back at work. Built onto a more traditional programme – but thereby lengthening it – action learning gives participants the opportunity to test out and decide what is useful and what is less useful, what they have forgotten, or what they may have misunderstood. It is, after all, what many professions and craft-based skills still require.

> You learn on various courses about relating, communicating, motivating, being assertive, and about management styles ... but you have to practise and practise to overcome years of doing things differently. And that's the value of action learning – the repetition and the constant building on what you've tried out once, to get it better.

Time therefore allows each participant to reflect on changes in themselves, and how those changes have come about – how they have learnt. The value in this is that once participants know how they best learn, they can re-create those conditions in the future.

152

Six months was not long enough for one participant: 'I became a great deal more aware. For me, it was all too short, I was just beginning to open out, learning, gaining the confidence to talk. I'm an introvert, and I'd just begun to come out of my shell ...'. In my presence, his set members gave him some feedback on how he was talking and participating much more than at the outset. He said this was being mirrored back in his department, where he was now talking to colleagues, and feeling much more relaxed. He was also talking more about work issues – and in greater depth – than before. He felt the quality of his work had improved as a result.

The 'unanticipated learning' that participants talk of (see Chapter 8) occurs as participants spend more time on their programme, for it is usually only with time, as participants realize that their learning isn't solely contained within their project, but will occur within the set – or, in fact, anywhere – that they emerge from thinking solely in terms of their 'role self' and allow their 'whole self' to become engaged (see Figure 7.1).

Others associated time with anchoring the learning: 'The length of the whole programme – nine months – was important. The opposite of the short, sharp shock soon forgotten ... and the longer you are there, the more committed you become.'

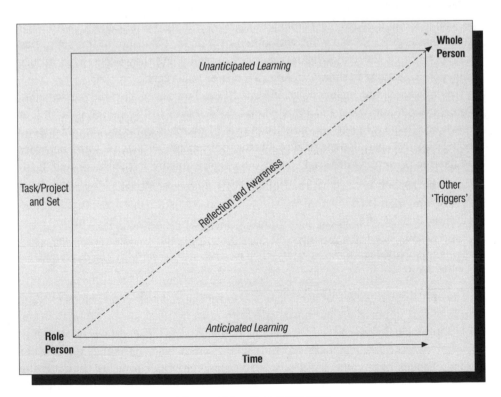

Figure 7.1   Time and its value

Many participants underlined quite emphatically: 'It takes time ... you must give it time ... giving up after one or two meetings when you feel not much is happening isn't giving it a chance. I'd say to anyone: give it time, hang in, don't be dismissive.'

MUTUAL SUPPORT AND TRUST, AS WELL AS INDIVIDUAL SELF-CONFIDENCE, DEVELOP WITH TIME

It usually takes time for participants to get to know each other and to trust one another. Only when set members have confidence in one another and feel safe enough to be honest can the set really begin to work.

The continuity of having the same set members (most of the sets I met had the same members throughout the programme) enabled the participants to begin to admit to emotions, or to not knowing: 'Over time, we began to talk much more about what we didn't know, or had done wrong,' grinned one participant. The observation that 'It takes time to develop trust you need in the set to allow you to work really well' was echoed frequently by participants, as was the sense that 'Real honesty was a long time coming, but when it did, the progress was incredible.'

Time showed them that 'Confidence is a moveable feast. As you get to know people, you see that they may feel confident about one thing, but not about another. Or their confidence came and went with different moods. The value of the set is that you can work on these moods and emotions as and when they occur. This in turn helps you to respond to them – in others – rather than react.'

The passage of time enabled participants to see how various people participated: some earlier, others later, and some when they felt they had some relevant skill or knowledge to offer. In one set, a relatively silent member came into his own when the set began preparing their final report for their client, because he was a designer and used to presenting material visually and professionally. It's worth noting, however, that this was also a set which did not work with a set adviser, who might have brought this silent member in sooner:

> I realized everyone had something to offer, given time. If you dismiss them early on, you may be losing a valuable resource ... It makes you realize that your preconceived notions of others are wrong – it makes you much more open in other settings. You cease to judge others instantly.

It was only through time that participants also recognized how impressions change, and how first impressions are not necessarily ones that last or should be built on. This applies particularly to action learning: many participants commented how anxious they were at the beginning, and how, initially, they behaved as they did in other groups, though often feeling it was 'out of character'. Over time, as they had the opportunity of observing their own behaviour, they felt more able to 'be themselves', and appreciate the value of this:

First impressions are often very wrong. That's the advantage of working with a set for a long time on lots of issues. You see people from different angles, and how over time they present all the different sides of their character.

What was valuable in having more time was the opportunity to study these issues, and discuss them and learn from them. In a more hurried programme, there would be less time for such learning.

SEEING TIME AS AN ALLY

From recognizing the value of time on the programme, it was an easy step for many to see time as valuable in other circumstances. They commented on how they began to view time in a different way: not something to battle against, or something which they 'lost'.

The metaphors – and hence the way people viewed time – changed. Time began to be seen as an opportunity for 'investment' in ideas and reflection on them. One participant commented: 'I gained the confidence to work with time ... to look at the long-term and marry it with the short-term. To acknowledge that we need more time, and need to stop constantly rushing, finding the quickest way forward.'

Another said: 'I see time as an ally – it gives me a sense of perspective. It's no longer a foe or enemy. Instead of "I must" or "I should", I now find myself saying "I will", which has a longer-term and more thought out ring to it.'

Where time is equated solely with money, there may be little time for action learning methods. As one participant commented: 'You need time at work to talk as we did in the set, but work pressures don't allow this.' Where learning – as opposed to assimilation of information or knowledge – is valued, time is normally found. We always have the time; we may choose to use it in different ways. It depends on what we value.

THREE CASE EXAMPLES

WORKING WITH CONSULTANTS

A major international consulting firm finding itself in an increasingly fast-changing, information-driven and competitive world felt there was a need for greater collaborative learning. But, said the training manager, 'The Western world finds collaboration difficult, since our culture emphasizes individual achievement, and also has great difficulty with the notion of reflection.' So the words 'action learning' were never used: 'It would be considered as jargon.' But the importance of learning over time, on real work assignments with a group of like-minded colleagues, was seen as crucial.

Senior sponsorship and support were vital – and eventually persistence, enthusiasm and convincing arguments began to pay off, in a culture that is driven by the notion of 'time equals money', where work pressures are immense, and where admitting you don't know is simply unthinkable.

An initial programme, made up of largely Training and Development and Marketing staff who wanted to experience action learning, took Peter Senge's 'personal mastery' (Senge 1994) as the theme they all worked on: first understanding the ideas, and then trying to apply them in their everyday work context.

A second, ambitious programme is planned – in conjunction with a university – for international senior consultants, to consist of three 'before, during and after' phases. The first, with participants on the job, will be preparatory and focus on their current issues and identify needs. The second phase will consist of three stages: knowledge-building, fieldwork (out in the world, applying the knowledge gained) and reporting back to sponsors. The third phase will again be on-the-job, and will focus on applying to ongoing issues and questions what was learnt in phase two. The sets will be active in all three phases, and will work throughout with set advisers.

FAST-TRACK MANAGERS IN A MAJOR RETAILER

The designer of this action learning programme for fast-track managers – with the aim of stretching them and broadening their experience of the business – was adamant that it had to include implementation by the participants of any projects undertaken and approved. Simply acting as consultants was not good enough, because: 'A manager needs to act, and react.' So all projects are business-driven, and must be resolved, actions implemented, and consequences – particularly for people – considered and dealt with.

Projects have included one about the retention of staff, and another about improving the logistics of the supply chain. Each participant identified his or her own development needs, and agreed them with their manager. What was important was senior managers' involvement and commitment, for 'action learning is risky, and empowering', and this was a culture characterized by power, control and little interest in new ideas. Why, then, was it prepared to commit to action learning? It was the training manager's own commitment and conviction that sold the idea – as well as her experience of running a successful large programme in another company. But given the culture, it felt, she admitted, 'like a white-knuckle roller-coaster ride with a blindfold on'.

There were no taught modules, but if participants expressed a need or interest in a topic, a meeting with an appropriate person – often a functional specialist within the company – was arranged, or participants organized a meeting or workshop themselves. On this programme they felt the need for inputs on project management, presentations and team development. Each set worked throughout with a set adviser: 'Nothing happens when there isn't one.'

A COMPUTER SOFTWARE COMPANY

In the past three years, three programmes have been run, largely for high-flying managers, in a major computer software company. All involved three elements. First, there were some taught inputs, which consisted largely of giving participants access to 'stimulating resources', usually someone with knowledge or insights who would engage their interest, but not through traditional taught means.

Second, each participant undertook a project. The development manager was adamant that 'it had to be something chosen by them, themselves, of real importance to their own business, and driven by a need to resolve a real business issue. I would never design a programme where projects are given by senior managers.'

Third, each participant had their own personal development plan, which identified his or her own development needs, which were then incorporated into the project they undertook. All sets were facilitated.

8 The learning

The learning on action learning programmes is very individual, and although much of it follows the path of the learning agreements made (see pages 71–72), a great deal of it cannot be anticipated: as participants become increasingly aware of the notion of learning from everything, they begin to gain insights which they could not have predicted.

This learning may be about:

- memorizing facts and information – gaining knowledge
- understanding intellectually
- doing something differently/changing – applying knowledge
- gaining insights, new beliefs, new values, and changing behaviour.

In action learning, the aim is to balance all four – but with a great deal of emphasis on the last two.

Much of the awareness of learning begins in the set, often prompted by the set adviser asking the question: 'So what did you learn from that?' It also emerges as participants begin, initially consciously, to use a learning spiral as a 'guide' to learning, and hear about what and how other set members are learning. Keeping diaries (see pages 167–170) helps them to recall and reflect on what they are doing, thinking, feeling and noticing – and what they can learn from this.

ACHIEVING LEARNING ALONGSIDE THE ACTION

One of the beliefs of action learning is that we learn best when we are committed to undertaking some action; another is that without action, there is no real evidence of learning. Thus, the emphasis in action learning is as much on achieving action as on gaining learning.

THE LEARNING EQUATION

Another tenet of action learning is that we learn best when we ask questions, probe, investigate and examine. It is thus a 'questioning' approach to learning, rather than a memorizing one.

Set members need to be aware of Revans's learning equation:

$$L = P + Q$$

For more on this equation, see pages 35–39.

THE LEARNING CYCLES

Participants also need to understand the notion of a learning cycle, or sequence:

1. We undertake an action (or something occurs).
2. Later, we recall what happened, and we reflect.
3. Having done so, we draw some conclusions, and hopefully have some insights.
4. Armed with these, we plan how to act in future, or what to do differently. Such an analysis is helpful when reviewing both our successes and our mistakes. We can learn from both.

But this sequence is purely to do with actions. If we are really to learn, we need to do more than go around this action cycle; we need to also ask ourselves some questions about our beliefs, assumptions and feelings, and how they impinged on our actions. We need to go around an inner experience cycle, acknowledging how all these affect what we do and say, and maybe deciding to tackle them – and thus to change what we say or do. This learning goes deeper and leads to greater changes than simply working superficially on actions. (For a more detailed discussion of these learning cycles, and diagrams, see pages 39–43.)

Such insights can also take place in the set, where participants have the opportunity to focus on learning about processes in a group, and communication in particular.

Figure 8.1 tries to pull together these three different learning cycles/spirals that occur in action learning: the problem-presenter's inner experiential cycle, his or her action cycle, and the set's processes (though these need not follow the sequence shown).

LEARNING STYLES

We need to be aware of different learning styles that we each have, and different approaches to learning that we adopt. Each set is likely to consist of members who have different styles and approaches, which point up differences in behaviours, and enable members to begin to understand – and maybe even value – these differences, while also seeing drawbacks in some of the styles and approaches.

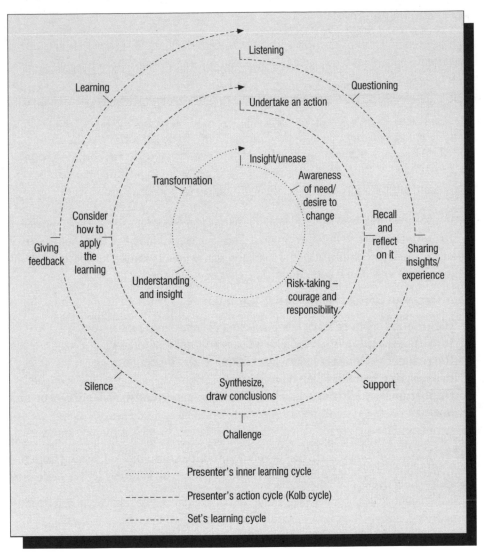

Legend:
- Presenter's inner learning cycle
- Presenter's action cycle (Kolb cycle)
- Set's learning cycle

Figure 8.1   Concentric learning cycles

The following learning styles have been identified:

- **Activists** prefer immediate action, and maybe stop to consider later (and may feel frustrated at the discussions and reflections in the set).
- **Reflectors** prefer to stop and think, and tend to be cautious (and will probably enjoy the time and space for this in the set).
- **Theoretists** integrate what they have seen or done into rational schemes (and will value some of the more theoretical discussions which may occur in the set).

TWO-COLUMN EXERCISE

One way of accessing the inner beliefs, thoughts and feelings that impinge constantly on our actions and behaviour is to keep a note – maybe as part of a learning diary (see pages 167–170) – firstly, of what we did and said, and secondly (and importantly) what we thought, felt, and wanted to say and do but didn't. In the left-hand column we note the former; in the right-hand column the latter.

In the right-hand column, we also need to note what was preventing us from doing what we planned, saying what we wanted to, or expressing our feelings. Such an analysis throws a great deal of light on us and our actions.

- **Pragmatists** are keen on trying out ideas or techniques – if they believe they make sense and will work (and may see many opportunities for learning about group processes, and communication, that occur in the set).

There are also different approaches to learning:

- **Incidental learners** learn when shocked or jolted into realization.
- **Intuitive learners** learn somehow, but aren't quite sure how.
- **Retrospective learners** learn by recalling and reflecting.
- **Prospective learners** plan their learning.
- **Opportunistic learners** learn from every opportunity, and both plan and review.

The aim of action learning is to create *opportunistic learners* – both within the set and back at work. Many participants commented that this shift of learning from the set to everyday situations took a bit of time. (For more on learning styles, see pages 44–47.)

THERE IS MORE TO LEARNING THAN LEARNING!

To paraphrase Dwight Eisenhower: 'To have learnt is nothing; learning is everything.' Learning is a process whose by-product is a final achievement. How we achieve is as important as what we achieve. We need to know what enabled us to learn, what happened to give us that insight. When we say, 'I've learnt,' what do we now do differently to justify that claim? Equally importantly, what difference is that difference making to those around us?

Some, but not all the programmes, concentrated on the 'how' of the learning as much as on the 'what' – the end-product. 'I've learnt to listen,' was one frequent response; 'I found that asking others questions made me think more about the issue and gave me insights'; 'Listening to others grappling with problems helped me resolve some of my own.' These are just a few instances of 'how' participants learnt. But even they are helpful: for those participants now have some ideas on how to re-create situations which help them learn.

For others, it was having to take a risk, do something they'd never done before, that provided insights – coming to terms with fear, recognizing it, and knowing that it was a sign of a learning opportunity ahead.

In set meetings, set members are asked to think about what has helped them gain insights and learn. Becoming aware of this means participants can re-create learning opportunities elsewhere, back at work.

Asked 'How do you learn?', participants' answers usually include:

- 'By talking things through with others.'
- 'By being listened to as I think out loud.'
- 'By reflecting.'
- 'By listening to others.'
- 'By helping others.'
- 'By practising and repeating.'
- 'By analysing and understanding.'
- 'By trying something out – even taking a risk.'
- 'By reviewing successes and mistakes.'
- 'By being asked questions.'
- 'By reading.'
- 'By getting feedback.'
- 'By writing.'
- 'By drawing/creating pictures.'

In answer to the question 'When do you learn?', the responses usually include:

- 'When I'm given the time and space.'
- 'When there is a sense of urgency.'
- 'When I am allowed to make mistakes.'
- 'When I am encouraged and supported.'
- 'When I'm "kicked".'
- 'When I'm appreciated.'
- 'When I'm challenged.'
- 'When I feel confident – and competent.'
- 'When I'm interested.'
- 'When I want to achieve something for my own satisfaction.'
- 'When I can see end results.'

Being aware of responses to these questions is useful, for it highlights for the future the circumstances and conditions in which you will best learn.

163

INTERNAL QUESTIONS EXERCISE[1]

An interesting way of trying to understand our willingness to learn is to see our-selves as two 'selves': a judger (judgemental) self and a learner (curious and open) self (Goldberg 1998). Each poses different 'internal' questions which pre-cede both our 'outward' questions and our behaviours, and are to do with our attitudes, thoughts and feelings. Below are a few instances of the different inter-nal questions:

The Judger	The Learner
Notices, judges and reacts	Observes, chooses, and responds
Thinking tends to be blame-seeking, self-justifying, and self-righteous	Thinking is inquisitive, accepting and open
Thinks in terms of control	Not overtly concerned with control; thinks in terms of choice
Black-and-white, 'all or nothing' thinking	'Shades of grey' thinking
Closed-minded. Tends to jump to conclusions	Open-minded. Resists premature conclusions or judgements
Thinks in terms of either/or: dualities, polarities; and opposites: right/wrong, true/false, good/bad, acceptable/unacceptable	Thinks inclusively in terms of both/and; of what might be useful, valid, workable and worthwhile
Tends to think in linear, cause–effect terms. Rarely open to systems thinking or multiple explanations. May not consider context	Thinks in terms of causes and explanations. Chooses linear, systems or contextual thinking, depending on goal
Considers own personal reality, opinion, interpretation is the only correct one, so is always 'right' (even about being wrong)	Looks for other points of view; recognizes simultaneous possible realities, opinions and interpretations
Paradox, contradiction, ambiguity, and/or confusion intolerable	Paradox, contradiction, ambiguity and/or confusion tolerable and acceptable

Overlooks or collapses distinctions, leading to over-generalizing, possible stereotyping	Habitual search for distinctions and new categories to think in. Actively seeks to understand, appreciate and utilize differences and exceptions
Accepts own assumptions, often	Habitually questions own assumptions
Thinking may be concrete and literal in relation to symptom or problem	Able to reflect on and think abstractly about own problems or symptoms
Thinks negatively of any person or position with divergent position	Think it's OK to disagree; may be curious and enquire about other viewpoints

Each of us exhibits both of these mindsets to a greater or lesser degree: 'These labels simply represent different ends of a continuum of human nature and human behaviour' (Goldberg 1998, p. 166). The judger self prefers not to learn. The learner self wants to learn, and is prepared to tackle the judger self.

EMOTIONAL INTELLIGENCE

Understanding emotional intelligence – and the neurological connections within the brain which allow the emotional memories and lessons stored in the 'emotional brain' to send useful signals to the 'thinking' part of the brain – is leading many people to place more value on emotions than hitherto. As Daniel Goleman has put it in his book *Emotional Intelligence*:

> The emotions, then, matter for rationality. In the dance of feeling and thought the emotional faculty guides our moment-to-moment decisions, working hand-in-hand with the rational mind, enabling – or disabling – thought itself. Likewise, the thinking brain plays an executive role in our emotions – except in those moments when emotions surge out of control and the emotional brain runs rampant ... In a sense we have two brains, two minds – and two different kinds of intelligence: rational and emotional. How we do in life is determined by both – it is not just IQ but emotional intelligence that matters. Indeed, intellect cannot work at its best without emotional intelligence ... This turns the old understanding of the tension between reason and feeling on its head ... The old paradigm held an ideal of reason freed of the pull of emotion. The new paradigm urges us to harmonise heart and head. (Goleman 1995)

He further defines emotional intelligence as our ability to motivate ourselves, to persist in the face of frustrations, to control our impulses and delay gratification, to regulate our moods, to empathize, to handle disagreements, to critique rather than criticize, to tolerate diversity, to overcome fear and stress ...

What's the connection with action learning? The value it places on honesty, openness and respect for others, plus taking responsibility for one's actions, coupled with helpful and challenging questioning by set members, leads many participants to acknowledge – sometimes for the first time openly – the place that their feelings have when they take decisions or make choices. The exercise on internal questions (see page 164) is one way of accessing these feelings.

WHAT IS EVALUATED IN AN ACTION LEARNING PROGRAMME?

Many participants asked in what way they would be assessed. Was there a 'pass' or 'fail'? Did they have to produce written material, and how and by whom would that be judged? And was it the completed project or the learning that would be evaluated?

The answers to these questions will be decided by each organization running such a programme. If the organization has an action-oriented culture, the measurable and visible results are what will probably be assessed primarily. In development-oriented organizations, the personal development may be viewed as at least equally important to any achieved 'actions'. Thus certain outcomes or criteria for success will have been specified and mapped out, and participants may have some form of a learning contract – for instance, evidence of leadership or improved team-working. Alternatively, they will have some personal targeted developments that they need to achieve. Areas for assessment might include whether someone now reasons differently, behaves differently, has a greater understanding of his/her motives, has altered some beliefs and values, and is able to acknowledge his/her feelings and their impact.

Participants remarked on the fact that assessing the action was easier: results of action could be observed – a task performed, a report prepared, measurable business improvements, a new team working well together, and (as we've seen) clients and managers being aware of, and impressed by, participants as they worked on the project.

For many participants, however, it was their learning – and how they had developed and changed – that became the most important element, and the one on which they preferred to be assessed. In other words, how they had changed as a result of their learning, and what they were doing differently, which inevitably had a knock-on effect on their day-to-day work, relationships and achievements.

HOW ARE ACTION LEARNING PROGRAMMES – AND PARTICIPANTS' ACHIEVEMENTS – EVALUATED?

There are a number of ways of assessing both an action learning programme and what participants have learnt:

- by asking participants to assess themselves and other set members, evaluating both 'action' achievements and behavioural developments – self- and peer evaluation
- by asking participants' colleagues and managers; those brave enough could ask participants' staff; a client or supplier may also have some insights about both
- by asking the Personnel and Training/Development Department for their observations, and using the next assessment centre to evaluate the change in the participant
- by asking the participants to write a report and/or a reflective document – the former would describe the actual achievements of the project; the latter would describe the journey of learning
- by asking participants to give a presentation to clients and other interested parties, including senior managers – such presentations might cover both 'action' achievements and learning.

If participants are on a qualifications-related programme, they will, of course, need to write a dissertation or some other 'academic' paper.

The important thing is to decide what form of assessment – if any – is going to be used, and to make sure that all the participants are clear about it at the beginning of the programme.

One set described in some detail their unhappiness at the lack of clarity over their assessment:

> We weren't told what exactly was going to be evaluated, nor who was interested in hearing it. All we knew was that we had to make a presentation of some sort. So we decided that, for us, our learning and development had been the key part of the programme. Our individual presentations covered our actual tangible project achievements, and then we began to get on to the learning part of the programme, but were stopped, and told that the managers had no interest in this!

The set went on to describe their unhappiness at this, and their feelings of disillusion with their managers – and the company – for being so uninterested in individual growth and change.

DO PARTICIPANTS KEEP NOTES OR SOME OTHER FORM OF DOCUMENTATION TO HELP FOCUS ON LEARNING?

Programmes differ. Some have a requirement – or encourage participants – to keep some form of reflective notes or a diary as an aid to learning.

Since one of the key elements of action learning is to go around the learning cycle – recalling what has happened since the last meeting, reflecting on it, being asked questions, beginning to understand better, and make plans for how to go forward – it is often helpful to keep notes about actions, thoughts, feelings and insights. Not only do they jog the memory for the next meeting, they are also a story in themselves of the journey of achievements and development that participants experience. We may think our memories will not let us down, but they do, and it is only by keeping a 'diary' or some other form of reflective document that we realize how much we forget.

Using a diary or learning log in this way – to see where we've been and where we are now – helps when we again face similar situations. It tells us what we did or didn't do last time, maybe what we wished we'd done, and gives us a wider repertoire of possibilities with which to progress in the future, as well as reminding us of what we should try to avoid.

On some programmes, sets may be required to produce a written report on their experiences, or individuals may be invited to write a short, reflective document on what they've learnt, more for themselves than for a formal assessment.

Others simply assess their learning as they go along – often at the end of set meetings. For instance, at the end of a meeting the set adviser might ask participants to note down their observations, reflections, what they have learnt from the day, and to share this with other members. This is also an opportunity for members to give each other feedback – a very useful commodity when learning!

Most of those not required by the programme to keep any notes didn't. One man remarked that he hadn't kept a diary because he wasn't sure what to put in it. 'I'm not a scribbler,' he added. Others similarly found writing difficult. Giving participants a form with a few basic questions can help those who feel stuck when facing a blank piece of paper.

THE VALUE OF A DIARY

Those who kept diaries found them beneficial. They acted as a memory – a way of stepping back into the event – part of the reflective element of action learning. It reminded them of what they'd done and felt, and what they'd thought, and what progress they were making: 'I always kept it. For me it was interesting to see what I did, and what I now do differently. You can see your own learning and progress. You begin to feel you're achieving something, getting somewhere. It shows up your journey.' Another diary-keeper commented: 'It was helpful in retrospect to see my feelings, both the successes and the moments of pain, and which ones were triggered off by what. I could then look to see if there was a pattern.'

'I found keeping a diary the most useful part of the programme,' said the young branch manager of a building society. A finance officer found that the learning log was the key for her – the insights and learning she recorded would, she felt, be of more use to her later, rather than a list of actions successfully accomplished.

One woman said that the actual writing had given her an insight: 'I found I couldn't write when I felt low – so I learnt that I don't learn at the moment when I'm low;

I do so later, when I'm able to reflect. But I could write when I felt good – and so could reflect and learn more quickly.'

A group of trainers/developers on a distance learning programme found it very helpful to keep 'learning logs', which chronicled their own learning and their discomforts at certain stages. They remarked that this rigour had given them helpful insights into how those they 'trained and developed' back at work might feel at times, and would make them more aware and more sensitive to the emotions being expressed.

For one participant, keeping the diary was 'an extension of the set, another way of talking', and an action learning veteran said: 'I keep notebooks with insights, questions, ideas, fragments, reflections and "bubbles" ... You might call it a learning log, but it's really more notes.'

A production manager – who prided himself as a fire-fighter, able to think on the move, no time to plan, stumbling from crisis to crisis, and coping – commented how the first entry in his learning log was: ' "Reflect and be planned" [a corruption of print and be damned]: not the best of entries, too vague, no actions, no review date, but when acted on was one of the most valuable learning experiences.'

Another manager noted that one entry in his diary went as follows: 'Lessons learnt: Stand firm, don't wilt under pressure. Senior managers, who on the whole are bright, can have significant weaknesses. Extremes of emotion destroy relationships, credibility and respect in a business environment. Never forget the other person's point of view. Do not be vindictive; it casts a shadow over future dealings with others.'

Several participants who kept diaries found they moved on from initially simply registering events to thinking about their reactions to them, what significance they had. One woman found the exercise an interesting experience: 'I found that as time went on, my diary changed from being an Adrian Mole diary to one more like Anne Frank's.'

'Maybe the word diary is the wrong word to use,' commented another participant. 'It's more of a daily portfolio of reflections – not so much of events and timing.'

If participants do keep diaries/logs, these headings and questions can be applied to projects, as well as to set meetings – or any other encounters:

- What I planned to do
- How I went about it
- What took place
- The outcomes/what happened
- Was it what I'd anticipated?
    - If yes, what went well?
    - If not, what could I have done/said differently?
    - My reflections on it
- What was I thinking?

- What was I feeling?
- Did I do/say what I'd planned?
  - If not, what was stopping me?
  - What did I choose not to say or do, and why did I make that choice?
- What have I learnt?
- What do I want to focus on next time?
- My thoughts on how my learning is occurring

KEEPING NOTES

To help these reflective moments, some sets would take time at the end of their meetings to write down their reflections and what they felt they'd learnt, then share them with others. They also noted their next action plans. Doing such reflection on the spot – at least of what they had learnt at the meeting – was, many found, the best way to keep track:

> At the end of every meeting we filled in 'action forms' – what we planned to do and how. I found I was approaching and tackling my project totally differently from any previous work project. I was doing very little hands-on. Implementing the project [a communication one] was always uppermost in my mind. I found I could change my mind – I gained the confidence to do so, I made mistakes (which I documented) – nothing too critical or life-threatening. I noted that I was no longer fobbed off by my manager. I considered lots of options before deciding. And I asked for feedback and ideas. I was making my own staff more accountable, and asking them: 'What have you done, and what will you do … and how?' Before, it was me who told them.
>
> I also wrote down questions going round in my mind, for instance: 'Can I say "I don't know," and not feel inferior?' And I'd keep track of what I was thinking and feeling. If I made mistakes, I'd go back to the point where things began to go wrong, and see what I could have done differently.

Many of those who did not keep diaries did take notes at meetings, which some of them then turned into something more coherent.

One company issued the participants with booklets in which to keep notes during set meetings. At the end of these were two pages: one to note their reflections on the day and what they thought they had noticed, felt at various times, and learnt; the second to evaluate the set processes, how they were managing them, and what they were doing well, and to consider how to improve for next time, and what to do differently. They spent about half an hour at the end of a meeting sharing their thoughts with one another.

THE LEARNING ISN'T ALWAYS EASY OR SMOOTH

These experiences of action learning may sound like a smooth passage. But, for many, it was difficult – even initially traumatic. Some felt like quitting after the first session, because the lack of structure upset them; the expectation of being open and honest frightened others; while some were anxious – even scared – about the prospect of having to complete a project: 'It felt like hell on the first day. A total culture shock, both in relation to work, and any other form of learning or education I'd experienced before.'

Many participants, all of whom lasted the course, admitted that much of the learning had not been easy – in some cases it was a struggle. Others had to overcome their fear of taking risks, or force themselves to talk about issues they'd prefer not to think about or admit to.

For some, these emotions were strongest at the beginning of a programme; for others, they continued until well into it. Several thought the hardest part was taking the plunge and admitting that an issue was troubling or puzzling them, and that they would like to discuss it: 'It's threatening because you can't hide – your colleagues won't let you ... they make you confront issues you didn't want to. But you don't half feel better once you've talked about them.' (The issue in this instance was how to 'energize' a management buy-out which was losing momentum, and facing up to what were the other managers' hidden agendas.)

Others talked of being 'nervous' at the outset, not so much of the people but, as one put it: 'of disclosing issues I wanted to work on ... Would the others be interested in it or would they be bored? But I grew to be fascinated by it, by the process, and in the end the time went all too quickly, and the others seemed genuinely interested.'

'At times it was really nerve-racking – like taking a driving test,' smiled one participant. Others felt daunted and nervous: 'How will we know when we're working in an action learning way?' was a question several participants asked themselves at the beginning.

At the beginning, participants had mixed feelings, and in many instances felt lost and confused: 'I nearly didn't come after the first set meeting, it was nothing but talk for an hour, but then something popped out of the woodwork, the set starting asking questions, and I realized that something very useful was happening.' This was the comment from one participant who now uses action learning in all his work.

'I was on my guard at the beginning – I didn't feel positive – and this wasn't helped by my missing the first introductory day,' commented one young bank manager.

Others spoke of feeling daunted, and a few of feeling cynical. One had asked himself, 'Was this just another fancy name for something very obvious. Now I think it's something very special.' Another participant said that in his set, 'We began by calling it therapy, then we realized it wasn't – it was considerably more than that.'

For a few, there was the concern, at the outset, about whether they were doing 'it' the right way and would eventually gain something. A young scientist was worried that 'It was just a lot of questions at the beginning – and I wondered how I would ever know if I was learning anything – would there be something tangible at the end?' Someone else described the experience as: 'dark at first, then grey, then, at last, it dawned'.

On the other hand, others felt elated at the beginning: 'I started on a high – this was something new, sounded interesting, and I'd been selected. Then my spirits flagged as I started work on my project and got bogged down. But my energy and enthusiasm rose again as I began to see results and began to learn.'

With time the emotions became more entangled. A senior manager talked of 'hard work, excitement, tiredness, frustration, renewed energy, fear ... you go through the whole gamut'.

A participant who admitted to feeling 'freaked' by the first meeting nevertheless was adamant: 'You must persist. It's later that the penny begins to drop.' Another said:

> My first feelings were ones of shock and horror: 'I'm not going to express my doubts and my feelings to someone I don't know.' It was all slow and tedious, and I saw the set adviser as being 'manipulative', constantly asking questions, prying. When he worked skilfully with one other set member, my worries went up one notch further. I didn't want to hear what I might have to say about my feelings. But then, gradually, as others took the risk, I began to think, 'It might be OK. After all, I've nothing particular to discuss, no issue of any concern. Why would I, and what I do, be of any interest to others?' Then suddenly it was my 'airspace'. I began to talk about the issue I'd decided to bring ... and next thing I knew an hour and a half had gone by. Others were saying, 'That was interesting,' and I began to feel valued. They'd given me their attention, but no judgements. That was a revelation to me – to say what you want to say, and not be judged.
>
> But at the end of the first meeting I decided I didn't want anything to do with it. I heard myself being sarcastic – which is a sign, I now recognize, of my fear. That evening, I wanted to go to the pub, and two of us went off to discuss our discomfort at what we called 'middle-class head-banging'. It was all too gentle for us hardened Eastenders. Nothing to do with the cut and thrust of managing.
>
> Slowly, though, I recognized that part of my fear was my lack of skill at 'it' – I didn't know how to ask helpful questions, so I didn't feel I could participate fully. Yet something in me chose to continue. The real breakthrough for me came when I challenged something the set adviser said! But it took four meetings before I plucked up the courage. And it was OK. That's when my 'apprenticeship' began, for I'd been a telecommunications engineer all my life until then.
>
> Now I sit fairly and squarely in management development, and use the action learning approach in all my work. I'm now convinced that when people work with real issues – the stresses, the delegating, the motivating and the decisions – they're learning and doing something about them simultaneously. That's the power of action learning: it works on the 'inside'. So it may be my attitude to a problem that is the problem, and not the stated problem.

One set reminisced how: 'We went up and down through the year – from excitement at the beginning, to frustration somewhere soon after – mostly at not being able to focus on a project, followed by more frustration at the rush, and not having enough time to concentrate properly on everything, followed by friction at the support that some members were getting back at work – and which others weren't.' A couple of participants remembered: 'It was a battle all the time, with our managers always fixing meetings for the day the set was meeting, and we were determined to come to the set meeting.'

An older manager with little formal education admitted that he came 'in fear and trepidation, convinced I'd be out of my depth; I'd spent twenty years in the building trade with little formal education'. But he soon found it was about experience and common sense, and he found he could easily hold his own with the other members of the set – all from different organizations. And at the end, he was proposing to introduce action learning back into his company, in support of an 'Investors in People' initiative.

Others talked of their frustration at the seeming lack of 'structure', milestones, goalposts, timetables to follow, and the lack of lectures. There were, they said, no obvious, stated measures of success or failure – was there such a concept as failure, in fact? There was no homework, either – except your next actions.

This unusual, novel approach to learning puzzled many: 'I asked myself, "What am I doing here? The facilitator gives me no answers – is this a waste of time?" I felt frustrated, and was convinced people there wouldn't be able to help me.'

Faced with a group of 'non-experts', one participant asked himself: 'Was it the blind leading the blind – how can we learn from one another? But that's not the case, the blind leading the blind, I mean. You don't have to have the answers – you need to know what questions to ask, which isn't always easy, and help others pinpoint who may be able to help them.'

'No books, no lectures – you have to find things out for yourself,' was how another summed up his first impressions. 'But then you begin to realize that the answers are in yourself, and you begin to wring them out with the help of others. It changes the way you work and approach tasks.'

'I wondered how I would know if I was learning anything at all,' commented one participant, echoing what many others had also voiced. 'There were just lots of questions at the outset – and nothing being taught. Would there be anything tangible to hold on to?'

One participant felt unable to participate fully, she said, because one of the fundamentals – confidentiality – was not being observed by set members and, worse still, by the set adviser. This participant – a new lecturer at a university – was very unhappy with the entire programme. Another participant pointed to the behaviour and attitude of the set adviser that upset her and other set members: 'The set adviser was arrogant, abrupt and condescending.' She knew advisers to other sets were nothing like this, and merely regretted she'd had the 'bad luck' to be in that particular set.

In spite of these initial doubts and fears, by the time they'd reached the half-way point, most participants were feeling much more confident, and were beginning to see the fruits of their work. The advice of even those who had expressed ambivalence, fear or disappointment at the outset, though, was: 'Hang in, don't give up after the first one or two sessions.' 'The longer you're there, the greater the benefits,' was another comment.

BEING THROWN IN AT THE DEEP END

All programmes should begin with an introductory session (see pages 215–216), and many participants commented on how important it was to be in on the beginning of such programmes – to participate in the introductory session, and any other exercises planned.

For those who had begun to work together on such introductory sessions, the arrival of a newcomer proved disruptive, because it meant starting from the beginning again. But, as one participant also pointed out, 'Although it does disrupt a bit, it's also a good insight into how groups and teams react to new members.' Everything that happened was turned into 'a learning opportunity' – another essential aspect of action learning. Everything is data to be learnt from.

Some participants complained that they were not reminded, once the programme had started, about the important elements of action learning – which happened particularly where the set adviser lacked experience – so that the group became 'just another talking shop, with little or no emphasis on the learning'.

Others were simply bemused: 'We're so used to plunging in with suggestions and advice, and thinking that is the way to help someone. I felt useless and helpless just asking questions,' was how one manager described his feeling after an introductory exercise of just half an hour. However, the presenter remarked to him how useful it was to have space to talk through his issue and not get suggestions and advice!

THERE WILL BE VISIBLE, TANGIBLE BENEFITS, WON'T THERE?

The tangible benefits will be many and varied. If the participant aimed to develop managerial and personal skills, these will be visible. If the participant aimed to achieve something more tangible – introduce a training programme, create a new system or process, introduce new ways of communicating, build up a new client base, resolve a production problem – then the results will also be clear to all.

In terms of wider development, it is impossible to specify what each individual will take away from such a programme – but the breadth and depth of the potential learning has been described earlier in this book. Any of these is possible.

Failure to achieve anticipated tangible results may not be the fault of the participant. It could be – and often is – a consequence of problems arising within the organization that preclude the hoped-for tangible results: departments are amalgamated, people are made redundant, a major restructuring occurs, and so on. But the unanticipated benefits of action learning remain.

WHAT IS LEARNT?

Each action learning programme – like any other – has its stated aims: both business outcomes and the behavioural changes needed to achieve them. Individuals also identify their own individual goals, stated in action and personal developmental terms. These formed the basis of participants' 'anticipated' learning. But what emerges from all the programmes is the breadth and depth of the 'unanticipated' learning (see pages 186–193).

ANTICIPATED LEARNING

Those organizations I spoke to which were running action learning programmes specified the following 'behavioural' outcomes they hoped for:

- good team-working
- introducing a new management culture
- engaging senior managers in management problems
- encouraging managers to take responsibility and decisions and to question; to be more energetic and pro-active; to coach and counsel their staff
- improved leadership and initiative
- supervision excellence.

In all instances, these outcomes were tied to business outcomes and results:

- recommending new business strategies
- delivering more customer-focused services
- introducing a new technology
- retaining staff
- tackling absenteeism
- cost-cutting.

(For other business issues addressed by action learning programmes, see page 89 and the case examples.)

Where the participants' learning outcomes were their own personal and managerial development, they talked of hoping to:

- challenge myself intellectually
- compare and try out new methods of working and managing

- learn how to motivate my staff
- learn about leadership
- become a better team member
- grow as an individual
- learn to influence and motivate
- empower others.

In some instances, individuals mentioned wanting to gain specific skills associated with communicating, implementing quality programmes, creating human resource development programmes, liaising with clients, implementing IT programmes, and so on.

Below are the main anticipated learnings, and what participants said they had achieved.

HOW TO ACHIEVE BETTER TEAM-WORKING

This was a stated outcome for three in-company programmes whose participants were interviewed. The reason why action learning was chosen, as opposed to a more traditional team-building programme, was that the organizations in question felt that working on a real project, and having the benefit of working as sets would add more depth to the learning – primarily because of the simultaneous emphasis on action and learning.

Nevertheless, participants could no doubt have gained this from other team-working programmes. What they said they gained through an action learning programme, however, was applying themselves to real-life, work-centred projects, which in two cases involved implementing their jointly agreed plans and ideas. They also valued the time they could spend on it, the discipline of the action learning processes such as having airspace and using questioning, the time for reflecting and the emphasis on their learning.

At the outset of the programmes, participants had all been introduced to Belbin's model of nine team roles:

- **Innovators/Plants** – original thinkers who provide new ideas
- **Resource Investigators** – bring in ideas from contacts outside
- **Co-ordinators** – social leaders of the group, guiding it towards its objectives
- **Shapers** – provide the energy and drive to implement ideas or projects
- **Evaluators** – appraise proposals, monitor progress
- **Team Workers** – provide and maintain contact away from team/meetings
- **Implementers** – translate plans into manageable tasks that team can get on with
- **Finishers** – make sure the team delivers
- **Specialists** – those with specialist knowledge

According to this model, each person will probably fulfil at least two roles.[2]

Most had completed the relevant questionnaire, and had been 'labelled'. Many participants were also familiar with the four learning styles defined by Honey and Mumford – activists, pragmatists, reflectors and theoretists – (see pages 44–47), and had completed the Learning Styles Questionnaire. This had helped them understand their own approaches to learning, and those of others – to accept, value and learn to work with them. They found these useful as reference points, and when they talked of how they had changed, many mentioned learning how to work with and 'use' people whom they now recognized as having complementary skills. In other instances, some participants talked of trying to develop different styles, such as becoming more reflective or more active. 'I've learnt,' said one manager, 'that there's more to learning than just being active.'

Participants in the three team-development programmes worked on group projects. In one instance, they selected a project to improve communications in one member's workplace, and each member worked on certain issues related to this. In the second programme, the set themselves chose to work on a group project, in this case, a 'consultancy' project – it did not have an implementing stage. In the third instance, there were two variants. In one, each set focused on one set member's issues, and acted merely as 'support' to that member. The outcomes here were not entirely successful, because the other set members felt uninvolved. In the second variant, one work section became a set, charged with reorganizing their own work area – a shop floor. This was a highly successful experience (see page 105).

In the first of these two programmes, the participants had never worked together before, nor were they accustomed to working in cross-functional teams; their only experience of team-working was with their own staff.

To summarize participants' experiences, they claimed to have learnt the following:

To work better with others, and be more understanding and patient

I listen far more, and am more than ever now committed to team work. I'm a 'shaper', so naturally I have a clear view of what I want, and am often tempted to impose it on others. Now I appreciate more where others are coming from, and can read their reactions better.

I'm now more aware that some team members' skills are more useful at the end of a project than at the beginning, and I've ceased to judge people in other teams I work with for not participating early on in the work.

I've learnt that my first impressions are often very wrong. That's the advantage of working in a set for a long time on lots of issues. You see people from many different angles, and you realize how wrong you can be, and how, if you act these out at work, you are likely to lose someone valuable.

During our joint project activities, I developed set ideas on who had worked hard, who had contributed most – because they'd talked most! But then at some stage everyone pulled their weight. I remember one member who had said virtually nothing, and I was ready to condemn him, when he suddenly offered some really useful insights on what we, as a team, were doing which wasn't leading us anywhere.

Others noted: 'Leaders emerge during team activities, and leadership swapped for different activities because of the different skills we needed at different stages of the project.'

Being more aware of what happens in teams and meetings

It taught me to be more aware and to concentrate on what was happening – particularly in meetings, or when I am with others. Before, I'd concentrate only on what was being said. Now I'm more aware of body language and silences. The 'task' isn't the sole important thing.

Many felt they were now more effective at other meetings. One man commented: 'I feel it's legitimate to comment on the processes in meetings, and not simply address comments to the chair about the agenda.'

How to let go of control

I'm normally frustrated when I'm not in control in a group. I've learnt that I don't have to 'own' and 'control' everything. I'm more tolerant of others, and they are then better able to work with me. I'm also more aware, more able to stop and see myself. Being a perfectionist is a problem!

For many participants, having the opportunity to observe, over time, the roles and the behaviours and communication patterns that went with them anchored the knowledge and theories they already had (gained on taught courses) in real life.

It also helped one manager who was, in her own words, an 'activitist' to become more pragmatic, and as she herself said, probably an easier person to work with. It was this young woman who also, almost in the same breath, added that as a result of this team-working experience, she had come to realize that being a manager was more than knowing all about her speciality (surveying) and simply talking loudly! This, she had not anticipated. 'Mind-blowing,' was how she described her experiences. 'This is my first managerial job. I've been given responsibility for making money in my department – a surveyor's department. In action learning I've realized that managing is much more than being good at the work of my department – and simply talking loudly. I have so much more to learn, and it isn't to do with the tasks we tackle, but with the processes we adopt when we work together.'

This 'jump' in thinking and awareness – these connections – is just one of the typical outcomes of an action learning programme.

How best to reorganize teams back at work

One of the more senior members of a set described how he was now using cross-disciplinary teams to work on departmental issues, thereby getting a wider range of perspectives and creating greater cohesion within the department. He went on to say: 'The best people for solving problems are not necessarily the most senior people ... the action learning programme encouraged me to reorganize my department and introduce a management team which isn't drawn solely from senior people. Involving people in a more consultative way can be uncomfortable, but it's worth it for the results.'

A marketing manager was excited about how he was now working in a totally different way:

> I run several projects at once. I now talk to as many people as possible. Before, my department had a bad reputation: we were told we never communicated. One of my current projects needs – to be successful – to involve operations, sales, marketing and finance people. I've decided to draw in people from various locations around the country and have them all work together, in the same building, for the duration of the project – more of a matrix-type of organization. Before, I'd have made assumptions about what each of these departments would say, or want, and how they'd view my suggestions. Now they have a direct input into any plans. I also work at a much 'deeper' level – mostly through questioning. It's important to overcome physical barriers to communication, as well as the 'psychological' ones – the beliefs and assumptions we have, bred by silence and distance. I'm really pleased because one of my main objectives in going on the programme was to improve my own and my department's communication.

Another participant remarked: 'I used to dread departmental meetings or team meetings I chaired. I've changed my style – modelling meetings much more on our set processes – and now everyone is contributing more freely. I've used the SWOT analysis as a tool, and I feel the team going with me. Even the doubters are beginning to participate and value the different way of working.'

Yet another described how her team: 'is now running as a set, because they're all experts. How can I go around telling them what to do? The way our set adviser used questions, and how he "managed" us in a quiet way, has now become more my style of managing.'

One young banker described how she had moved to a new job since the programme, and was now the quality manager: 'I've moved the teams away from having a structured approach to their meetings, and they're now using an action learning approach. So, although we go through what has been achieved (for an agenda and report to be written) we give everyone "airspace", and we use questions rather more than a general discussion.'

HOW TO EFFECT A CULTURE CHANGE

Two programmes specified 'culture change' as an anticipated outcome. What they meant by this was 'creating a more energetic, pro-active, responsive environment'

179

and 'to build a strong team-working culture and increase team performance'. But neither detailed what different behaviours they hoped to see; nor did they anticipate the fact that changes would have to be made in structures, systems and procedures for a so-called 'culture' change to have a chance of occurring.

Of the two, the first company appeared to succeed, at least in part. It had introduced an action learning programme at all its sites, with the stated aim of improving team performance across the company. This arose out of a realization that communication within the company was sadly lacking, and this was resulting in limited communication with customers.

In the words of one senior manager:

> We were natural fire-fighters, but not good at planning: we set no deadlines and did little monitoring. Our staff were beginning to lose confidence and respect for management. What they wanted was strong managers who took decisions ... without discussion. But we're a US company, where team-working is important. So we selected teams to work on issues, and by using action learning we were saying to our staff: 'If you have a good idea, go ahead and tell me and do it.' At first there was a lot of cynicism, that this was a new gimmick that wouldn't last ... a waste of time. But what we did was, rather than span the gap instantly, begin to build small pack bridges.

Another manager said he noticed a definite difference in how his staff were working – with him – after the programme:

> My staff are more aware of what is happening, both inside and outside our own group. It's made it easier for me to let go and give them the tasks to work on, because I've seen that they're able to do it. Before, I'd be telling them what to do; now I involve them in decisions. And they're asking me more questions – that's part of the improved communication – more listening and more talking. It's the process of action learning that has helped. Before, we would fire from the hip; now we stop and take stock.

The second company which set out to achieve a culture change was less successful, largely because the programme involved only a handful of people. So, although those on the programme changed their way of thinking and acting, the rest of the company – not only the staff, but all the systems and procedures – remained unchanged.

Culture change is achievable through action learning programmes, but they do need to be organization-wide, and possibly even begin with senior managers – they, after all, create the culture the others follow.

HOW TO BE A MORE EFFECTIVE MANAGER AND INDIVIDUAL

Participants on every kind of action learning programme, whether in-company, mixed-company or academic, were eager to improve their effectiveness as managers. What they had in mind were the normal managerial needs: to create better relations with staff, to motivate staff, to communicate more effectively, to learn to delegate. Organizational terminology usually states such projected outcomes in terms of 'creating more responsive and energetic managers', and 'learning to empower staff'.

Participants' comments showed that they had achieved in no small measure what they had set out to learn.

Increased understanding of what managing is about

A manager's role is to manage the business, and not carry out the tasks. It's really made me think about prioritizing my time.

People – your staff – respond more to what you do and how you do it than what you say. By changing your behaviour, you begin to change the culture.

If you don't have authority to do something, get it. Get senior managers to help you make things happen ... don't sit around, or moan, or behave like an ostrich.

More skill in relating to staff

I have a better understanding of my people – I don't walk all over them, and people respond more favourably to me ... I'm more aware of my staff.

'I've realized,' said one departmental head in a university, 'that I don't feel threatened by having my staff ask me questions and give me their opinions. Before, I feared I'd find that threatening, so resorted to being autocratic, and not being my natural self which wants others to share and be motivated. So I've learnt to motivate others, while simultaneously having to take tough decisions about resources or people.'

Another said he had learnt: 'to involve people more, ask their opinions. Before, I was quite dogmatic. Now I realize I was often wrong – the problem of having power! Now I listen more.'

One young woman commented: 'I've learnt not to jump in so quickly with responses and ideas, suggestions, comments or criticisms.'

Another comment was: 'I've learnt the need to challenge – which is not the same as confronting. At work challenge is often interpreted as confrontation, and the person so "challenged" often gets defensive or angry, rather than considering what has been pointed out or asked.'

Another woman spoke at length of how she had become aware of assumptions she made about others' behaviours, and the origins of such behaviour, which on further investigation had proved to be unfounded. She talked particularly of people being aggressive, negative and cynical, and how she had taken 'evasive' action where she thought someone might react this way. In other words, she was adapting her behaviour to fit with assumptions she was making. If she was behaving this way, perhaps others were, too? She summed up these experiences and her increased understanding of her own behaviour, by saying: 'I have begun to practise a more open-minded approach ... I have also learnt by my own personal behaviour that a positive attitude is infectious.'

And another commented: 'Confidence is a moveable feast. People's confidence at work varies – it jumps up and down. Sometimes you take on the world, other times you can't. I now recognize this, which of course helps me when I'm dealing with my staff or colleagues.'

Delegating: Giving staff more opportunities

One woman said that she was giving her staff: 'more opportunity to "give". I'm delegating more to them and they're enjoying it. I've learnt that there are good ideas out there ... even someone you've mentally dismissed has them.'

The art of delegating was not a stated outcome for a young manager in retailing. But she had found that the programme was taking up so much of her time that she had to delegate! As she put it:

> This was not one of my learning objectives. I was learning how to work in a team. But I simply didn't have time to do everything at work once we started to work on the project. I didn't know how to delegate. So we – my staff and I – learnt together, an offshoot, so to speak of what I was doing on the programme! I didn't initially give my staff enough background or guidance on what they were to do. And they didn't at first ask me either – they were afraid of my reaction. So I'd phone and give them detailed instructions on what to do, and then phone to check how they'd managed. But then, as they began to cope better, I created a tape of tasks they need to carry out, but not how. And they managed. Soon I found that all I was doing was phoning to reassure them, praise them and tell them what a great job they were doing. They are so pleased, since it's given them much more responsibility – and they've proved they can do it.

Another manager commented on how he had become aware of the difference between managing and leadership: 'In the latter, you set standards and lead from the front, take on board conflicts with others, don't retreat. They're challenges, and as you resolve them, you feel a sense of achievement. I appreciate my staff much more and take on board their suggestions as well as their feelings. And I'm more aware of the effect I have on people.'

Empowering staff: More open relationships with them

'I give my staff more positive feedback because I feel more confident,' said one participant. 'A manager's skill should be to listen. I've certainly learnt to do this better,' commented another.

Another young manager pondered: 'Before, if my staff asked me how to do something, I'd have told them. Now I say: "What do you think?" But I'm aware that asking a question isn't always the best way. Making a statement may be better, or showing them what I think is best, and then next time asking them to generate ideas.'

I wanted to learn how to manage – and I've achieved it, or at least begun to understand. Before, I'd 'mother' my staff and tell them what to do. Now I give them more rope. I ask them what they've done, how they think something should be done ... if they're puzzled, we work it out together.

At the end of the programme, I sat down with my staff and said: 'Let's start doing things differently. Let's try and be more open, and give feedback, and use mistakes to learn from' ... and then I started doing it. Staff found it a bit uncomfortable – it's often comfortable to remain passive. And this way of working can also be frustrating, because everything takes longer to accomplish – but what we do is better.

I'm more tolerant of my staff. I have a tendency to be pedantic – action learning has made me reflect more, and allowed me to allow my staff to make mistakes, with me as a support to see where they went wrong, and what to do differently next time – learning from the last time. It's the learning cycle again – reflect, evaluate what you've done, and think what you could have done differently, and why you did what you did in the first place.

Another manager had achieved a greater appreciation of his staff's different styles at work: 'I now respect those differences. But I'm also more able and confident to do so because I've acquired a wider repertoire of skills and interventions – in particular how to ask good questions.'

An older manager, who had been rather timid, found it had made him 'much less hesitant ... I find if I sound convinced, people take me more seriously! I'm delegating more to my staff, and they are enjoying me more – I get invited out to drinks and lunch. If they do something wrong, I work through it with them, encourage them, and act more as a consultant and guide than as a reprimanding manager. And the more confidence I have in them, the better they do things. It's also improved my relationship with my daughter at home. I get her to suggest things – before, *I* would!'

A manager whose entire company was going through a programme, his own staff included, spoke of more visible communication with his staff: 'I'm more aware of them coming to talk to me, and they're asking me more thoughtful questions. They're more aware generally. '

BEING MORE ORGANIZED

Participants listed the following:

Being more organized, writing lists, structuring what I'm doing. Before, I was pretty chaotic.

Managing and organizing my time. It's been vastly more useful than the time management course I recently went on!

Since the programme, I've had to do a major re-seating of people – in terms of computers and phones. I spent hours thinking – talking – working out how various schemes would work. Before, I'd have piled in and made mistakes as I went along – at some considerable cost and with lots of aggro. I was a pragmatist! Now I've become a 'reflector' as well. The problem is, there is no thinking time allowed on our time sheets! So, I still at times feel guilty when I'm sitting and thinking, and not rushing around and 'doing'.

HOW TO TAKE ON RESPONSIBILITY, AND A MORE ACTIVE ROLE AT WORK

This was another category of learning that participants and their organizations hoped to gain from action learning – with a view to creating more energetic, proactive and responsible climates in the organizations.

Again, judging from participants' comments they managed to achieve much of this:

> I've created an open style office to go with the more open style of management I've introduced into the department.

> We're a very traditional company, but I now have ideas on what we can be doing differently – I was in a set with four people from different companies, and you hear them talk, and you get ideas. I'm hoping to free people up in my department, to get them to take initiative rather than blindly follow rules.

> The processes of the set have helped me intervene more effectively in other meetings – and run them better. I now feel it's legitimate to comment on the processes I see happening, and not simply work on the 'task'.

> It's generally heightened my sensitivity back at work. Everything is data – memos, interviews, group discussions. I begin to recognize what is happening, and it helps my responses and reactions.

> I spot more opportunities, and I'm less inhibited. Action learning could be a really powerful way to get cross-functional groups working together, and understanding each others' point of view.

'I now respond rather than react,' said one manager, and talked of his greater ability to stop and think, and thus respond, rather than jump in fast, which he saw as a knee-jerk reaction. In a similar vein, another participant said: 'I know I don't have to blindly accept what I'm told to do, and that I can go back and redefine the issues.' And a third commented: 'I'm no longer the passive recipient of information to regurgitate.'

'It's made me stand on my own two feet, take responsibility for myself and my work much more, analyse my problems, rather than run for guidance. And I help others do the same – using the well-worn action learning technique of asking questions!' said yet another participant.

Said one young woman: 'I'll now ask my managers why they're proposing to do something in a certain way. They don't – as I'd thought before – bite your head off. In fact some now treat me with more respect, probably because I do ask, in a constructive way, not aggressively. You need to say things, and ask, in the right way.'

A training manager related how he couldn't get the notion of action learning accepted on programmes, so he was introducing 'action projects' on his programmes, and then taking participants into a realization of what they were learning from doing them.

HOW TO CHALLENGE MYSELF AND OTHERS

Interestingly, the meanings of 'challenging' and 'confronting' were frequently compared, and participants made clear distinctions between them. The former was seen to describe a non-judgemental approach, the latter involved criticism. The former was an action learning approach; the latter was what participants talked of encountering all the time at work:

> Challenging can be developmental – both as you challenge others and they challenge you. It brings you up face to face with your assumptions and prejudices ... and if you're pushed you have to explain them, not justify them. That's much harder.

> I'm better now at challenging myself, asking those awkward questions ...

> I've learnt to think more laterally and see the broader picture in everything I do.

> I found I enjoyed the intellectual challenge of some of the issues that arose – the depth of thinking that was required to really penetrate to the crux of the matter ... something we don't do enough of.

And back at work? Participants talked of the difficulty of being 'challenged': 'Exposure to constructive criticism in the set makes you aware of its absence at work. I seek it, though, and encourage it, and try to give it myself.'

A number said they were trying to introduce an 'action learning way of working' with those around them – but it wasn't always proving easy: 'It's become a way of life for me, but at first it created difficulties because my staff – and others – expected instant answers, usually from me. In fact, I infuriated them because I kept asking questions and pushing and challenging them to find their own answers. I know, though, that you have to be aware of not going to the other extreme – and have no opinions and no responses.'

'Why don't we have more challenging – rather than confronting – back at work?' asked several participants.

HOW TO CONSULT AND FACILITATE

This outcome was specified for two programmes only – in one instance with sets of young managers identified as 'blue-eyed boys'; in the other with bright young managers who had little or no 'consulting' experience. In both instances, the learning vehicles were group projects which required them to act as 'consultants': their task was not to carry out an 'implementation' of their recommendations, but ended with presenting them. In 'purist' action learning terms, implementing proposals is an important element. Interestingly, one of the sets did, almost by accident, have the opportunity to implement one of their recommendations, and this provided a major insight: that when you have the responsibility of implementing, you are more realistic and thoughtful over your recommendations.

They felt they had learnt:

> How to look at issues in a more strategic way; how to gain people's confidence when you're suggesting change.

> Learning to cope with a manager's non-availability – when we're consulting him but also needing to get information from him in order to help him ... we learnt to keep him involved and updated on what we were finding, we scheduled regular meetings with specific agendas and questions. Our client even told us that he was learning from the project and the process!

> I've just been coaching a sales team back at work, and I got them to consider more options, look at what might stop them achieving what they set out to, and think about how best to approach the issue – by having a contract with one another, and working as a team with individual responsibilities.

None of the participants talked of what they were doing differently back at work in terms of 'consulting'. They had all returned to their managerial roles, and 'consulting' as such played no role. But they had gained insights on team-working, their own styles of managing, and had learnt to delegate to their staff – mostly by default, and from necessity, since the programme had made more demands on them, and kept them away from work for longer, than they had anticipated.

However, one participant on an 'academic' programme, who was in the process of changing jobs to become a consultant, related how, in her project, which was simultaneously a 'consultancy' for a real client, she was using the processes of action learning: 'My consultancy project – and how I work with my client – is mirroring my working and learning on the programme.'

SOME TANGIBLE RESULTS

In addition to the learning and development, there were also some real success stories with tangible and visible results: departments restructured to take account of client liaison, participative communication systems introduced, new marketing strategies put into place, cost-cutting exercises implemented, consultative projects implemented, a workshop reorganized, a personnel department given a new lease of life, greater staff involvement and motivation in many departments, and so on.

There were no instances of projects being shelved. They were all found to be useful – even though in a few instances implementation took time (to many participants' frustration).

UNANTICIPATED LEARNING

In addition to the anticipated learning gains, participants reported numerous and valuable unanticipated learnings. This will come as no surprise to people who have participated in or managed action learning programmes.

This unanticipated learning was often a shift away from the learning focused on skills, behaviours and knowledge, into learning based around values, beliefs and awareness. This in itself is an interesting learning for participants, for it indicates how, when we think of learning, we so often focus initially on those more concrete items.

Of these unanticipated learnings, four stand out in particular, in that a majority of participants referred to them:

- gaining greater self-confidence
- gaining greater self-awareness
- learning to network
- learning how to communicate more effectively.

Much of this learning emerged from the way the sets worked, and from the participants' increased ability to apply those same methods elsewhere. When asked, 'How did you learn?', many participants replied: 'By being pushed by the set', 'By overcoming my fear', 'By taking a plunge', 'By being asked questions I was avoiding' and 'By stopping to reflect more.'

Some found that helping others in the set was a major step towards their own learning, as was simply listening to others working hard on their own issues, and using the spaces and silences to think and reflect. One set, in two consecutive meetings, listed what they were learning:

- 'We're asking more challenging questions.'
- 'We're giving each other better and more direct feedback.'
- 'We're asking more "how" [process] questions, and not simply "what" [content] questions.'
- 'We're sharing more of the things that go wrong.'
- 'We're placing our questions more into a context, rather than firing from the hip.'
- 'We're listening more to what isn't being said.'
- 'We're picking up more on unspoken feelings underlying what is being said.'

They commented that at each set meeting, they were improving.

Often, this unanticipated learning – which is powerful, and is where much of the change in participants occurs – is left undocumented except in personal diaries or learning reports (if the programme asks for them). It will in part, of course, be captured at the end of set meetings, when time is given over to reflection and sharing of insights on the day's meeting, and also in part be captured by colleagues and managers who notice change, and by set members who see the personal transformations as they occur.

It is worth reiterating comments that participants made.

INCREASED SELF-CONFIDENCE

Almost everyone mentioned this. The range of manifestations of this greater self-confidence that emerged is striking: from something as simple as giving a presentation and offering their own ideas to taking on new tasks and having the confidence to disagree (see Figure 8.2).

Participants talked of developing the confidence to be themselves, to admit to feelings, to have, as one of them put it: 'the confidence to say I don't feel confident'.

Others talked of confidence in their own views and opinions, and thus to feel able to challenge what they were told. 'I'm prepared to be controversial,' said one. 'I know I don't have to accept blindly what I'm told to do – I can and do go back and redefine issues,' said another.

> I'm more forthright. I'm not afraid of saying what I think, even to my manager. It's given me the confidence to disagree constructively, and as he gets louder so I just quietly repeat my disagreements.

> I've learnt not to accept blindly what I'm told, but think about it and question it – and go back with a different/better suggestion. Managers don't bite your head off. You have to do it in the right way, though.

> I'm crisper, more forthright, less amenable, more challenging – and my manager and colleagues have remarked on this. Before, when my manager suggested something which I thought was ludicrous or outrageous, I wasn't able to respond – through fear and doubts. That's gone.

> I'm more confident, and my boss has more confidence in me. He's delegated a larger budget to me, and asked me to prepare a report for him – for the board.

Others felt relieved that they could admit to not knowing everything, to having gaps in their knowledge, to not having instant solutions or answers to problems posed or questions asked – even to having made mistakes!

> I don't feel I always have to be good at something – or even everything. I can say I don't know – and that's OK. I know I'm good at certain things.

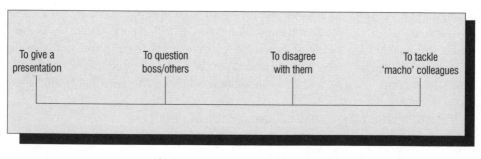

| To give a presentation | To question boss/others | To disagree with them | To tackle 'macho' colleagues |

Figure 8.2   A spectrum of confidence

I can now admit to having made a mistake – to be honest, in fact. That's what's required in the set. From that I also learnt the confidence not to be overly diplomatic, conciliatory or accepting.

Another participant talked of: 'listening to my own "inner voice" more – call it gut or intuition, but I know what should be done or said because I have an inner voice that tells me ... Only before, I'd ignore it, until someone else confirmed what I was thinking.'

With this new confidence often went what many referred to as a change in thinking: 'The mind set changes – and your thinking becomes more positive.'

It increased my confidence that I could tackle and resolve any problem I was presented with. Before I'd have shied away and thought 'Oh no.' Now I feel positive.

If I'm faced with a problem, I say, 'Right, I'll take it away and consider it.' Before, my reaction was 'Oh no,' and negative. So it's a subtle change, but actually a very powerful one. It's to do with: 'I may choose not to do X, but I know I can do X.'

I now discuss real work issues with colleagues. Before, I bottled them up and had merely superficial chats or discussions with them – even if they were work-related issues. Or I'd sit with a problem ... or avoid it.

And then there were more elusive examples of growing confidence: 'I can cope with silences. I no longer have to fill them,' said one. Another felt she had acquired 'the confidence to work with time – not to always be rushing', and a third that: 'I don't readily accept others' accusations, or feel guilty if something doesn't work out, or isn't successful or has failed.'

I always had good ideas, and would mention them to others, or at meetings, but they were never noticed. Now I repeat or say things more forcibly. I also didn't know how to react when people said 'no' to me, or disagreed. I now have a wider repertoire of responses ... the set helped me with that.

An older manager grinned: 'I've learnt more in the past eighteen months on the programme than in the last twenty years. I participate more in meetings, I stand my ground, and my manager is now giving me much more responsibility.'

AN INCREASED AWARENESS ABOUT MYSELF AND HOW I LEARN

This aspect of learning, probably more than any other, came as a result of the amount of emphasis that was placed during the programmes on reflecting and learning – and not simply on actions. Reflecting, in this instance, as one participant put it, is 'making an honest assessment'.

The source for this emphasis was normally the set adviser – at least initially. Once sets became more accustomed to stopping to check on what they were learning, such awareness began to emerge as part of each participant's 'story'. For some, it became the main focus:

> I have discovered that I learn best in a social environment where others are willing to share their learning experiences ... sharing in this way adds a richness to the learning, by hearing others' views, and making the experiences more memorable ... I have also learnt that by allocating serious thinking time to reflection on action and all that is involved has made me more aware. In particular I have seen patterns in my own behaviour. This has made me better equipped to question my behaviour, and to adjust it if necessary.

Thus, for one participant, 'The light bulbs went on.' Another observed: 'It brings you conscious awareness. It makes your brain work at a different level and speed.' A third commented: 'It's taught me to be honest with myself, and see my emotions as part – a valid part – of the picture. So if I'm genuinely feeling frightened, threatened, hassled or uneasy ... that's part of the equation and needs to be looked at, as well as what's causing the feelings.'

Others became aware of how and when they learn: 'I've learnt that I learn best when I'm challenged by others. I have a tendency to dismiss things quickly.' Another spoke of the realization that 'learning is evolutionary. I now expect to learn from every situation I'm in.'

Several remarked: 'Challenging others can be developmental – both for them and you.' One or two found that 'Only when you admit you're stuck can others help you.'

Some saw awareness as linked to the benefits of 'being my natural self' – not playing games, and not pretending or, as one or two put it, 'wearing a mask'.

'I've learnt to be my natural self – to be direct, friendly, blunt when necessary,' said one participant. Another commented: 'It's created a radical change in how I operate – it was very personally challenging. The onus is on you as a person, rather than you as a role player, and it resonates with how you want to be.' And a younger participant remarked: 'It's taken away my naivety.'

Some became more pragmatic as a result: 'A bad experience is simply that – just one bad experience. It needs to be reflected on, but not colour one's subsequent actions or beliefs.'

HOW TO NETWORK, AND USE OTHERS AS A VALUABLE RESOURCE

Learning how to network was a major gain for most participants. Many had not considered doing so before, for a variety of reasons – the most commonly stated were fear, scepticism as to the value, and 'Never thought of it.' Experiencing the value of working closely with others, in the set, often from different functions to their own, proved to be an eye-opener for most participants. The support of the set also encouraged those who were nervous of the idea of networking to try it out.

Furthermore, participants gained a better understanding of each others' work, and of the work of the organization as a whole. And they were able to provide each other with access to even wider networks through their own contacts.

As a result, many discovered a new confidence about networking:

I lost my fear of approaching people. I may still be apprehensive, but I know that if I'm clear about what I want, it'll be fine. I had to go to talk to senior managers as part of my project. It forced me to network, particularly with those senior people, as well as with the marketing department which I'd always been a bit scared of (I'm only a scientific researcher)! But I realized I had as much knowledge as them, and as much ability as others, and it gave me a great sense of my own 'power'.

I've realized how much help others can – and are willing to – give you. I'd always feared people would be dismissive or would find excuses.

Networking also gave participants a wider picture of their company (particularly if they were participating on an in-company programme), and helped them begin to understand 'how things hang together'. The majority felt more committed as a result, simply because they understood better:

Networking broadens your perspective, widens your horizons and gives you the bigger picture. I think more laterally now.

In our set, we've had people from different departments, and you see them grappling with different problems, and you begin to have much more understanding of them and their problems. Also, communication is bad in our company, so the set is making up for it. We can now pick up the phone to so many people in different parts of the company – and they can give us contacts beyond – so it's tentacles spreading out further.

Another participant was more philosophical: 'Managers, on the whole, are somehow meant to know, to be aware of what's happening elsewhere in the company, only there's often no mechanism for this to happen, merely informal contacts and lots of "technology", as if the existence of this technology means things happen differently. But after action learning, and when you know other people, maybe the technological wires will hum more.'

One Dutch set, which began after a residential programme, ran for several months without a set adviser, and at the end of their 'programme' listed the following thoughts on what they had gained and learnt (reproduced with kind permission of Tricia Lustig and her colleagues, Lasa Management Training):

- 'It enables me to hold up a mirror and see what I am doing.'
- 'I have to order the case (project report) in order to explain it, which is good for me as it helps me to see things more clearly.'
- 'Questions! The questions are fantastic and really help us to think things out. Quite often questions we would not have thought of ourselves.'
- 'When we don't see the forest for the trees, explaining the case to someone else, together with their questions, helps us to regain perspective again.'
- 'We all have different experiences which we can share.'
- 'It gives me freedom to think, to be inspired.'
- 'It's a wonderful mental game.'
- 'You come out stronger than when you went in.'

- 'All the wonderful hints we get from one another!'
- 'Our self-confidence and self-esteem increases after each session.'
- 'We role-play different scenarios so that when the day comes, the right scenario gets played out.'
- 'Support from all the group members. This is not just that we are friends. We call each other regularly to check progress, and if someone is having a difficult time we will make sure one of the others speaks to him/her at least once a week.'
- 'This is a group of people who really listen to what I have to say.'
- 'It gives an opportunity to look into other companies and other sectors, a sort of benchmarking.'
- 'Friendship.'
- 'Learning both from one another and together in a synergy where we learn quicker and better.'
- 'We define concrete "truths" which can be used again and again.'
- 'We can distil a lot out of the notes we took at previous meetings; they are still relevant, even several years later. Still right on the mark.'
- 'Core competences.'
- 'Shared learning experiences.'
- 'It gives the ability to look at a case as an outsider, objectively.'
- 'We all read different things, so we keep each other informed about interesting developments in management and such.'
- 'We create more effective processes.'
- 'We always discuss learning points, both individually and as a group.'

COMMUNICATING MORE EFFECTIVELY

On the whole, what struck participants was how valuable it was to simply listen and relate questions to what the speaker was trying to do, rather than cutting across or going off at tangents – in other words, having a genuine dialogue with another person.

'It's taught me to listen, and not just to hear,' was a comment almost everyone made in one way or another. 'I now really talk to others,' was something many also remarked on: 'Action learning forced me to talk in a way I had never talked before.'

Often, participants described how difficult it was to really listen, and understand, and ask for clarification.

Responding to questions, rather than answering them – not feeling the need to give reasons or justifications, but rather using questions as an invitation to reflect – was another major learning that many participants commented on. It made them feel less pressurized and reactive.

And then there was the giving and receiving of feedback – and seeing that as useful, rather than as criticism. As several participants said wishfully, they would welcome such openness at work.

One phrase that seemed to sum up much of what participants were saying about the value of better communication was: 'The more you share, the more you learn.'

One participant's lasting impressions of action learning included:

- being challenged by questions to honestly review situations as they are
- listening to other people's experiences
- sharing knowledge and techniques and examples of their implementations (practical solutions)
- the caring and support of the set, which helped me through difficult situations.

He went on to say:

> The process is less disruptive than a course, as it allows you to actively work on issues and reflect during the process, and does not deflect your attention as on some courses, where action planning and reflection only happen on your return to work. The key learning from the programme for me was:
>
> - Managing myself is as key as managing resources.
> - Development is all about taking actions, not just understanding theories.
> - Sharing problems and concerns allows you to better visualize situations and plan/develop appropriate actions.
> - Good facilitation is key to effective group work
> - Reflection is one of the key tools to development.
>
> I am looking to use action learning within the new organization I will be joining soon. Its first use will be within the development programme for first-line supervisors, where I see it supporting a current education programme.

SOME PARTICIPANTS FELT THEY HAD GAINED LITTLE

Of those I interviewed, five individuals said they had learnt little; they were unhappy, disillusioned, and felt the exercise had been a waste of time. Three others were non-committal. Two of these admitted they had come on the programme to investigate whether action learning had any use back in their organizations. Although both had gained, they were unsure about its value for their organizations.

The five who were unhappy identified the reasons as follows:

- no confidentiality in the set
- lack of interest and 'empathy' with the action learning process, in particular with the set
- incompetent and unhelpful set advising
- irrelevance of the 'group' project to that individual's work
- unhelpful set members
- their own emotional state
- the nature of the project.

The three who were unsure identified various sources of their disquiet: it was too vague; it might be more useful with everyone from the same function; the project chosen by one participant had focused on an issue in which she alone was powerless to influence the company in the direction she wanted (both these latter individuals were in mixed-company sets, and I couldn't help wondering if their views would have been different if they had been on in-company sets).

VERY SENIOR MANAGERS' EXPERIENCES

One group of participants – the more senior managers and managing directors – warrant separate attention, because the programmes they attend are focused slightly differently: such senior people do not work on defined projects in the way that more junior participants tend to. Rather, their responsibilities for the organizations they manage become their 'projects', so they each came with the anticipation of discussing issues of strategies, decisions, relationships, and any attendant questions, dilemmas, worries, and so on.

Because such senior managers have few if any 'peers' in the organizations they manage, they normally participate in mixed-company sets. This is the only feasible – and safe – way they feel able to discuss their problems, and 'gain from our cumulative wisdom', as one put it. Another chief executive said: 'Many of us have got these senior positions by convincing others we can walk on water!'

One managing director remarked: 'Action learning is a management development process. The issues you bring are ones of the moment, and usually inter-personal ones. The people you might have been able to discuss issues with are often precisely the ones you are having difficulties with.'

WHAT DID VERY SENIOR PEOPLE GAIN FROM SUCH PROGRAMMES?

Asked what they had gained and learnt, and what they were now doing differently back at work, they talked of benefiting from working openly with a forum of peers, valuing time to take stock – a time for themselves, a place to admit to doubts, a place to be challenged, and a place to share and to hear others.

The brief accounts below give some flavour of the insights and learning, although, as always, there were some dissenting voices. One managing director felt that the set was too polite. She described how, in 'this gathering of competitive, high-achievers', she was concerned that at one meeting she had 'let myself down by talking about a particular issue that concerns me'. She went on to ponder whether this emphasis on sharing, useful though it was, didn't in fact encourage a slight veneer of civilization: 'We rarely go for each other's jugular. Much as I appreciate people who are prepared to reveal themselves in this setting, I still sometimes think I might not like them in other situations. Is something "real" missing from sets?'

A time to be 'me' and 'human': To step out of role

At the outset, they valued the time and space to be themselves. Many talked of the pressures of being 'at the top' and not being able to be 'human': 'It's an opportunity to meet on human terms – not in a role. At work, I sometimes forget I'm human, too!' laughed one senior woman executive.

Another talked of having to sustain an image at work: 'There is a perceived image of people at the top being totally confident. But we're full of doubt.' The set allows these doubts to be voiced and explored: 'I was comforted, and surprised, that all these other managing directors and chief executives are not super-human.' It had given one chief executive the opportunity to see that other very senior people were not necessarily 'all brilliantly successful, and only me struggling ... I've discovered that's not the case.'

One senior manager's response to the question 'What aspects of action learning do you value in particular?' was:

> One aspect is that the reporting back to the set can be quite searching, *if* the set is doing its job and being challenging (a very big 'if'). You ought not to be able to get away with doing a snow job, and the weakness of your position – if it is weak – should become apparent and give you the opportunity to rethink. Better to be exposed among friends than when you go public!
>
> The second aspect is the insights you get while working on someone else's problem. It is almost as if when you are the focus of the slot, you are so busy giving and receiving information, responding to questions and 'defending' your position that there is no opportunity to reflect. However, I get some of my most creative insights when it is someone else's slot and I find there is time to reflect during the comparative eddies and back-currents surrounding the work on someone else's problem. I frequently scribble things down which I pick up on later.

A managing director felt that the most important lessons he learnt were:

- Managing yourself is as important as managing others.
- Development is all about taking actions, and not just understanding theories.
- Sharing problems and concerns allows you to better visualize situations and plan/develop appropriate actions.
- Good facilitation is vital to effective group work.
- Reflection is one of the key tools in development.

Taking action learning back into the organization

> The set was fascinating – a great mix of people, including the contrast of an army guy who did everything by numbers and a psychiatrist who was very reflective.
>
> We discussed mainly professional issues – although the psychiatrist did once bring up the issue of having only seen his wife three times in the past fourteen days.
>
> For me, it was interesting because it brought so many different perspectives to each issue. There were some crunch points on which I was stuck and looking for guidance. We

195

spent ninety minutes at one meeting on my issue, and it was really helpful. I began to find myself thinking, 'I want to discuss such-and-such an issue with my set.' It helped me particularly with group work – as a senior manager, so much of my work is group-based, with me chairing. I know I gained confidence from seeing that everyone else was in the same confusion and muddle as me. But I feel that less senior people on the teams are now more responsive than they used to be.

And the luxury – and benefit – of having one problem on the table at a time, with the space to tackle it! I've introduced this idea back into our organization. I'm getting people to work in small groups and run our projects on action learning lines. The time and the rigours of action learning are particularly useful. More thought and effort now goes into our initial exploration of questions, into the preparation, things are more focused, better designed, and commitment to our projects is greater, because it's given people more opportunity to go into more depth.

We've extracted, and used, some core elements: an initial question is floated in, the group looks at it and reshapes it, then we design our next steps ... an action learning approach.

Gaining and learning from others' experiences and perspectives

I'm a one-company man with no experience of other companies or other industries. What I've learnt is that the more you talk to others, the more you realize there are the same basic threads and themes ... which comes as a great comfort! You realize you're not, after all, working for the worst company!

The other set members ask you searching questions that colleagues might never find the guts to ask you, or aren't able to because of my seniority, and fear of how I might react. So I have a chance to explore, and exchange experiences and get second opinions. The decisions are still mine, but I've not damaged people in the process. I have little to lose by such an opportunity, and much to gain. I know I've come to decisions differently.

The programme also forms part of my time for *me* – to step back from everyday things that drive me, and take stock. I can use the set to experiment and try things out ... without crossing boundaries with people I work with every day ... and then I can walk away from the set. But at the next meeting, I update them – which is important, because that way we learn from everyone, not just our own stories.

However, for this to work, you do need a professional facilitator – knowledgeable about processes, and sensitive as well.

I'm now watching people more carefully, and listening to what's being said, and don't assume that everyone is agreeing with me. When you're the boss, you can sometimes think they're nodding like dogs – but now I know they're not. I look for signals over and above the words. I'm more aware of my effect on people, especially as I'm very task-oriented, and can tend to forget others.

The managing director of a small engineering company talked of expecting the programme he attended to 'sharpen up my thinking', which it had done. Moreover, he said it had completely changed it: 'I now appreciate the complex symbiosis between me and the business. I realize that business growth requires other skills besides analytical ability, and that building relationships is very important.'

THREE CASE EXAMPLES

A CROSS-COMPANY PROGRAMME FOR MANAGING DIRECTORS OF SMALL BUSINESSES

This programme was the result of a group of managing directors of small businesses (with up to 75 staff) asking for something more than a one- or two-day course, since they had found that there was not enough transfer of learning back into work. Their prime goals were to work on their own business strategies, but they wanted a confidential environment in which to do so. They resisted an expert consultant, and were looking for something 'practical'.

The set adviser, who designed the programme, was himself the managing director of a small business – a necessary credibility, he felt, with this particular group, for although he avoided giving advice (true to action learning principles), he was able to ask the pertinent questions.

The six managing directors came from a chemical company, graphic printing company, an IT training company, an engineering production company, a plant company, and a company running homes for adults with behaviour difficulties.

The issues they worked on were: investment decisions; marketing strategies; recruitment and motivation of staff, and everyday problems and quandaries that they felt they could not share with anyone in their own companies: 'Managers at the top are a lonely group of people ... It's difficult to admit to weaknesses or to not knowing ... so this forum gave them a structured approach to resolving what was worrying them. Besides, managers in small business are all interested in what others are doing, how they are coping and resolving problems ... Action learning provides a way of looking over the fence.' If individuals wanted any information or formal 'input', they either went on a short course, read appropriate literature, or asked whether someone in the group had some relevant experience.

A PROGRAMME FOR REDUNDANT/UNEMPLOYED SENIOR MANAGERS

There were just four members of this set: a managing director, a finance director, a human resources director and a training and development manager. The goal of each was to become 'employable'. They worked on their needs, their desires, their dreams, their values, as well as their skills, and 'reality out there'. The ex-managing director had a massive debt that needed to be addressed; the finance director was feeling very hurt and angry; the human resources director was an older man, but wanted to continue in some form of work, and the training manager wanted to become self-employed.

By the end of the programme, the human resources director had become a steward at a racecourse (always a secret wish of his!); the managing director had received three offers of work, but had in the mean time decided that the quality of his life – and where he wished to live – were as important as simply finding a job, any job; the training manager had become self-employed; and the finance director was becoming involved in venture capital schemes.

A 'SMALL TOWN' PROGRAMME STILL AT THE 'IDEAS' STAGE

Many small towns are experiencing economic and social problems, partly because of the drift of people to larger cities, and partly because of the building of out-of-town shopping centres. Revitalizing town centres is a major aim.

The plan was to gather together a small number of such small towns, identify who within them has the interest, power and authority to bring about change, either through undertaking actions, or influencing others (Revans's classic trio of identifying 'who knows, who cares, and who can'), and to create an action learning set from those interested in beginning to resolve this common problem.

NOTES

[1] Adapted from M.C. Goldberg (1998) *The Art of the Question*, New York: John Wiley.
[2] M. Belbin (1981) *Management Teams*, London: Heinemann.

9 Overcoming some reservations

As discussed in Chapter 8, some participants did not find action learning useful, and mentioned a number of problems which those involved in action learning have met on various occasions. The trick is to ensure that, where possible, they do not occur. It is also important to recognize that some organizations are not yet ready for, or may not be suited to, action learning, with its questioning processes and democratic values, and that some individuals will be unsuited to it, for temperamental or other reasons.

SOME FREQUENT RESERVATIONS

It's too time-consuming.

This will often be the case when the project or task is not directly related to a participant's work. Where it is, it becomes a part of participants' everyday tasks, is linked to their own developmental needs, and hence is likely to be considered less 'time-consuming'.

It seems to advocate a matrix-type of organization, but most organizations – ours included – are hierarchical.

This is true! But it offers skills to deal better with hierarchical impedimenta.

It's too nice and cosy – not challenging enough. This company is largely run by macho managers. Our department seems to be different, but we're not typical.

Many participants do not see action learning as sufficiently challenging. Several say that set members are too anxious to be supportive. However, a good set adviser will ensure there are challenges, even if set members try to avoid them. If anything, action learning challenges participants in ways that they have not been challenged before. And challenge should not be confused with being confrontational – the latter may be less useful.

However, there is some truth that if participants are self-selecting, more macho and aggressive people are less likely to put themselves forward, because they will be less in sympathy with action learning's values and philosophy.

> We didn't seem to move on. Maybe it was because we were all engineers.

Some sets may have trouble in developing new ways of working together, of asking questions, and changing their mind-sets – their way of looking at things – particularly if they all come from the same discipline or function. This is why it is often useful to have mixed-discipline and mixed-functional sets.

> It's too vague for money-minded managers. Its benefits are not concrete enough – too hit and miss, not specific enough.

Action merely to create action, regardless, is something that action learning tries to redress. And using money as the sole or even the most important criterion by which to judge progress is a journey on the road to disaster in the long term. It is true that not all the benefits of action learning are instantly visible, since learning and changing are not instant. But its results are concrete, although they may not always be easy to spell out in advance. The same criticism can, of course, also be levelled at any taught course or programme, but the value of action learning is its broad remit.

However, it is precisely concerns such as these which have led many who introduce what they call 'action learning programmes', to focus mainly on the 'action' and ignore the other elements. The question then is: in what way do such programmes differ from, say, project-management programmes?

> It needs some taught inputs to really catch on.

Many programmes do include some, but only where it is strictly relevant to the programme's aims, and often at the request of participants who identify a need. But care should be taken that such taught input does not take over the programme, and push the action learning to the sidelines.

One way to link action learning to taught courses is to build in the action learning as an integral part of a programme – an opportunity to test out what really *is* being learnt!

> It claims to change culture – which it would do. But you'd have to involve everyone – in particular senior managers – and they back away.

True, it can change culture, and several organizations have used it as first step in this direction. And although if senior managers do not initially become 'actively' involved, small changes can occur among staff, and filter upwards. Ideally, though, culture changes need to start at the top.

> It doesn't seem to help with the politics that infest most organizations.

It does, and it doesn't. It can't remove politics, because where there are people, there will usually be politics. But it does give participants a greater understanding of it, and some tools for working around it. For a start, set members can form a network, and create their own 'political' grouping of those who want to change things!

> It advocates sharing, but doesn't address the other individualistic and competitive aspects in most organizations: the reward system, primarily.

It will do, if those designing and supporting the programme have the courage to address these individualistic and competitive issues in the projects worked on by participants.

> The problem is, we've created a working environment in the set, and we've worked on projects – been given responsibility – but when we get back to work, it won't be like that.

This is undoubtedly true in many organizations. But a well-designed and managed programme will have made clear to those who send participants on it that they will not get back the same people who were sent on the programme. Indeed, many participants do get promotion after such programmes – either through their own initiative or because they are now ready to tackle new challenges. Organizations which fail to recognize the changes that have occurred will probably sooner or later lose valuable employees.

10 The future of action learning

Action learning has its devotees, and those who decry it. Yet it is – after some years on the sidelines of management development and training – coming back to a point at which it is, if not exactly centre-stage, then at least widely recognized for what it has to offer. In fact, one journal recently stated: 'Action learning is the latest buzzword in training.' In the mid-1990s, some fifty articles on action learning were published in business and management journals alone.

Its role in the workplace has been the main focus of this book, and it has a continued future there, as organizations – those edifices which control the destinies of those who work within them – are constantly seeking to create ways of involving staff, giving them an opportunity to contribute, to gain a sense of achievement during the eight or so hours per day spent at work. As organizations set about dismantling some of the old hierarchical structures, adapt to new market demands and face competition worldwide, there may be further opportunities for action learning. But action learning also has much to offer outside the workplace (see pages 208–210).

DOES ACTION LEARNING MOVE US CLOSER TO CREATING LEARNING ORGANIZATIONS?

Yes, it would appear to do so. The concept of the learning organization has been around for a number of years, and a number of the progenitors of this elusive idea are themselves action learners, no doubt influenced in some of their thinking by their experiences of action learning.

Thus, in *The Learning Company*, the authors state:

> In a learning company managers see their primary task as facilitating members' experimentation and learning from experience. It is normal to take time out to seek feedback, to obtain data to aid understanding. Senior managers give a lead in questioning their own ideas, attitudes and actions. Mistakes are allowed – if not exactly encouraged – for it is recognized that we will never learn if we don't try out new ideas, new ways of doing

things, and these won't always work. We need to recognize that there is no such thing as a failed experiment – as long as we learn from it. (Pedler, Burgoyne and Boydell 1991)

Peter Senge, in his book *The Fifth Discipline*, says: 'organisations learn only through individuals who learn. Individual learning does not guarantee organisational learning'. What is important is team learning, which he claims starts with 'dialogue', the capacity of members of a team to suspend assumptions and enter into a genuine thinking together, where the dialogue enables the group to discover insights not attainable individually, as well as the patterns of defensiveness that undermine not only how the team operates, but how it learns. Much of this sounds familiar to those acquainted with action learning. And 'personal mastery', the life-long process and discipline which is the cornerstone of Senge's learning organization, is, as he puts it: 'the phrase my colleagues and I use for the discipline of personal growth and learning ... People with a high level of personal mastery are acutely aware of their ignorance, their incompetence, their growth areas' (Senge 1992, pp. 238–248).

And Bob Garratt, in an article entitled 'The power of action learning', states that action learning:

> is a very powerful organisational tool for the reform of working systems and the subsequent restating of organisational objectives. Its power derives from releasing and reinterpreting the accumulated experiences of the people who comprise the organisation. The combination of this released energy and the act of moving the authority for problem solving to those people who must live with the consequences is a deliberate devolution of organisational power. (Garratt 1997)

Other writers seem to concur. They talk of the trust that is needed; the particular 'energy' that comes from an organization becoming a complex of individual energies flowing together; and a re-evaluating of the notions of power and politics, to take a different approach to tensions and conflicts. One (who is also an action learner) has a metaphor for a learning organization:

> a building entirely constructed of glass, a 'crystal palace', airy and spacious, into which streams light of a pale and piercing quality. A feeling of spaces replaces that of claustrophobia, a feeling that I could spread my arms wide and take a deep breath. Since the building is made of glass it is entirely transparent and I can see through into other rooms where others live and work. This transparency encourages me to think that there is nowhere in this building that I cannot go and nowhere where I would not be welcomed. (Phillips 1994)

All these descriptions ring bells for action learners. The values and vocabulary are so similar. Action learning may well be a powerful way of creating a learning organization. And participants' experiences of action learning back up these more 'academic' musings.

Gareth Morgan talks of creativity and innovation thriving, and systems having shared meanings, where there is 'ambiguity, uncertainty, questioning, risk ... openness, quest and challenge' – words immediately recognizable to action learners.

However, he also raises a note of caution: 'You can't create a learning organization. But you can enhance people's capacities to learn and align their activities in a creative way' (Morgan 1997). Further, he warns that you can't make massive changes all at once. Incremental changes are what each and every one of us can make, and he maintains that we can each 'leverage' 15 per cent of our work – we have sufficient control or authority over only 15 per cent of what we do in order to bring about change. The rest is too bound up with other people and systems to be over-ruled simply by ourselves.

Returning to action learning: each of the six or seven members of the ideal set is, in a sense, 15 per cent of the whole set. Between them, even as each only attempts to change their own attainable 15 per cent – be it their behaviours, assumptions and beliefs, or the procedures they work with, or structures within which they work – they will be achieving much more in organizational terms because of the learning ethos within the set. Take a number of such sets in an organization, and you begin to have a movement – and maybe a real cultural change!

LEARNING BEHAVIOURS FOR A LEARNING ORGANIZATION

Peter Honey (1994) has defined what he thinks are the ten learning behaviours that organizations need to have present in their culture and their staff, if they are to become learning organizations. Those behaviours are (and many would happily fit into Morgan's 15 per cent):

- asking questions
- suggesting ideas
- exploring options
- taking risks/experimenting
- being open about the way it is
- converting mistakes into learning
- reflecting and reviewing
- talking about learning
- taking responsibility for your own learning and development
- admitting to inadequacies and mistakes.

Many of these sound remarkably similar to behaviours that participants on the action learning programmes in my survey claim to have learnt! Action learning is a step towards a learning organization because it develops people who:

- listen
- question themselves and others
- have a sense of self-awareness and confidence
- are willing to be open

- are willing and able to share, and to learn with and from others
- value and respect others
- understand the value of networking
- have a sense of energy, of being motivated, and wanting to achieve
- are aware of their own, and others', ability to change and develop.

I would add one further quality – what Peter Honey and Alan Mumford have called 'being an opportunistic learner' – someone who learns from any situation they find themselves in. Action learning certainly develops opportunistic learners. In the words of one manager quoted earlier: 'I've realized that everything is data from which I can learn.'

In addition, participants in action learning acquire two other important skills that are indispensable to an organization that is using all the accumulated experience of its staff:

- an increased ability to network
- recognition of the need for – and valuing – time and space to stop and reflect.

Of course, these behaviours alone do not create a learning company. What is also needed is a will to use them: a culture which genuinely values them, structures which encourage them, systems that reward them, and opportunities that will call for them. Many participants doubted whether their organizations could or would reach this stage.

But where organizations are willing to take the step, the model of the set could be a beginning – for in many ways the set is a learning company in microcosm. The way it values every member, allows airspace, gives space for thinking, reflecting and sharing, acknowledges mistakes as much as success in order to learn from both, builds people's confidence and self-awareness, and encourages a generally democratic and hence 'flat', non-hierarchical, non-authoritarian type of organization – these are all elements that a learning company needs. Can small beginnings lead to greater things?

WHAT ARE THE IDEAL QUALITIES OF OPPORTUNISTIC LEARNERS?

Action learning aims to develop opportunistic learners, who:

- can describe the learning process
- review experience
- recall details
- share experiences
- respond flexibly
- invest effort in learning
- ask questions

- listen patiently
- express thoughts
- are open to new angles
- identify their own development needs
- convert ideas into actions
- take risks
- see connections
- adjust to the new/unfamiliar
- are intrigued by criticism, and convert it into suggestions for improvement
- ask for feedback
- accept responsibility for themselves
- accept all situations as learning opportunities
- believe you're never too old to learn
- explore alternatives
- accept praise
- analyse successes, as well as mistakes
- feel exhilarated by change
- sit and think – without guilt or rush
- cope with ambiguity
- feel confident with strangers.

For more on opportunistic learners, see Honey and Mumford (1995).

OTHER ORGANIZATIONAL OPPORTUNITIES

There are other opportunities for action learning processes to be used in organizations. Here are just three instances.

Companies working in different cultures across the world need to help their staff understand and work with different behaviours and expectations: bringing them into action learning sets to listen and learn, and go away to practice new ways of doing things could ease what are often initially fraught and unhappy encounters.

Companies are becoming more involved in the needs of the communities in which they are based, offering their staff's expertise, or simply their time and energy. One merchant bank, for instance, gave its employees a day off every few months to work for a charity which created sports opportunities for deprived inner-city children. This could in turn have been an opportunity to bring those who volunteered together with the 'youngsters', to share with each other their feelings and insights, and maybe seeing how they could continue to play – and work – together, and learn.

Information overload is creating worries and stress among an increasing number of people. As we begin to drown in information, more technology is not necessarily the answer. People increasingly need an environment in which they can acknowledge their inability to absorb – let alone process – all the information and knowledge that is around, while simultaneously coping with the time pressures imposed by 'downsizing'. They need to be given space to seek insights from others, and be helped with asking the right questions – to be given 'permission to not know', if they are to avoid ever higher levels of stress. The sharing and co-operation of action learning is one way forward.

OPEN SPACE AND ACTION LEARNING

Open space has become an increasingly popular form of group exploration – often as part of more traditional conferences. But in contrast to traditional 'presentations', it is a space to which participants come with questions and uncertainties, saying: 'I don't know how to ...' or 'I'd like to explore ...'. It offers an opportunity to have a focused, questioning type of discussion with a group of people who have expressed an interest in exploring a subject. It offers the focal person in particular, but others as well, suggestions about how to pursue the ideas generated during the exploration.

It is in this admission of not knowing, and in the emphasis on asking questions, that open space resembles the ethos of action learning. Action learning's stress on questioning and on supportive challenge, avoiding the giving of advice, might be a useful adjunct. The two activities could also be blended in an interesting way by adding action learning on, so to speak, after an open space gathering: participants could pursue the ideas generated as the basis of a project to work on and bring to the set.

OTHER APPLICATIONS OF ACTION LEARNING

It must by now be clear to most readers that action learning has much wider applications than simply in our working lives. Below are a few examples.

One of its earliest applications was to explore the needs and wishes of a community in a housing estate in Melbourne, Australia. Those taking part were residents who between them decided on the type of environment they would like to live in, and established the means of beginning to create such a community. More recently, a similar approach was explored in a landlord–tenant relationship (Goldberg 1998).

Reg Revans himself introduced the idea into a school – again in Australia – where it became known as the 'Q factor'. The headmaster wrote: 'Everyone [is] amazed that we have no school rules nor any vandalism. Why is it, they ask, that so many staff members are involved far beyond their job descriptions and work long hours without remuneration? ... The answer is action learning ... [and] the upward communication of doubt in our administrative style.' The head girl added: 'in order for the school to run efficiently and effectively there needs to be a lot of team work, not just between the students themselves, but between the students and the teachers. There needs to be mutual respect and co-operation' (*IFAL Newsletter*, 1992, vol. 11, no. 2).

Even parents have discovered that working with other parents can help to cope with the difficulties of, say, bringing up teenage children – and it doesn't have to be called 'action learning'. Parents have met to discuss the 'hows' of parenting: how to cope with the mess they leave around the house; how to communicate with adolescents who have mood swings; how to cope with that minefield, the curfew? Too often, parents said, they had felt alone, with no one to discuss their everyday problems and challenges. In groups, as they reported on how they coped at home, and tried out new methods, parents discovered that what was important was to: 'listen , really listen, to your children, but also to yourself and your partner ... [In the group,] I was listened to and acknowledged, I could sort out my ideas. It opened up all sorts of avenues to doing things differently.' Another parent discovered: 'There are no magical answers, no right or wrong ways of doing things.'

Groups of women wanting to return to work have found regular meetings with one another helpful. From initially sharing their fears of not having any skills and abilities (and not realizing that running a household is a highly skilled administrative task!), they move on to discussing how they can each tackle the search for work, the interviews, how they can brush up on old skills, or learn new ones, how to find childcare help, and a hundred other relevant issues.

In Tanzania, many small businesses run by men and women – often simple market stalls by the roadside – have formed themselves into self-help organizations (SHOs) to work on issues they all face, such as: how to reduce the influence of the powerful old, ultra-conservative man; learning to deal with officials; how to protect their space; caring for the sick in their families; holding funds for emergencies; doing deals with confidence. Their 'set advisers' are often more experienced businessmen and businesswomen, as well as a few graduates, who in turn are also formed into action learning sets, to share their experiences with their SHOs, and to gain insights into how to help their groups further.

In all these instances, whether or not the process was called 'action learning', participants had some concrete actions to carry out between meetings, thus maintaining the importance of having a task to work on and learn from. In meetings, they gave each other individual airspace, and they spent time sharing with the group what they found useful and helpful.

The opportunities for an action learning approach are endless: anywhere where searching, questioning, doubting, needing to find new ways, using and sharing knowledge and insights, building confidence and learning to value and respect differences is needed:

Let us enquire together. In a world increasingly overwhelmed with information, we can ask learner-centred, solution-seeking questions about what to do with all we know. As learners we can join in creating an age of enquiry, rather than merely living in an age of information ... Taking advantage of the question-driven nature of choice and responsibility, we can dedicate ourselves to speak, listen, and act together in enlivening the spirit and expression of genuine community. (Goldberg 1998)

THREE CASE EXAMPLES

A LEARNING COMMUNITY EXPERIMENT IN A MAJOR LOCAL GOVERNMENT AUTHORITY

Fitting people into permanent sets was becoming increasingly difficult because of work pressures, which were resulting in non-attendance at meetings. Participants at a set meeting had the following discussion, from which emerged a new idea.

The city local authority was searching for the answer to the question, 'Who is our community?' 'What is a community,' asked one participant. 'A group or groups of people looking to make life in their local community better, or to improve things,' was one response. 'Well, isn't that what we, here, are about?' came a comment. 'So why don't we think of ourselves as a learning community?'

With about fifty people in the authority already involved in action learning programmes (and with newcomers appearing regularly), the decision was to have six community days a year, two months apart, for 'old-timers', and three for new enquirers to learn about action learning. Participants would attend community days for a morning or afternoon, and would participate in sets formed on the day, to work on a topic they each brought (as in a usual set).

INTRODUCING CULTURE CHANGE IN AN IT COMPANY

An IT company used action learning to 'change the management culture and create a more energetic, pro-active responsive environment'. The candidates chosen for the programme – just one set – were the young high-flyers (the 'blue-eyed boys and girls'), selected by senior managers.

It was not clear whether this was a trial programme, or the beginning of something larger.

The group project – the restructuring of a customer service department – was initially to be a purely 'consultative' project. However, many of the recommendations were implemented, some by the set themselves, which they themselves pointed out was a major point of learning for them. For it was only when having to implement their suggestions that they realized what they had omitted to consider, how they had ignored the insights – and needs – of people working in the department, and how unrealistic some of their targets had been.

However, the programme was fraught with problems. The set adviser was replaced in the middle of the programme because of his lack of competence. And although ostensibly a culture change programme, the participants felt they were constantly impeded in their work by 'old-style' managers who refused them access to information, were unhappy at being asked challenging questions, and generally made their life difficult. The choice of project was largely unrelated to the learning needs of the participants, and was a classic case of a senior management 'hijacking': here was a group who could work on a pet project.

At the end of the programme, the participants felt they had learnt a great deal, but the management culture remained unchanged. This is not because the culture – 'how things are done around here' – isn't an ideal candidate for an in-company action learning programme, for it is! But it must involve a wide range of people, preferably beginning with senior managers, who themselves need to change if any culture change is to be maintained.

A CULTURE CHANGE PROGRAMME IN A UNIVERSITY

A university planned to 'engage senior managers in senior management problems, with the aim of increasing managerial effectiveness and changing the culture, creating a sense of ownership'. Participants on this programme were senior departmental managers, who tackled group projects – largely of an administrative nature – with a view solely to offering recommendations. The set advisers' roles were played by departmental heads who had had minimum training, and fell back into old habits such as running sets like staff meetings.

According to the participants, the anticipated outcome was not achieved largely because there was no senior management commitment to, or participation in, the programme. Participants had the strong impression that there was little senior management cohesion. However, participants did report many insights into how to handle their own staff and departments, they learnt many new approaches to team-working with staff, and several commented that they gained useful insights into their own preferred style of management.

Many expressed their individual commitment to further management development, though at the same time they felt little engagement in senior management's problems.

11 How to design an action learning programme

This final chapter contains guidelines and notes on how to set up a programme. The guidelines assume a programme lasting approximately six months, with sets meeting for a full day on each occasion, and participants focusing on tasks and projects for their learning.

BEFORE THE PROGRAMME

If action learning is new to the organization, and to avoid being disappointed, or having participants who feel let down, the person proposing to run a programme (usually someone within Training and Development, who may also be a set adviser) should first conduct a 'diagnosis' on whether the organization is ready for action learning (see pages 18–20).

Next, to gain maximum support for – and hence benefit from – the action learning, the person proposing such a programme should:

- Understand its nature, be clear why he/she is proposing action learning, agree on the objectives for the programme, communicate them to all who are concerned and will be actively involved, and most importantly, gain the commitment of senior managers to the programme.
- Be involved in 'selecting' who will participate – who will benefit from the design, coupled with the programme's objectives and hoped-for outcomes.
- Discuss the programme and its intention with potential participants, their managers and the clients:
  - Ensure that everyone knows that the programme will last for a minimum of four to six months, and is aware of what other commitments it will involve (regular and relatively frequent set meetings, the need for projects – when they are selected – to be implemented to resolve real business needs while simultaneously meeting the learning needs of participants (and not some personal agenda of a senior manager!), and possibly a final written report).

213

- Ensure everyone understands how participants will change, and what qualities – and expectations – they will have at the end of the programme.
- Design the programme with care, being clear whether it will be part of a 'taught' programme, whether it will be a free-standing programme, whether participants will be given access to resources during the programme, such as taught inputs, books, videos, visits, or simply money which participants themselves decide how to spend.
- Determine:
  - what will be evaluated – the action implemented, the participants' development and its effects
  - how the programme will be evaluated – by written reports, by some 'bottom-line' measurement
  - by whom it will be evaluated – participants themselves, their managers, clients, or even their staff. Everyone involved then needs to be informed.
- Find a convenient location (or locations) for all set meetings, and ensure that all the necessary administrative arrangements are made (timing, rooms, food and refreshments, and so on).
- Be available to sort out any misunderstandings that may arise during the programme.
- Liaise closely with the set adviser(s).

One organizational development manager, who was involved in designing a programme for a major oil company, commented that, with hindsight, she would have formed an action learning set of those colleagues involved in working with her on the design of the programme.

PARTICIPANTS

Potential participants:

- should be selected/invited in good time, and given a brief idea of the nature of the programme, and the reason why they have been selected/invited
- may be selected/invited by their managers, by the personnel or training/development department, or by some other person who has a stake in their development; in some instances, they may self-select
- should be given the choice of participating or not
- should, by and large, if they will be working together, be of approximately the same level of responsibility; there may, however, be instances where vertical or diagonal slice sets are highly appropriate
- may be from the same function or different functions (and this may vary, depending on the objective of the programme)
- should be involved in selecting the task/project they will focus on during the programme; if they are working on a project, they should have identified it at the latest by the second set meeting.

CLIENTS AND OTHERS WHO NEED TO BE INVOLVED

Every participant (or set, if they work on a group project) needs to have a client (unless they are senior managers who are addressing their own tasks or quandaries):

- Clients should be senior managers who are in sympathy with the programme, will champion it and the participants, and step in to resolve any misunderstanding over the programme between participants and their immediate manager.
- Managers whose staff will participate in the programme need to be told what action learning is about, and be involved in selecting a project for the participant. It is crucial that they understand both the amount of time that participants may need to spend on the programme, and the commitment required from participants to attend set meetings.
- Participants need to agree with their managers and clients what their project will be, and in what way it will offer opportunities to develop themselves – they need to be clear about their intended learning. Agreeing these points should take place either just before or following an introductory day/days to action learning (see below).
- Development/training personnel, who may be instigators of a programme, may be responsible for development programmes or have some responsibility for helping individuals develop themselves, or may have identified, through assessment, individuals who would benefit from action learning.

EVALUATION

Participants need to be told how they will be evaluated. Those responsible for running the programme should therefore:

- be clear and agree on – at the beginning of the programme – what form the assessment will take – will it be by written document, project report, a learning/reflective document, or some verbal presentation; and will both 'action' and learning be assessed?
- be clear who will be carrying out the evaluation – the participants, their managers, their staff, or someone else?
- communicate all this to everyone concerned – participants, their clients, the set adviser, the participants' managers, and possibly the training/development department (if someone other than them is responsible for the programme).

INTRODUCTORY SESSIONS

At the beginning of every programme, there should always be an introduction to action learning. Such introductions may last just a few hours, others a day, yet others might include a couple of days on some team-building exercise. Those who experienced the latter said it was most useful, as it helped gel the set together.

Although on such days it is necessary to point out how working in a set differs from working in any other group, and to highlight the values that underpin action learning, some participants commented: 'There was too much theory at the beginning – all about change and projects and the philosophy of action learning.'

Clients also need to be introduced to action learning, and to their role as client to the project(s) and champions of the participants and their learning.

At the introductory session, participants and clients, and maybe even participants' managers, need to agree – if this is feasible – on the intention and scope of the project(s), and on the focus of the learning. It may be helpful if the clients for some programmes attend part of the participants' introductory days, to publicly agree to their project.

Introductory sessions should involve:

- a brief (one- or two-hour) introduction to action learning
- a short experience of it; if the numbers are small, participants can go into sets; if there are more than six or seven, a fishbowl or 'triad' exercise is a good alternative (see below)
- possibly other elements, such as mind maps (useful for mapping out participants' relationships); lifelines (for focusing participants on their most effective learning experiences to date, and what they involved); transactional analysis (to alert them to how certain behaviours trigger complementary behaviours in others), or brainstorming (to show the benefits of group creative thinking).
- if the purpose of the programme is to build team-working, an outdoor exercise, and maybe an introduction to Belbin's nine team roles (see pages 176–177)
- Honey and Mumford's Learning Styles Questionnaire (see pages 44–47).

A Myers-Briggs Questionnaire for participants is another useful tool (for those qualified to administer it).

THE ACTION: PROJECTS/TASKS

What constitutes a project is described in detail on pages 88–89. To summarize:

- Each participant needs to have an individual project or task, or a mini-project within a larger group project.
- These projects should be ones that participants will implement, or be involved in helping to implement – research projects, simply involving reports to be written up at their conclusion, are not suitable for an action learning project.
- Projects may fall within a participant's own work area or elsewhere (see Figure 4.1, page 86); or be a current work-based quandary.

A FISHBOWL

Five or six of those present form a 'set' and, sitting in a circle, they work with a set adviser while everyone else sits around the circle and observes the process. An empty chair is left in the inner circle; anyone from the outer circle wishing to participate on a point may join the inner circle by sitting in the empty chair.

At the conclusion of the exercise, the set and the presenter are asked to comment on their experience, and then the discussion is open to everyone.

A TRIAD EXERCISE[1]

Put participants into threes or fours, and ask one member to present an issue – a quandary, challenge or irritation – but nothing too large.

Ask the problem-presenter to hold onto their airspace for 15–20 minutes. Meanwhile the others try and focus on asking questions, giving feedback or reflecting, and turning ideas or suggestions into questions.

When the time is up, ask each group to discuss the experience, beginning by getting the views of the presenter. Then bring everyone back into the larger group and discuss. Ask the presenters first what it was like to be the focus. Then ask the others how they experienced their role.

- Where they are outside a participant's immediate work and function, they should centre on/be directly related to issues they may be involved with in the future, or in their next career moves.
- A project should relate to, and give participants the scope to work on, their identified learning needs.
- Projects should involve the participants in tackling something new to them, something of importance to their section, department or their organization, and something that will stretch them and develop them in identified ways.
- If projects include an implementation stage, the participants must be given authority to carry this out.
- Projects need to be large enough to last for the length of the programme. If they are not, the participants will need to identify new projects/quandaries to work on.
- Each individual and group project must have a client who expects results.
- Participants need to be told at the outset whether they will be expected to produce a written report of their project and/or their learning, or how their efforts will be evaluated.

- On programmes for senior managers, their projects are normally their own managerial issues, decisions, responsibilities and dilemmas, with no clients involved.

An action is a project, a task or a management/personal developmental issue, with a work focus. Participants should ask themselves the following questions to clarify their project:

- What do I plan to do? What tasks do I intend to undertake? What experiences do I want to try out?
- What result/outcome am I anticipating/hoping for?
- How do I plan to go about it?
- How do I plan to review/evaluate it?
- What do I hope to learn?

THE SET

The sets' membership will depend on the objective of the programme. They may consist of people from different functions, or just one. But members are most likely to be of approximately the same level of responsibility, unless they are working on a group project which would benefit from having a vertical-slice set. Sets should:

- consist of no more than five or six participants
- be formed at the very beginning of the programme, during the introductory session(s)
- be told that they will retain the same membership for the duration of the programme
- be told that they will be working with a set adviser (initially, at least)
- be told that they will be meeting for (ideally) a full day, approximately every month for a period of four to six months
- be aware of what are helpful behaviours by both problem-presenters (in their airspace) and by other set members (see pages 111–112).

THE FIRST MEETING

The first set meeting may take place during the introductory session(s), or shortly thereafter. At it, the set members should:

- create their own ground rules (see pages 70–71 for an example)
- agree on future dates for set meetings
- create a learning agreement (if the programme demands one)
- help members think about a project, if they don't already have one

- be told if they are required to – or if the set adviser thinks they would gain if they – keep a diary or learning log (see pages 167–170)
- be reminded of the evaluation (if any) that will take place at the end of the programme
- be told if they are expected to write reports or some other form of document on their project and/or their learning.

The first set meeting is unlike the subsequent ones, for participants don't yet know each other, nor are they familiar with the action learning processes. Here are some guidelines on how to work at the outset of that first meeting:

- In their airspace, each person needs to describe the project he/she has chosen, or the task to be addressed. There may need to be quite a lot of detail, for the other set members to get a full picture and be able to help.
- Try not to interrupt the person, for maybe five or ten minutes, so that they can give you both the 'history' of the project and their own 'story' within it.
- Don't be seduced by a presenter who, after two or three brief sentences, asks the set to share any relevant experiences they may have. It is too early for anyone to contribute helpfully. Instead, ask the presenter questions such as:
  - 'What are the challenges or opportunities?'
  - 'What would be the most useful thing to work on?'
  - 'Where would you like to start?'
  - 'What concerns or worries do you have?'
  - 'What have you thought about already?'
  - 'Who have you involved so far?'
  - 'Who do you need to get agreement or commitment from?
- Maybe give the presenter some feedback on what you're hearing: not just about the picture they're painting, but how they appear – pleased, energized, worried, unclear.
- Ask them what are some of the first steps they need to take to get their project started, and what action they will be taking, to report on at the next meeting.

Thereafter, the set meeting will proceed until the end of the day, leaving time for reflections before the close of the meeting.

STRUCTURING THE SET MEETINGS

It's important to keep to a timetable at each set meeting, to ensure that each participant has an equal amount of time (if everyone is to have equal airspace, which is ideal). If there is time for each member to have one hour, it may be useful to split this time along the lines of:

- 10–15 minutes to 'regroup' and share events and news, and establish the air-times for the day (ensuring the person who went last at the previous meeting isn't last this time!)
- in individual airspace, 10 minutes for feedback on what's been done or achieved since the last meeting, and what has been learnt (very important, for this ensures that the learning cycle is observed)
- around 30 minutes on whatever the presenter wants to work on that day
- 5–10 minutes on 'next actions'
- 10–15 minutes on reflecting on that session – asking the presenter first how he or she felt it had gone, and then inviting each set member to comment. It is important not to return to the 'content' at this stage, but to focus on the processes in the set, and any learning.

At the end of each day's meeting, it is important to have time – say 30 minutes – for the participants to reflect on, and share, what they have learnt during the day, how they think they are working as a set, and what they need to do differently/better at the next meeting.

PROCESSES IN THE SET

These are the elements:

- airspace for everyone, ideally an hour at every meeting; if time does not allow this, then one or two people per meeting, in a rota, or as and when someone needs airspace (the two latter options are not ideal)
- focusing on asking questions (see pages 122–124 for the different types of questions)
- giving/asking for feedback
- giving insights/ reflecting
- sharing ideas and suggestions (in question form)
- trying out new behaviours (the set can be used as an 'experimental bubble')
- studying, and learning from, set processes
- brainstorming; using mind maps, etc. – at the presenter's request and for a limited period only.

It is important to avoid:

- giving advice
- having a general discussion
- criticizing and passing judgement.

Some programme organizers produce documents for participants to read: simple explanations of action learning; guidelines on the processes, and suggestions on how to structure the set meetings and the individual airspaces.

Here are some options for the content of the set meetings:

- focusing on shaping/progressing with the project
- focusing on 'self':
  - How am I doing?
  - How am I feeling?
  - How am I learning?
  - How am I changing?
- focusing on the set:
  - How can I/we use it?
  - How is it helping me/us?
  - What can I/we be doing differently?
  - What are we learning?
- focusing on the processes:
  - What am I finding useful?
  - How are we working?
  - What are we learning?
- discussing other issues of mutual interest, and deciding on the way of working – whether to have a discussion or dialogue (see page 39), or ask for short taught inputs, or other resources
- deciding on other processes that would be helpful, such as brainstorming ideas.

THE SET ADVISER

The role of set adviser is discussed in Chapter 6. The set adviser's main responsibility is to be present for the set meetings, and adhere to the principles of action learning throughout. The set adviser should:

- be 'trained' and understand his/her role to be that of a facilitator (not chairperson, group leader, tutor or lecturer)
- have had some experience of action learning
- observe the ground rules of the set
- organize, if appropriate, short taught inputs on specific subjects of relevance to the set and their projects or their learning/developmental needs
- have the qualities and skills that a good set adviser needs (see pages 138–140)
- be competent and confident to work with the processes that are basic to action learning, such as airspace for every member, a focus on the tasks/projects, a questioning approach, attention to listening, time for reflection, emphasis on learning, and avoidance of advice and judgement.

The set adviser should also remember that he/she is *not* to act as:

- a subject expert
- a tutor
- a chairman
- a group leader.

Some guidelines for set advisers are given on pages 139–140.

THE MEETINGS AND THE TIMING

Meetings should:

- be at a place convenient for all participants – preferably away from work (to avoid phone calls or being called to other meetings)
- be regular, with the timing established at the beginning of the programme, adhered to, and attended regularly by all set members
- last for a full day, to give every member their airspace.

The processes of the set should be observed at every meeting, unless the set – with the acquiescence of the set adviser – decides otherwise.

THE FINAL MEETING

Most programmes have a final wrap-up meeting to:

- review the programme
- possibly give verbal reports to clients and any other interested parties
- evaluate the programme's successes – as well as shortcomings – and propose changes to any future programmes
- to formally end the programme, and invite participants to continue working with their set, either on a formal basis, or as a looser network.

WHAT CAN GO WRONG?

From all that has been written so far, you – the reader – will probably now be able to list the potential pitfalls:

- an ill-trained, unprofessional set adviser
- the wrong choice of project
- the lack of support in the company
- the lack of time

- the mix of participants
- lack of commitment by participants
- all action and no learning
- the set dissolves into a talking shop.

These pitfalls can be eliminated or avoided by observing the following rules:

- Use only trained set advisers; do not think you can train up a line manager or even a trainer within the space of two days to be a competent set adviser.
- Make sure the project lies within the authority, and scope of responsibility, of the participants. The project should be neither so large as to swamp the participant, nor too small and simple. It needs to be something to get one's teeth into, something moderately difficult, and something the participants haven't tackled before.
- Make sure there is senior management support for the programme and for the participants. Revans's dictum of ensuring you pinpoint 'someone who knows, cares and can' is very relevant here.
- Ensure that the importance of time is taken on board at the designing stage of a programme. A programme should allow time for at least three or four (preferably more) set meetings, each to last a full day. There must be adequate time for the project to go from the incubation period to implementation, or at least for proposal stages to have been reached and further implementation agreed.
- Ensure that set participants are compatible and match each other, more or less, in terms of years of experience and level of responsibility. Consider having mixed-function and mixed-discipline sets.
- Make sure participants are aware that it is in their own interest to commit themselves to the programme and all its elements if they are to gain from it – and be able to give to others.
- Ensure that the emphasis is on learning, and not just on action. In other words, ensure that projects (actions) are geared to participants' needs, and are not hijacked by senior managers for their own ends.
- Make sure participants are reminded of the 'action learning way of working' and keep to the processes of airspace and questioning in particular.
- Ensure that participants' managers – and, if necessary, senior managers – are aware of, and committed to, the programme and its stated outcomes.

NOTES

[1] Adapted from a note given to me by Liz Beaty of Brighton University.

Useful addresses

THE INTERNATIONAL FOUNDATION FOR ACTION LEARNING (IFAL)

The International Foundation for Action Learning, a membership organization, aims to identify and encourage a network of enthusiasts to support and develop the work of action learning worldwide. It has active 'chapters' in the UK, Canada, Italy and the USA, and other members in countries across the world. Membership includes both individuals and organizations, and provides opportunities to meet with and learn from others engaged in practising action learning.

In the UK, IFAL collects and disseminates information, promotes research and case histories, publishes a newsletter three times a year, maintains a library of articles on action learning, runs a number of workshops and meetings during the year, and welcomes telephone and letter enquiries.

IFAL is based in the UK, and can be contacted at: The Department of Management Learning, The Management School, Lancaster University, Lancaster LA1 4YX, tel./fax: 01524-812254; e-mail: p.wright@lancaster.ac.uk; its home page on the Internet is: http://www.mentat.co.uk/park/ifal. IFAL is also strengthening an IFAL Worldwide network, to create links with other action learners. Further contact with this network is possible through:

Jean K Lawrence (Worldwide): tel./fax 015394-44671; e-mail Jean.Lawrence@intal.net1.co.uk

Peter Smith (Canada): tel. 905-853-9553; fax 905-853-1954; IFAL Canada website http://www.tlainc.com/ifalcan.htm

Judy O'Neil (USA): tel. 401-737-9997; fax 401-737-9668; IFAL-USA website http://www.metalearning.com/ifal-usa

References and further reading

Beaty, L., Bourner, T. and Frost, P. (1993) 'Action learning: Reflections on becoming a set member', *Management Education and Development*, vol. 24, part 4.

Boddy, D. (1981) 'Putting action learning into practice', *Journal of European Industrial Training*, vol. 5, no. 5.

Boddy, D. and Buchanan, D. (1992) *Take the Lead: Interpersonal Skills for Project Managers*, Hemel Hempstead: Prentice-Hall.

Bohm, D. (1993) 'For truth try dialogue', *Resurgence*, no. 56, January/February.

Borzsony, P., Dadge, R. and Hunt, K. with Daly, J. (1997) *Practical Magic: How to Create Learning Organisations*, Maidenhead: Peter Honey Publications.

Casey, D. (1997a) 'The role of the set adviser', in Pedler, M. (ed.) *Action Learning in Practice* (3rd edn), Aldershot: Gower.

Casey, D. (1997b) 'The shell of your understanding', in Pedler, M. (ed.) *Action Learning in Practice* (3rd edn), Aldershot: Gower.

Chawla, S. and Renesch, J. (eds) (1995) *Learning Organisations*, Portland, OR: Productivity Press.

Dixon, N. (1994) *The Organisational Learning Cycle: How We Can Learn Collectively*, Maidenhead: McGraw-Hill.

Fritz, R. (1991) *Creating*, Oxford: Butterworth-Heinemann.

Garratt, B. (1994) *The Learning Organisation*, London: HarperCollins.

Garratt, B. (1997) 'The power of action learning', in Pedler, M. (ed.) *Action Learning in Practice* (3rd edn), Aldershot: Gower.

Gaunt, R. and Kendall, R. (1985) *A Short Manual for Set Members*, Greater London Employers' Association.

Goldberg, M.C. (1998) *The Art of the Question*, New York: John Wiley.

Goleman, D. (1995) *Emotional Intelligence*, New York: Bantam.

Honey, P. (1994) 'Establishing a learning regime', *Organisations and People*, vol. 1, no. 1.

Honey, P. and Mumford, A. (1986) *The Manual of Learning Styles*, Maidenhead: Peter Honey Publications.

Honey, P. and Mumford, A. (1995) *The Opportunistic Learner*, Maidenhead: Peter Honey Publications.

Inglis, S. (1994) *Making the Most of Action Learning*, Aldershot: Gower.

Lawrence, J. (1986) 'A questioning approach', in Mumford, A. (ed.) *Handbook of Management Development* (2nd edn), Aldershot: Gower.

Lewis, A. (1994) 'Action learning in Prudential Assurance', in *Authors and Authorities in Action Learning*, MCB University Press.

Logan, A. and Stuart, R. (1987) 'Action based learning: Are activity and experience the same?', *Industrial and Commercial Training*, March/April.

McGill, I. and Beaty, L. (1994) *Action Learning: A Practitioner's Guide*, London: Kogan Page.

Meehan, M. and Jarvis, J. (1996) 'A refreshing angle on staff education', *People Management*, 11 July.

Morgan, G. (1997) *Imaginization*, Thousand Oaks, CA: Sage.

Mumford, A. (1993) *How Managers Can Develop Managers*, Aldershot: Gower.

Mumford, A. (ed.) (1997) *Action Learning at Work*, Aldershot: Gower.

Pedler, M. (1996) *Action Learning for Managers*, London: Lemos and Crane.

Pedler, M. (ed.) (1997) *Action Learning in Practice* (3rd edn), Aldershot: Gower.

Pedler, M. and Boutall, J. (1992) *Action Learning for Change: A Resource Book for Managers and Other Professionals*, NHS Training Directorate.

Pedler, M., Burgoyne, J. and Boydell, T. (1991) *The Learning Company*, Maidenhead: McGraw-Hill.

Phillips, A. (1994) 'Creating space in the learning company', in Burgoyne, J., Pedler, M. and Boydell, T. (eds) *Towards the Learning Company*, Maidenhead: McGraw-Hill.

Reeves, T. (1994) *Managing Effectively: Developing Yourself through Experience*, Oxford: Butterworth-Heinemann.

Revans, R. (1982) *The Origins and Growth of Action Learning*, Bromley: Chartwell Bratt.

Revans, R. (1998) *The ABC of Action Learning*, (2nd edn), London: Lemos and Crane.

Senge, P. (1992) *The Fifth Discipline*, London: Century Business.

Special issues of journals on action learning

Education and Training (1996), vol. 38, no. 8 (UK): special issue on action learning in higher education.

Journal of Workplace Learning/Employee Counselling Today (1996), vol. 8, no. 6 (UK): special issue on action learning.

Performance Improvement Quarterly (1998), vol. 11, no. 1 (USA): special issue on action learning.

The Journal of Management Development (1987), vol. 6, no. 2 (UK): special issue on action learning.

Index

A Systematic Approach to

Getting Results

Surya Lovejoy

Every manager has to produce results. But almost nobody is trained in the business of doing so. This book is a practical handbook for making things happen. And whether the thing in question is a conference, an office relocation or a sales target, the principles are the same: you need a systematic approach for working out:

- exactly what has to happen
- when everything has to happen
- how you will ensure that it happens
- what could go wrong
- what will happen when something does go wrong
- how you will remain sane during the process.

This book won't turn you into an expert on critical path analysis or prepare you for the job of running the World Bank. What it will do is to give you the tools you need to produce results smoothly, effectively, reliably and without losing your mind on the way.

Gower

The Goal

A Process of Ongoing Improvement

Second Edition

Eliyahu M Goldratt and Jeff Cox

A Gower Novel

Written in a fast-paced thriller style, *The Goal* is the gripping novel which is transforming management thinking throughout the Western world. Alex Rogo is a harried plant manager working ever more desperately to try to improve performance. His factory is rapidly heading for disaster. So is his marriage. He has ninety days to save his plant - or it will be closed by corporate HQ, with hundreds of job losses. It takes a chance meeting with a colleague from student days - Jonah - to help him break out of conventional ways of thinking to see what needs to be done.

The story of Alex's fight to save his plant is more than compulsive reading. It contains a serious message for all managers in industry and explains the ideas which underlie the Theory of Constraints (TOC) developed by Eli Goldratt - the author described by Fortune as 'a guru to industry' and by Businessweek as a 'genius'.

As a result of the phenomenal and continuing success of *The Goal* there has been growing demand for a follow-up. Eliyahu Goldratt has now written ten further chapters which continue the story of Alex Rogo as he makes the transition from Plant Manager to Divisional Manager. Having achieved the turnround of his plant, Alex now attempts to apply all that Jonah has taught him, not to crisis management, but to ongoing improvement.

These new chapters reinforce the thinking process utilised in the first edition of *The Goal* and apply them to a wider management context with the aim of stimulating readers into using the technique in their own environment.

Gower

The Management Skills Book

Conor Hannaway and Gabriel Hunt

From managing employee performance to chairing meetings, and from interviewing staff to making retirement presentations, the list of skills demanded of today's manager seems endless. How can you be effective in all these areas?

If you are a practising manager, this book is for you. It is designed to answer your need for support in your day-to-day work.

Over 100 brief guides cover essential management skills. Each guide gives you all you need to know without cumbersome technical details. Look up the subject you need, and apply the ideas immediately.

The Management Skills Book was written with today's busy managers in mind. It is an ideal introduction for new managers, and a great reminder of the essentials for the more experienced.

Gower

Managerial Consulting Skills

A Practical Guide

Charles J Margerison

The advisory role in organizations is more important today than it has ever been. To perform effectively, managers and professionals need the skills of the consultant.

This book has been designed to provide practical help for all advisers, whether working within or outside the organization. It covers every aspect of the process from interpersonal skills to organizational context, from planning to follow-up. Each chapter concludes with guidelines summarizing the content, and questions designed to help the reader to apply the material to his or her own activities. Fascinating real-life cases from Professor Margerison's own experience are included, as well as examples drawn from the work of many well-known consultants.

Gower

The Motivation Manual

Gisela Hagemann

Improved productivity, flexible work practices, low rates of
absenteeism, commitment to quality, ever-higher standards of
customer service - these are the benefits of a well-motivated
workforce. In this prize-winning book the author takes modern
motivational theory and shows how any manager can apply it to
create shared vision, develop mutual trust and involve employees in
the decision-making process.

The text is enlivened throughout by examples with which
managers will identify and there is a unique final section
containing twenty seven exercises designed to strengthen
interpersonal skills and improve creativity.

Gower

The New Unblocked Manager

A Practical Guide to Self-Development

Dave Francis and Mike Woodcock

This is unashamedly a self-help book, written for managers and supervisors who wish to improve their effectiveness. In the course of their work with thousands of managers over a long period the authors have discovered twelve potential 'blockages' that stand in the way of managerial competence. They include, for example, negative personal values, low creativity and unclear goals.

By means of a self-evaluation exercise, the reader first identifies the blockages most significant to them. There follows a detailed explanation of each blockage and ideas and materials for tackling the problem.

This is a heavily revised edition of a book that, under its original title, *The Unblocked Manager*, was used by many thousands of managers around the world and appeared in ten languages. The new edition reflects the changed world of management and owes much to the feedback supplied by practising managers. In its enhanced form the book will continue to provide a comprehensive framework for self-directed development.

Gower

Problem Solving in Groups

Second Edition

Mike Robson

Modern scientific research has demonstrated that groups are likely to solve problems more effectively than individuals. As most of us knew already, two heads (or more) are better than one. In organizations it makes sense to harness the power of the group both to deal with problems already identified and to generate ideas for enhancing effectiveness by reducing costs, increasing productivity and the like.

In this revised and updated edition of his successful book, Mike Robson first introduces the concepts and methods involved. Then, after setting out the advantages of the group approach, he examines in detail each of the eight key problem solving techniques. The final part of the book explains how to present proposed solutions, how to evaluate results and how to ensure that the group process runs smoothly. With its practical tone, its down-to-earth style and lively visuals, this is a book that will appeal strongly to managers and trainers looking for ways of improving their organization's and their department's performance.

Gower

Professional Report Writing

Simon Mort

The ability to write reports that really convince is an invaluable management tool, yet it rarely features amongst the list of skills managers need to be effective. Simon Mort gives that skill the attention it deserves, in the most thorough book on the subject available.

As well as helpful analysis he provides practical guidance on such topics as:

- deciding the format
- structuring a report
- stylistic pitfalls and how to avoid them
- making the most of illustrations
- ensuring a consistent layout

The theme throughout is fitness for purpose, and the text is enriched by a wide variety of examples drawn from business, industry and government. The annotated bibliography includes a review of the leading dictionaries and reference books.

Simon Mort's book is an indispensable reference work for managers, civil servants, local government officers, consultants and professionals of every kind.

Gower

Project Leadership
Second Edition

Wendy Briner, Colin Hastings and Michael Geddes

The bestselling first edition of this book broke new ground by focusing on the leadership aspects of project management rather than the technical. This radically revised edition is substantially reorganized, to introduce much new material and experience and bring the applications up to date.

Project leaders now exist in many different types of organizations, and they and their projects extend far wider than the construction work where traditional project management began. This new edition begins by explaining why the project way of working has been so widely and enthusiastically adopted, and provides new material on the role and key competences of project leaders in a wide range of different organizations. The authors provide invaluable guidance to senior managers struggling to create the context within which project work can thrive as well as be controlled. A new section, 'Preparing the Ground' reflects their increased emphasis on getting projects off to the right start, with new insights into the scoping process designed to ensure all parties agree on objectives. It also demonstrates the importance of understanding the organizational and political factors involved if the project is to succeed in business terms. Part III shows how to handle the issues that arise at each stage of the project's life including a whole new section on the critical process of project team start up. The final section contains a thought-provoking 'action summary' and a guide to further sources of information and development.

Project leadership and the project way of working has moved on. This book will provide both a conceptual framework and a set of practical tools for all those who find themselves permanently or occasionally in the project leader role, as well as an invaluable guide to setting up and maintaining project activity.

Gower

Unlocking Peak Performance

Christie Kennard

Smart Management Guides Series

Today's managers and team leaders face tough personal, departmental and organizational goals. To meet and surpass these goals, you need to:

• inspire your people to make things happen
• give them the determination to continuously improve
• instil them with the confidence and commitment they need to succeed
• earn their trust, loyalty and respect.

This book shows you how to unlock your people's full potential. It's full of short, pragmatic ideas and techniques that go beyond the traditional motivators such as money and job security to explore the real reasons why people work.

Unlocking Peak Performance offers any aspiring manager or team leader a starting point for building a team of creative, happy and productive high-achievers.

The *Smart Management Guides Series* offers practical guidance, with helpful tips and checklists, in a range of essential business skills. With each title providing an instant grounding in a key area, they're ideal for today's busy manager. Other titles in the series include: *Managing Through Change, Empowering the Self-Directed Team, Essentials of TQM, Managing Your Boss, Assert Yourself!, Essential Delegation Skills, Managing Stress, Motivation and Goal Setting*, and *Essential Presentation Skills*.

Gower

What Every Manager Needs to Know About Health and Safety

Ron Akass

New legislation introduced as a consequence of the Single Market reinforces the accountability of managers for the health and safety of their staff. And contravening the regulations can have serious personal consequences.

Ron Akass has written this book to provide all managers of people with the information they need to know. The focus is upon the key statutory health and safety requirements that affect every business, and every manager, in the European Union. He highlights ways in which organizations can manage these responsibilities with confidence and the knowledge that they are doing all that is 'reasonably practicable' to comply. 'Management action checklists' at the end of each chapter summarize the principal requirements for each area.

Any manager responsible for staff will find the book a stimulating, even enjoyable, guide to this area.

Gower

Unlocking Peak Performance

Christie Kennard

Smart Management Guides Series

Today's managers and team leaders face tough personal, departmental and organizational goals. To meet and surpass these goals, you need to:

- inspire your people to make things happen
- give them the determination to continuously improve
- instil them with the confidence and commitment they need to succeed
- earn their trust, loyalty and respect.

This book shows you how to unlock your people's full potential. It's full of short, pragmatic ideas and techniques that go beyond the traditional motivators such as money and job security to explore the real reasons why people work.

Unlocking Peak Performance offers any aspiring manager or team leader a starting point for building a team of creative, happy and productive high-achievers.

The *Smart Management Guides Series* offers practical guidance, with helpful tips and checklists, in a range of essential business skills. With each title providing an instant grounding in a key area, they're ideal for today's busy manager. Other titles in the series include: *Managing Through Change, Empowering the Self-Directed Team, Essentials of TQM, Managing Your Boss, Assert Yourself!, Essential Delegation Skills, Managing Stress, Motivation and Goal Setting,* and *Essential Presentation Skills.*

Gower

What Every Manager Needs to Know About Health and Safety

Ron Akass

New legislation introduced as a consequence of the Single Market reinforces the accountability of managers for the health and safety of their staff. And contravening the regulations can have serious personal consequences.

Ron Akass has written this book to provide all managers of people with the information they need to know. The focus is upon the key statutory health and safety requirements that affect every business, and every manager, in the European Union. He highlights ways in which organizations can manage these responsibilities with confidence and the knowledge that they are doing all that is 'reasonably practicable' to comply. 'Management action checklists' at the end of each chapter summarize the principal requirements for each area.

Any manager responsible for staff will find the book a stimulating, even enjoyable, guide to this area.

Gower